ULTIMATE X-MEN

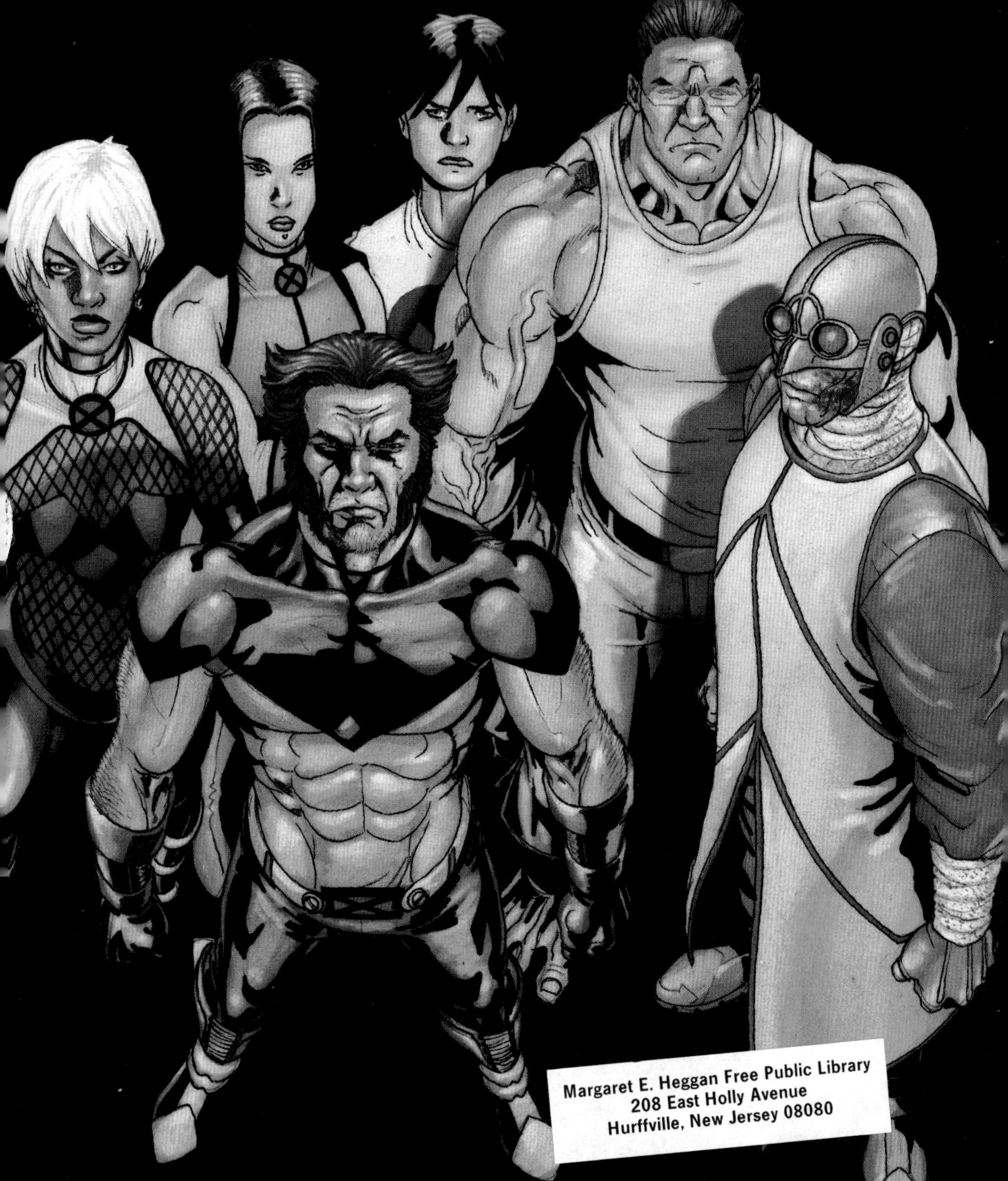

APOCALYPSE

ULTIMATE X-MEN

APOCALYPSE

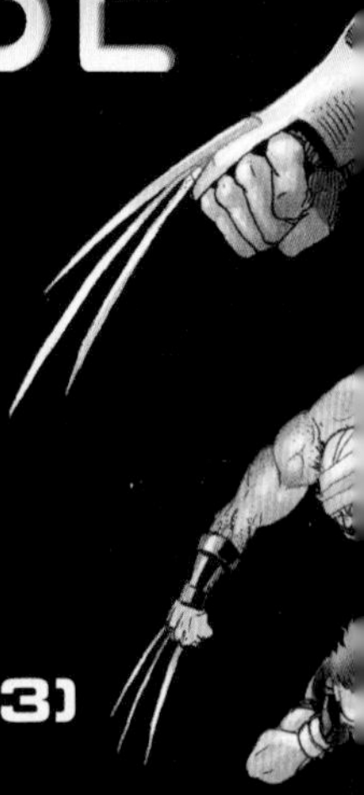

WRITER:
Robert Kirkman
ARTIST:
Salvador Larroca
with Harvey Tolibao (Issue #93)

COLORISTS:
Stephane Peru
with Paul Mounts (Issue #92)
& Jay David Ramos (Issue #93)
LETTERERS:
Virtual Calligraphy's
Joe Caramagna with Cory Petit
COVERS:
Salvador Larroca
with Paco Roca
& Stephane Peru
ASSISTANT EDITOR:
Lauren Sankovitch
EDITOR:
Bill Rosemann
SENIOR EDITOR:
Ralph Macchio

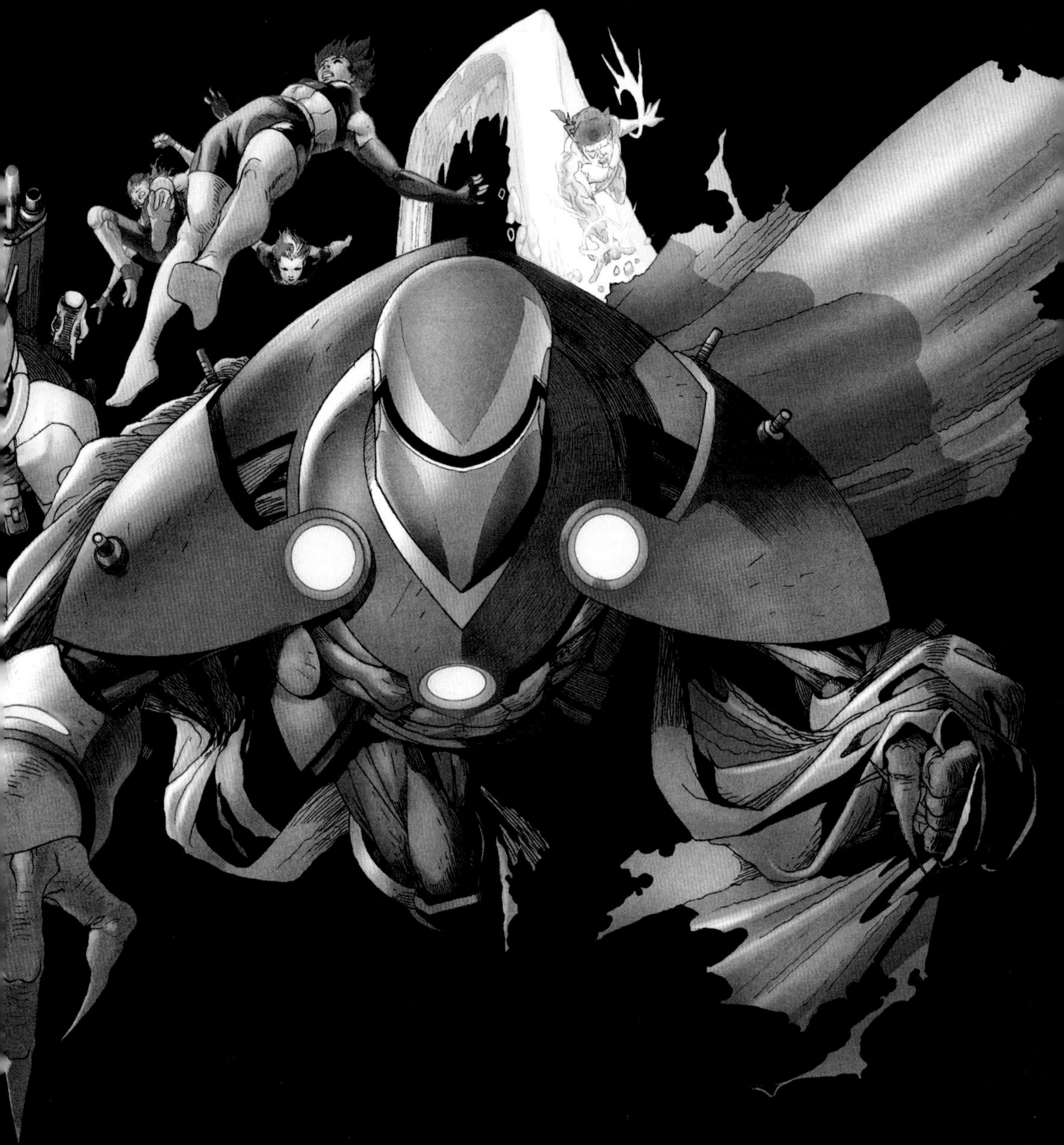

COLLECTION EDITOR:
Jennifer Grünwald
ASSISTANT EDITORS:
Cory Levine & John Denning
EDITOR, SPECIAL PROJECTS:
Mark D. Beazley
SENIOR EDITOR,
SPECIAL PROJECTS:
Jeff Youngquist
SENIOR VICE PRESIDENT
OF SALES:
David Gabriel

PRODUCTION:
Jerron Quality Color
VICE PRESIDENT OF CREATIVE:
Tom Marvelli

EDITOR IN CHIEF:
Joe Quesada
PUBLISHER:
Dan Buckley

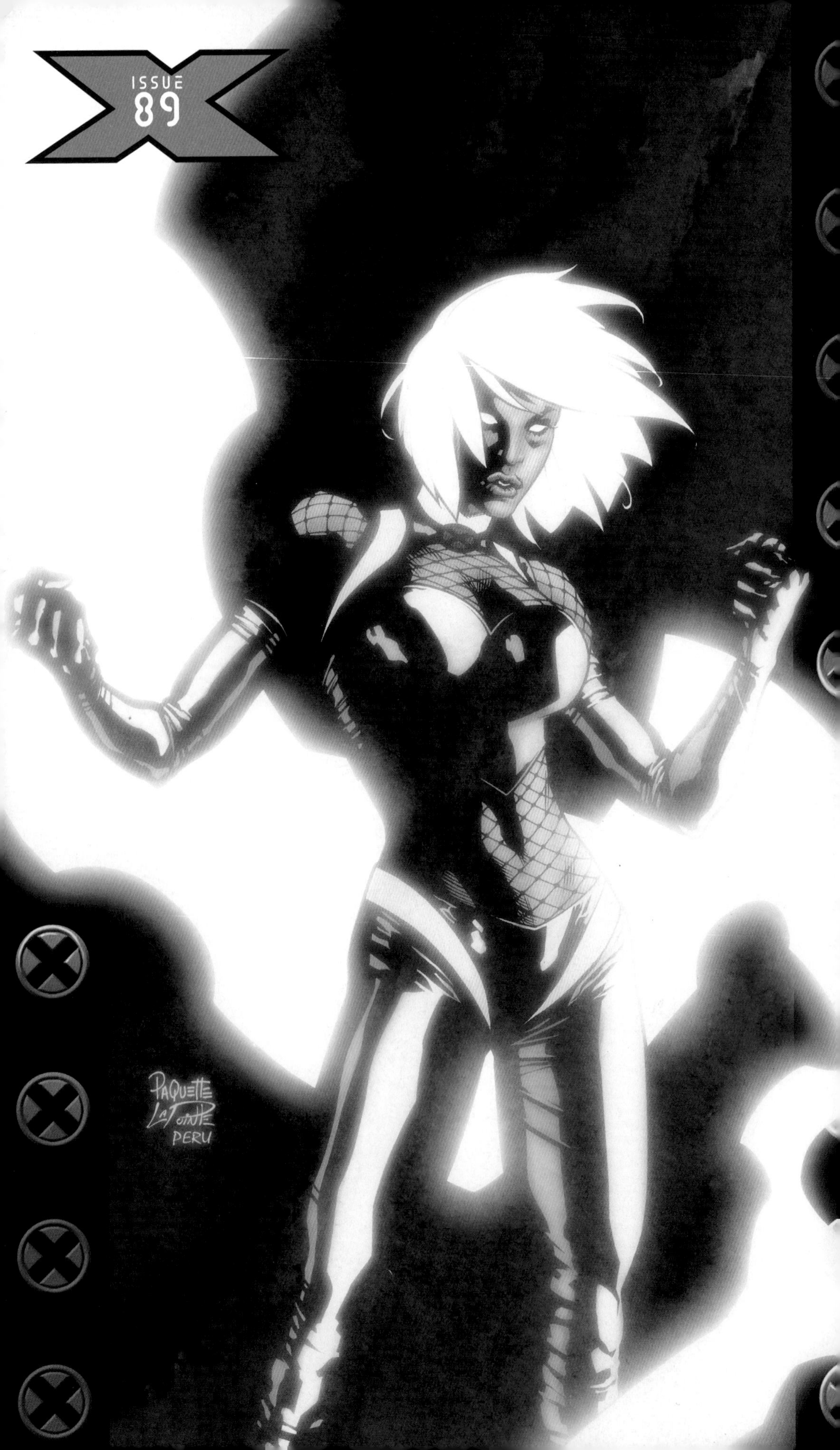
ISSUE
89
PAQUETTE
LAPOINTE
PERU

PREVIOUSLY IN ULTIMATE X-MEN:

n with strange and amazing abilities, the X-Men are young mutant heroes, sworn to protect a world that fears and hates them.

Since she first came to Xavier's mansion, Storm had been using the Danger Room as a creative outlet, designing programs for the X-Men to train with.

Later, she revealed she was working on a play entitled "The Shadow King." This play was inspired by extremely vivid dreams she'd been experiencing.

Recently, her dreams have become more vivid--and are even occurring while she's awake.

Something is definitely amiss.

the Wolverine side of things, Sabretooth revealed that he believed himself to be Wolverine's son, and used this startling moment to violently extract a tissue sample from Wolverine for use by Doctor Cornelius, the former head of WEAPON X.

What his plans for that sample entailed are as of yet...unknown.

SHADOW KING

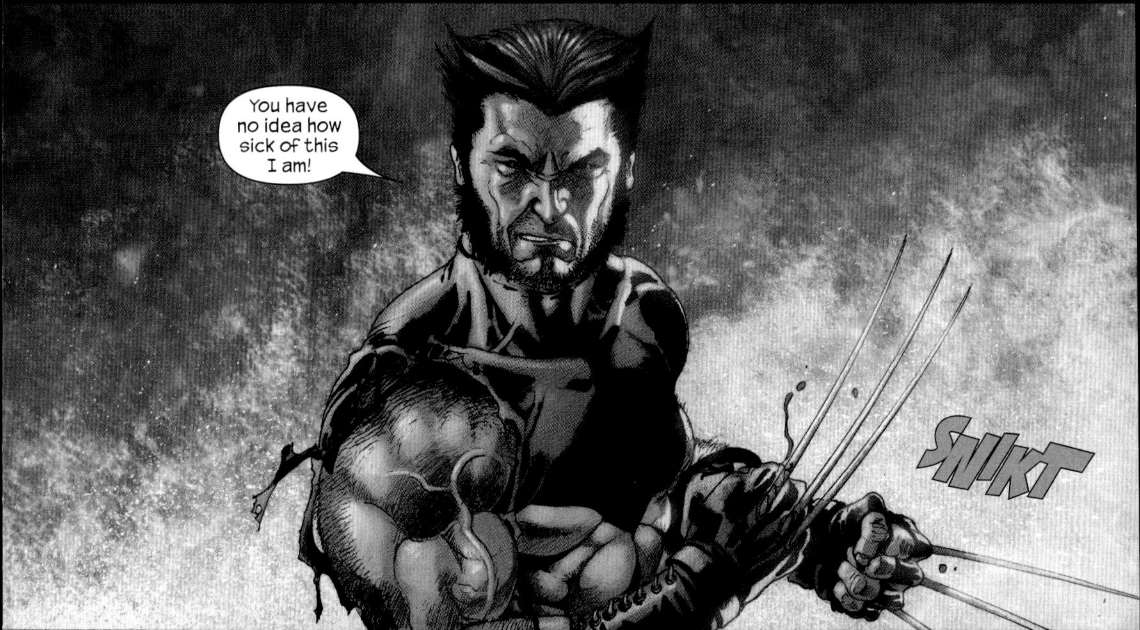
You have no idea how sick of this I am!
SNIKT

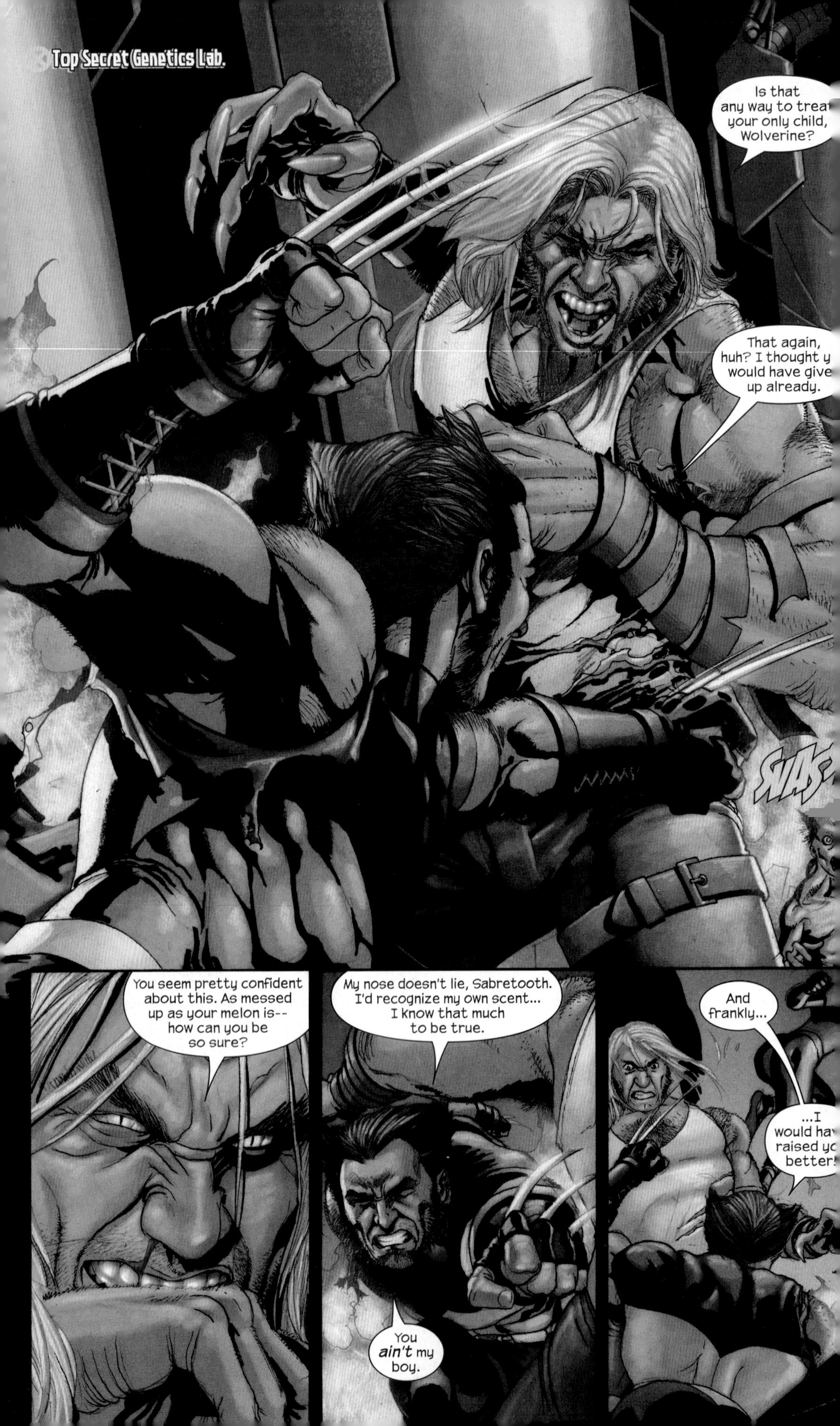
Top Secret Genetics Lab.
Is that any way to trea your only child, Wolverine?
That again, huh? I thought y would have give up already.
SWAS
You seem pretty confident about this. As messed up as your melon is--how can you be so sure?
My nose doesn't lie, Sabretooth. I'd recognize my own scent... I know that much to be true.
You *ain't* my boy.
And frankly...
...I would ha raised yo better!

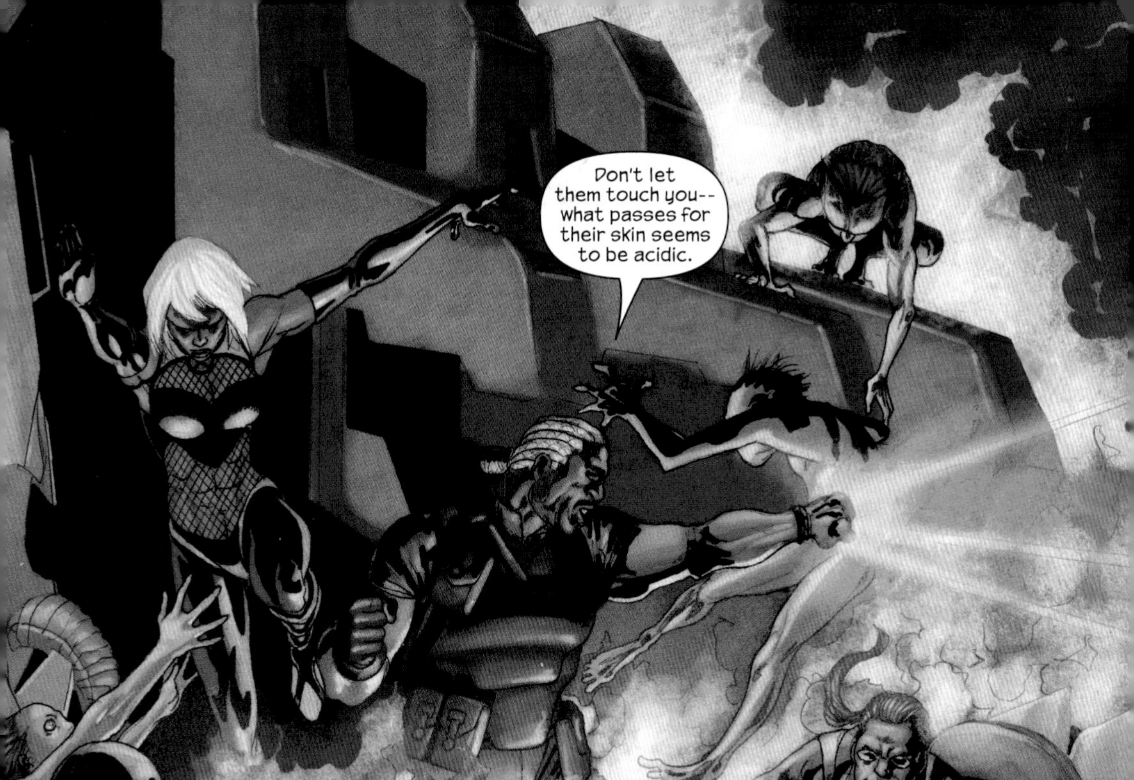
Don't let them touch you-- what passes for their skin seems to be acidic.
Get back!

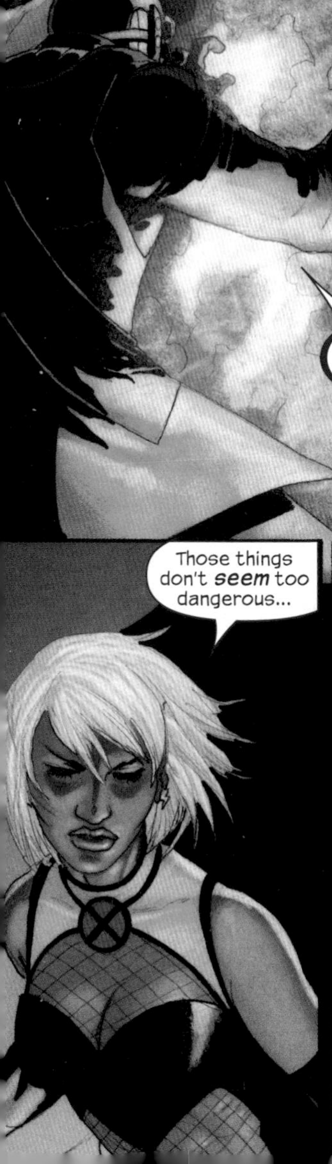
Those things don't *seem* too dangerous...

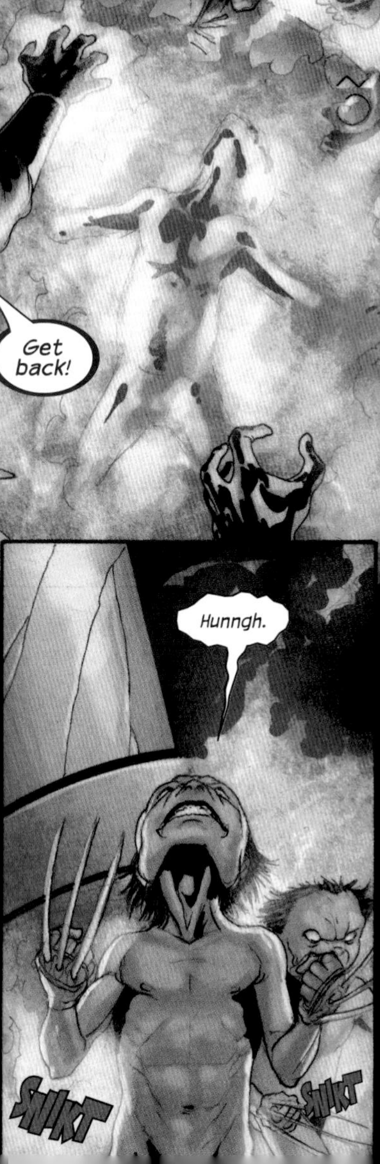
Hunngh.
SNIKT
SNIKT

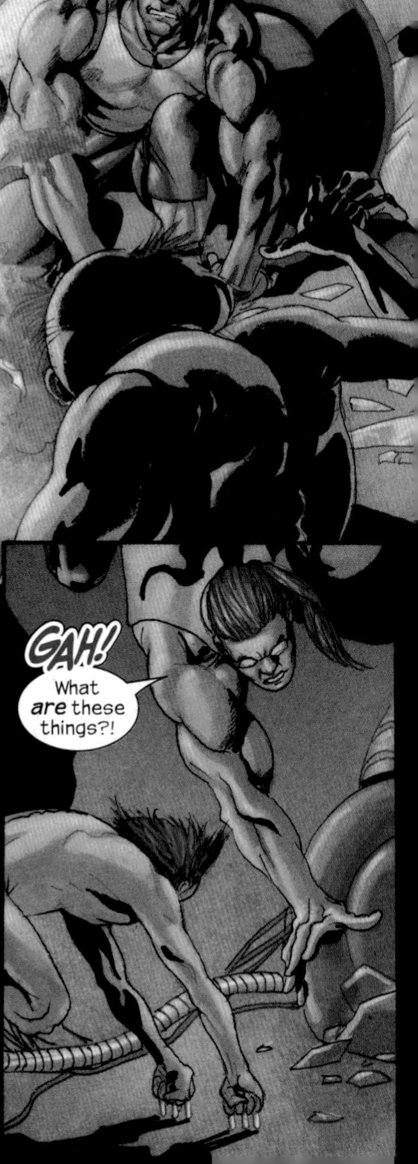
GAH!
What *are* these things?!

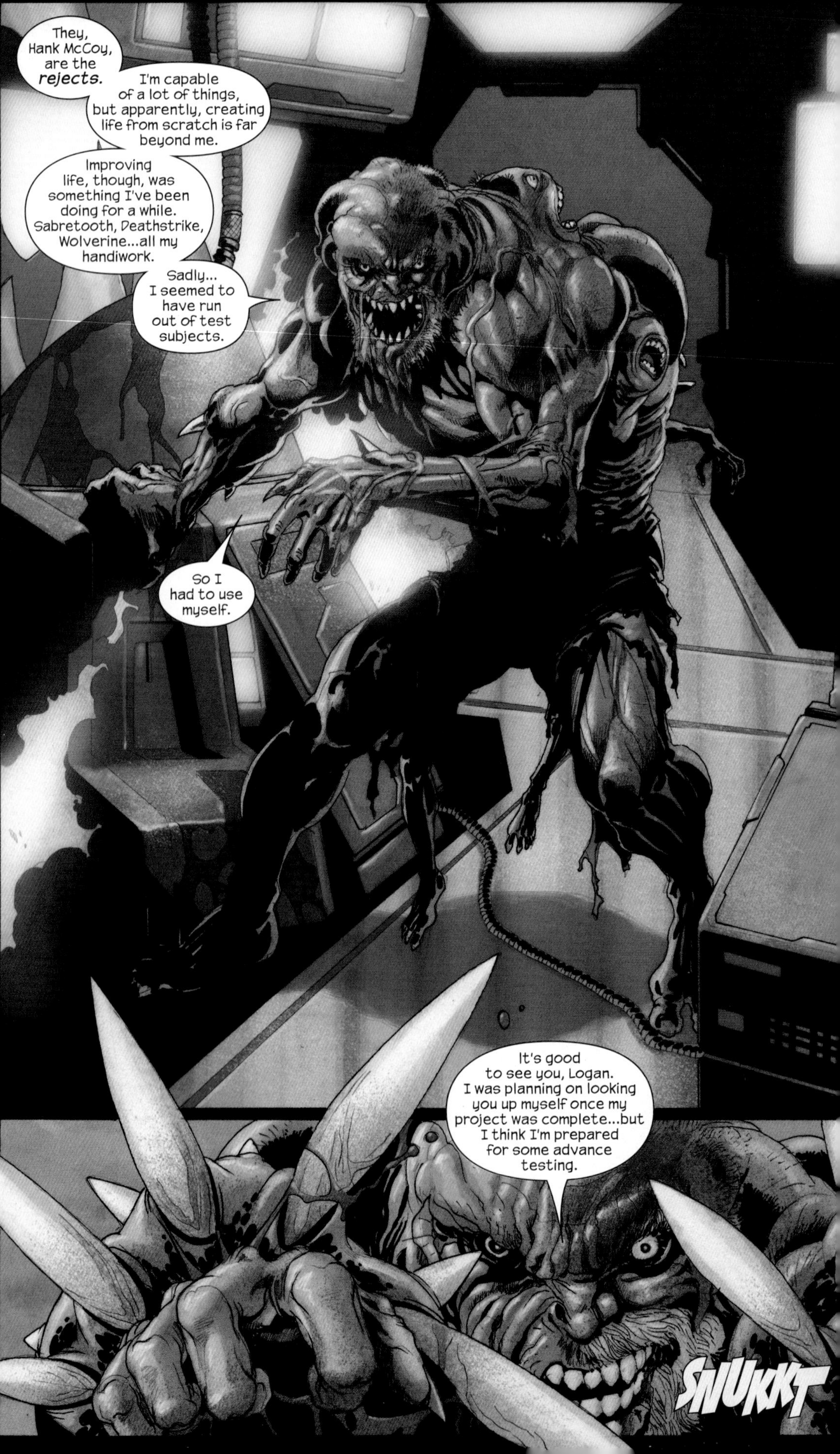
They, Hank McCoy, are the *rejects.*
I'm capable of a lot of things, but apparently, creating life from scratch is far beyond me.
Improving life, though, was something I've been doing for a while. Sabretooth, Deathstrike, Wolverine...all my handiwork.
Sadly... I seemed to have run out of test subjects.
So I had to use myself.
It's good to see you, Logan. I was planning on looking you up myself once my project was complete...but I think I'm prepared for some advance testing.
SNUKKT

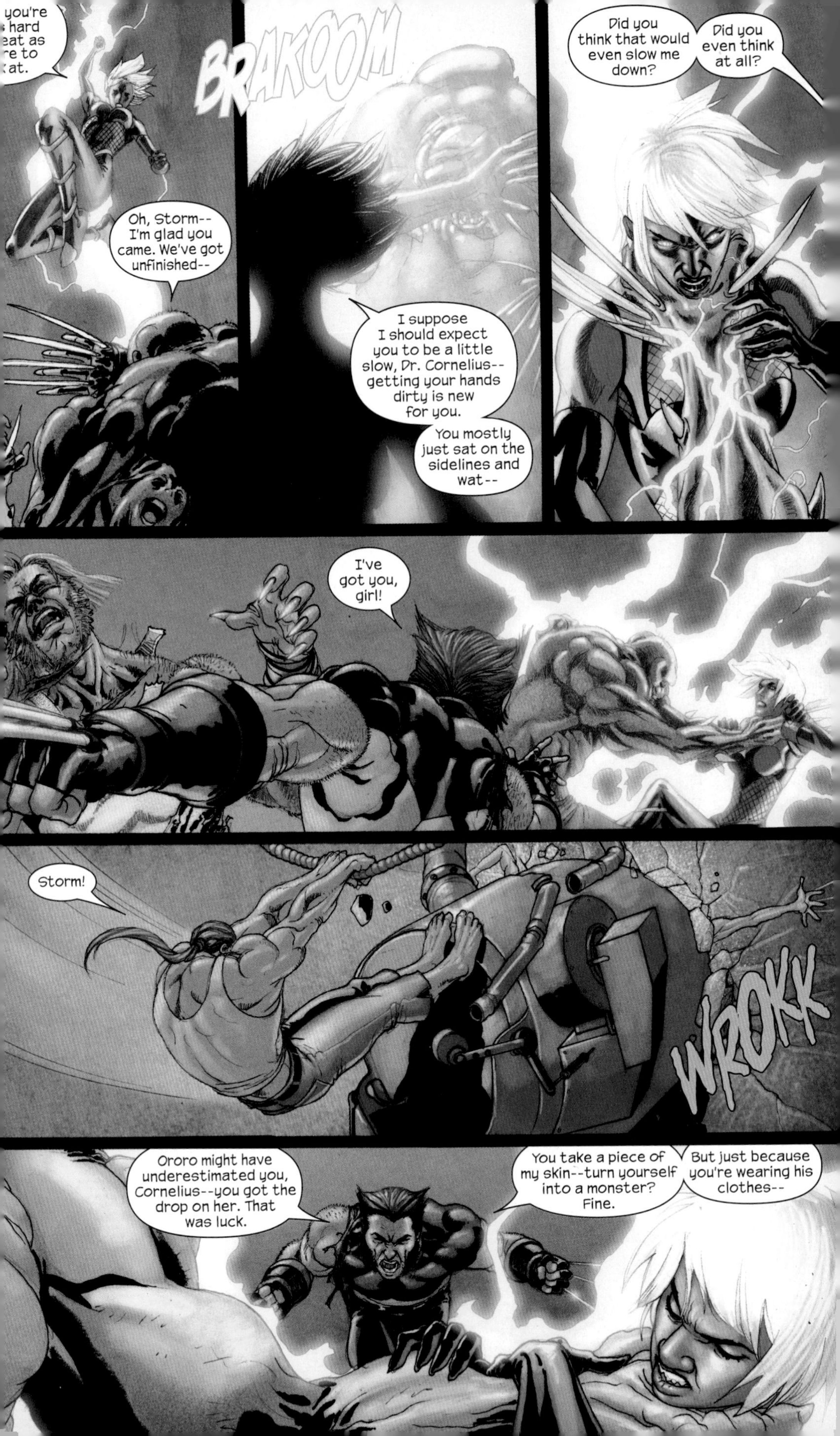
you're
hard
eat as
re to
at.
BRAKOOM
Did you think that would even slow me down?
Did you even think at all?
Oh, Storm-- I'm glad you came. We've got unfinished--
I suppose I should expect you to be a little slow, Dr. Cornelius-- getting your hands dirty is new for you.
You mostly just sat on the sidelines and wat--
I've got you, girl!
Storm!
WROKK
Ororo might have underestimated you, Cornelius--you got the drop on her. That was luck.
You take a piece of my skin--turn yourself into a monster? Fine.
But just because you're wearing his clothes--

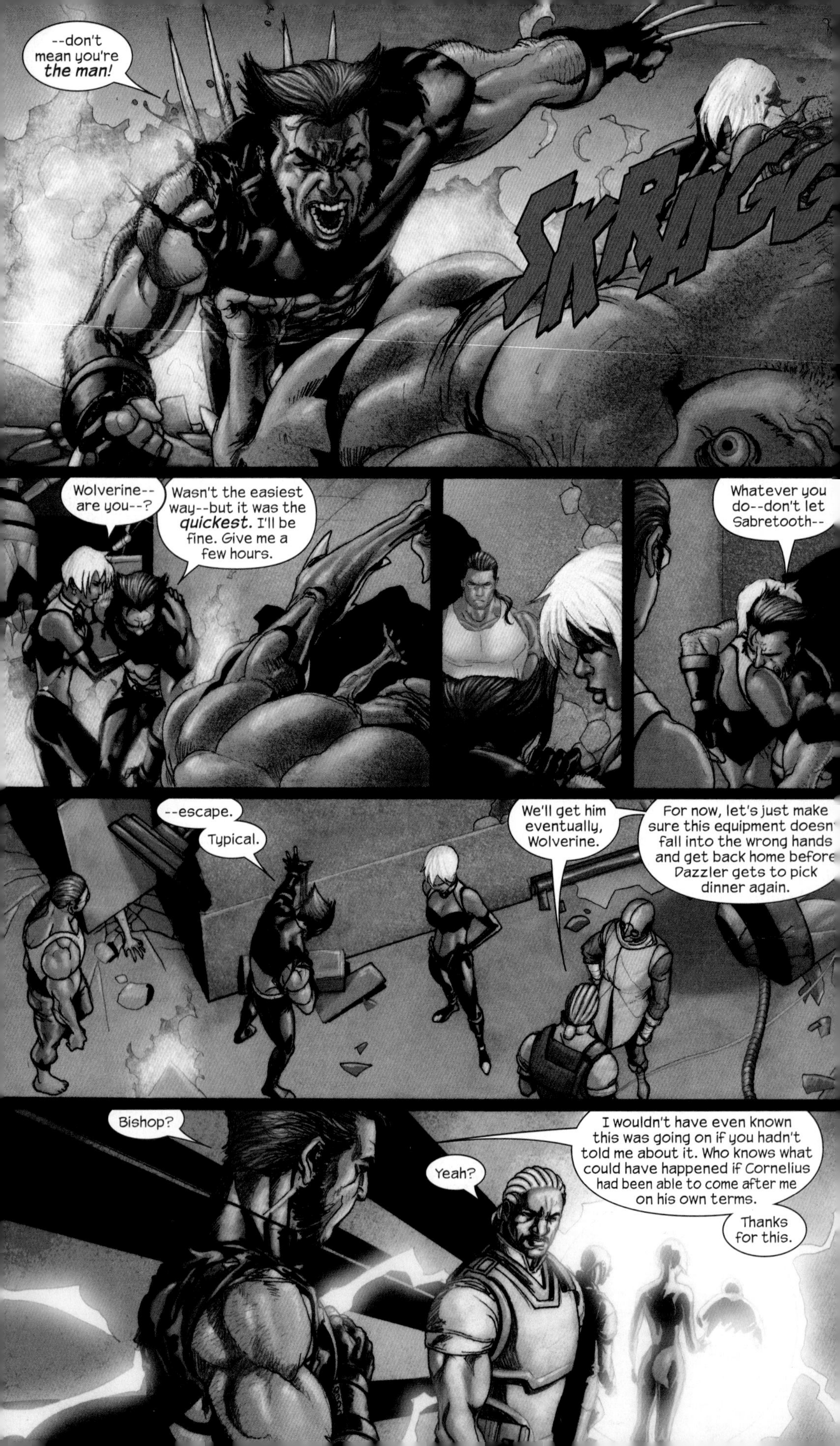
--don't mean you're *the man!*
SKRAGG
Wolverine-- are you--?
Wasn't the easiest way--but it was the *quickest.* I'll be fine. Give me a few hours.
Whatever you do--don't let Sabretooth--
--escape.
Typical.
We'll get him eventually, Wolverine.
For now, let's just make sure this equipment doesn't fall into the wrong hands and get back home before Dazzler gets to pick dinner again.
Bishop?
Yeah?
I wouldn't have even known this was going on if you hadn't told me about it. Who knows what could have happened if Cornelius had been able to come after me on his own terms.
Thanks for this.

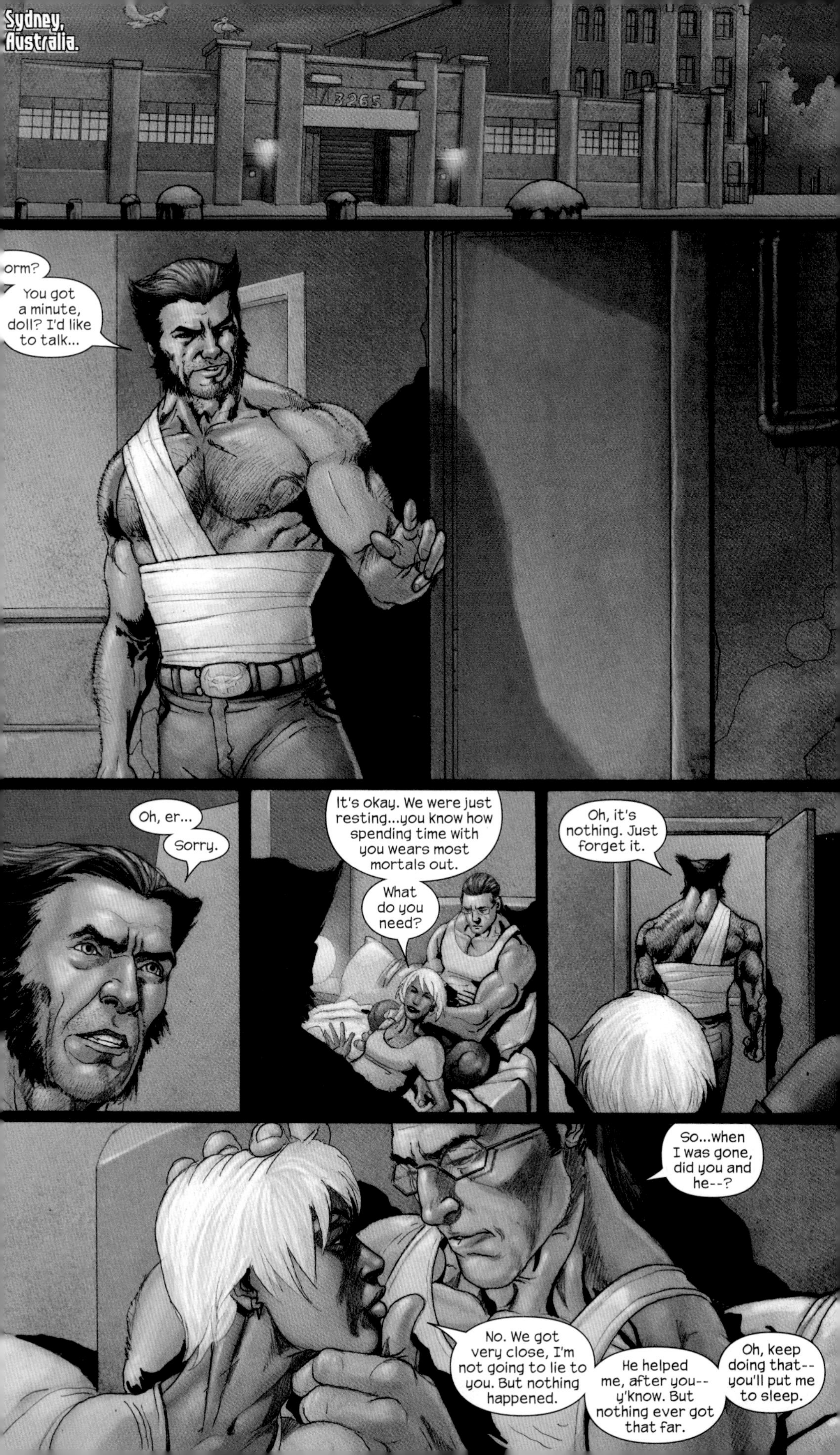
Sydney, Australia.
3265
orm? You got a minute, doll? I'd like to talk...
Oh, er... Sorry.
It's okay. We were just resting...you know how spending time with you wears most mortals out.
What do you need?
Oh, it's nothing. Just forget it.
So...when I was gone, did you and he--?
No. We got very close, I'm not going to lie to you. But nothing happened.
He helped me, after you-- y'know. But nothing ever got that far.
Oh, keep doing that-- you'll put me to sleep.

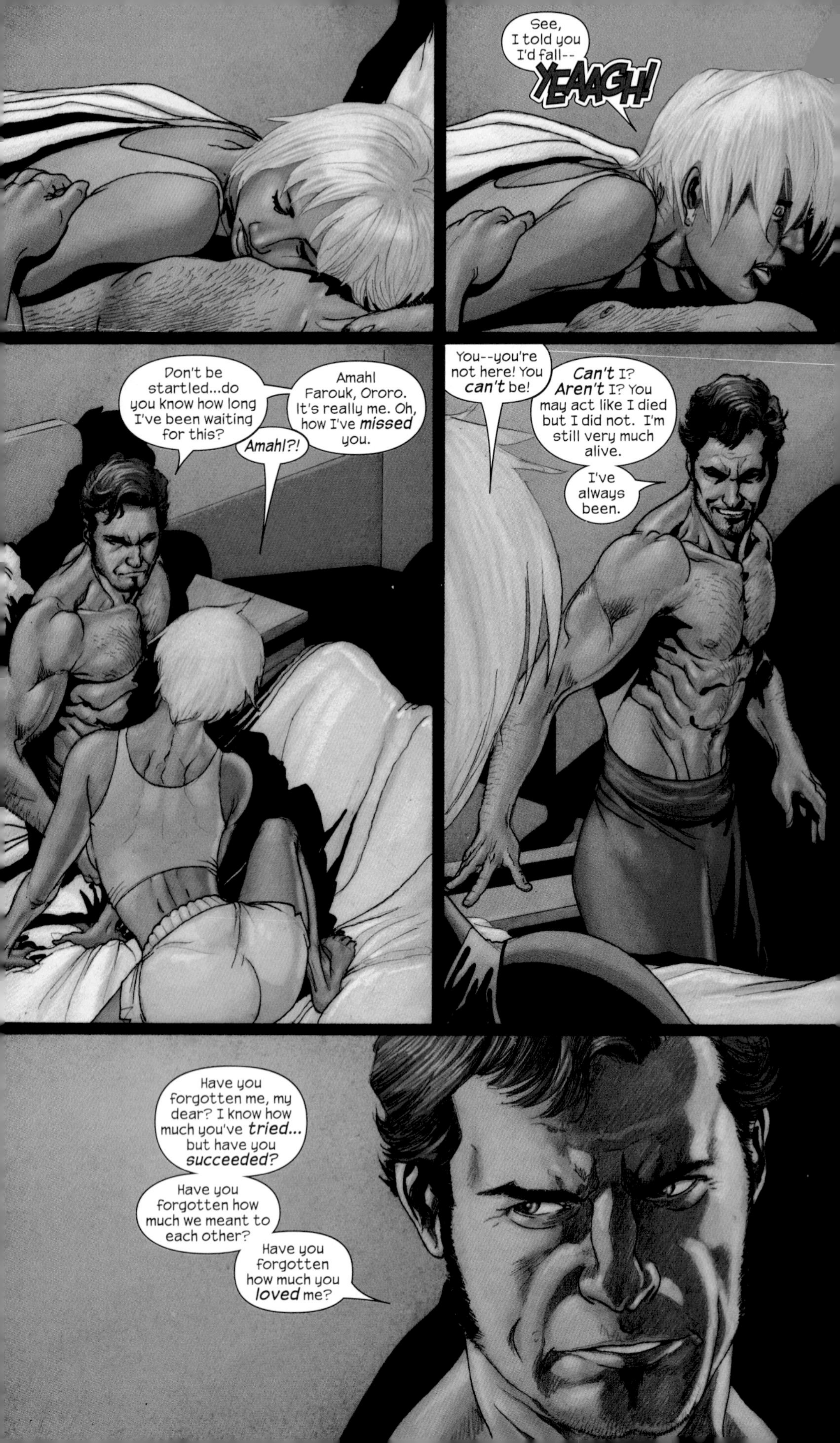
See, I told you I'd fall--
YEAAGH!
Don't be startled...do you know how long I've been waiting for this?
Amahl Farouk, Ororo. It's really me. Oh, how I've missed you.
Amahl?!
You--you're not here! You can't be!
Can't I? Aren't I? You may act like I died but I did not. I'm still very much alive.
I've always been.
Have you forgotten me, my dear? I know how much you've tried... but have you succeeded?
Have you forgotten how much we meant to each other?
Have you forgotten how much you loved me?

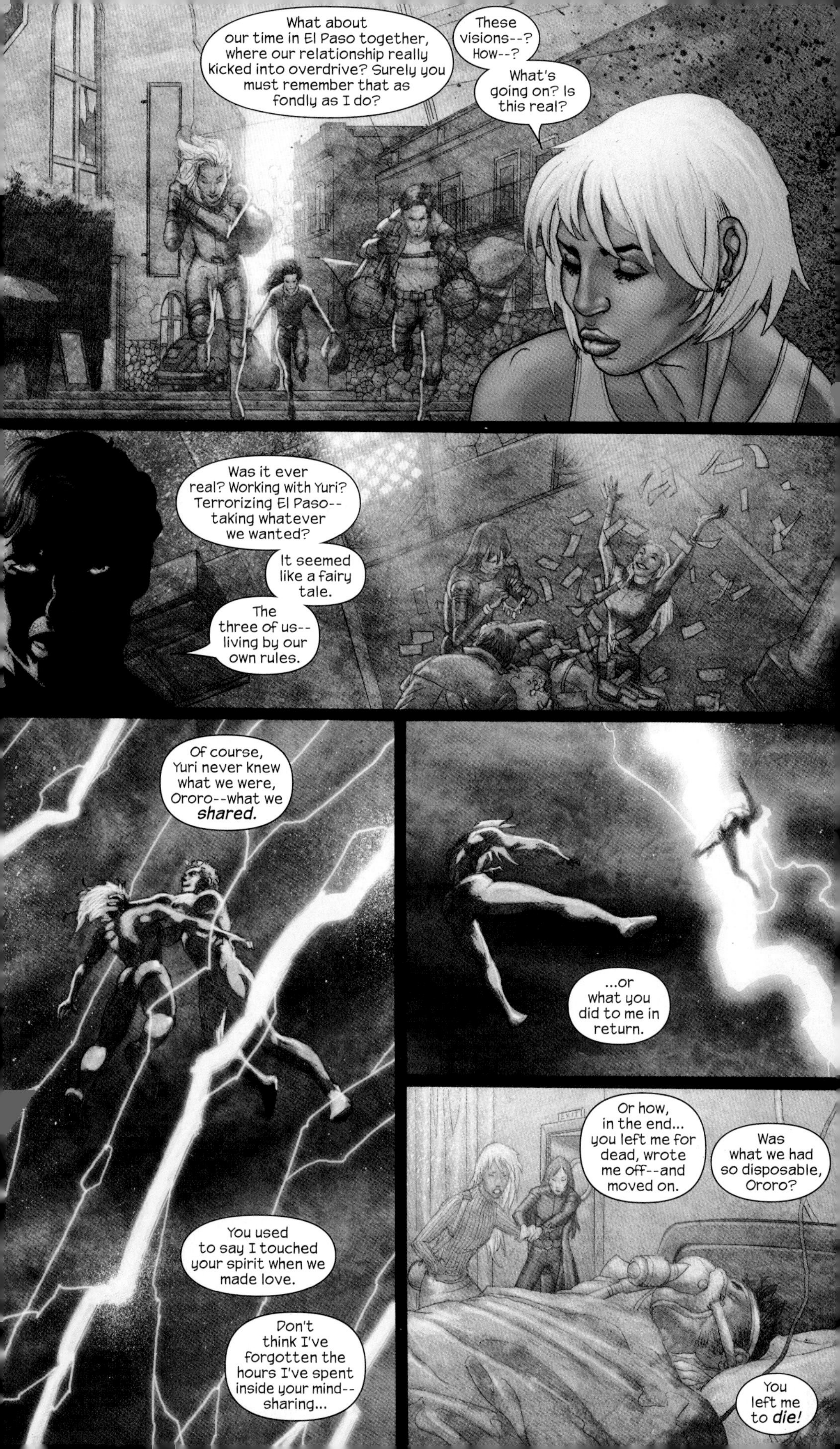
What about our time in El Paso together, where our relationship really kicked into overdrive? Surely you must remember that as fondly as I do?
These visions--? How--?
What's going on? Is this real?
Was it ever real? Working with Yuri? Terrorizing El Paso--taking whatever we wanted?
It seemed like a fairy tale.
The three of us--living by our own rules.
Of course, Yuri never knew what we were, Ororo--what we *shared.*
You used to say I touched your spirit when we made love.
Don't think I've forgotten the hours I've spent inside your mind--sharing...
...or what you did to me in return.
Or how, in the end... you left me for dead, wrote me off--and moved on.
Was what we had so disposable, Ororo?
You left me to *die!*

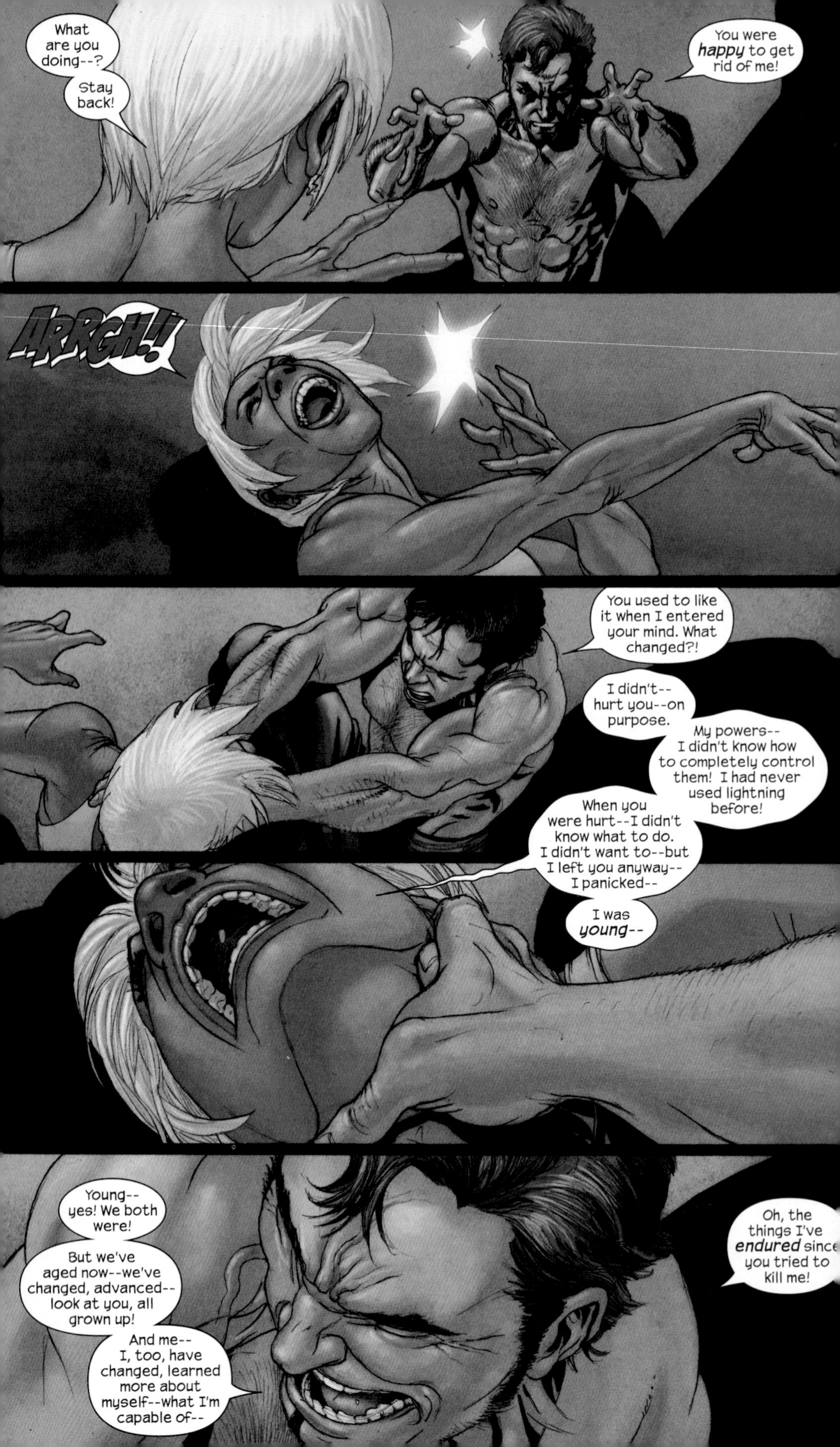
What are you doing--?
Stay back!
You were *happy* to get rid of me!
ARRGH!!
You used to like it when I entered your mind. What changed?!
I didn't--hurt you--on purpose.
My powers--I didn't know how to completely control them! I had never used lightning before!
When you were hurt--I didn't know what to do. I didn't want to--but I left you anyway--I panicked--
I was *young*--
Young--yes! We both were!
But we've aged now--we've changed, advanced--look at you, all grown up!
And me--I, too, have changed, learned more about myself--what I'm capable of--
Oh, the things I've *endured* since you tried to kill me!

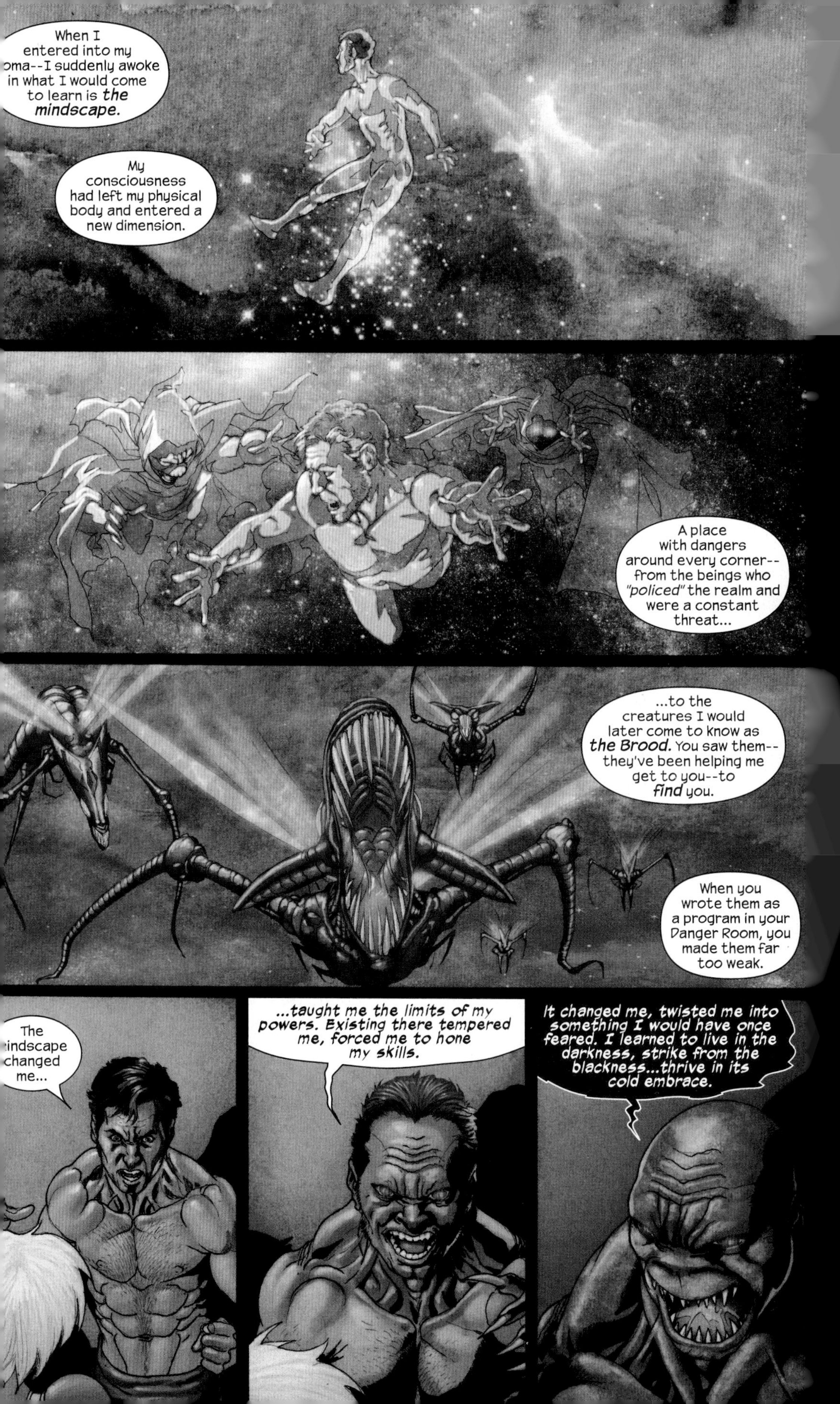
When I entered into my oma--I suddenly awoke in what I would come to learn is *the mindscape.*
My consciousness had left my physical body and entered a new dimension.
A place with dangers around every corner--from the beings who *"policed"* the realm and were a constant threat...
...to the creatures I would later come to know as **the Brood.** You saw them--they've been helping me get to you--to *find* you.
When you wrote them as a program in your Danger Room, you made them far too weak.
The indscape changed me...
...taught me the limits of my powers. Existing there tempered me, forced me to hone my *skills.*
It changed me, twisted me into something I would have once feared. I learned to live in the darkness, strike from the blackness...thrive in its cold embrace.

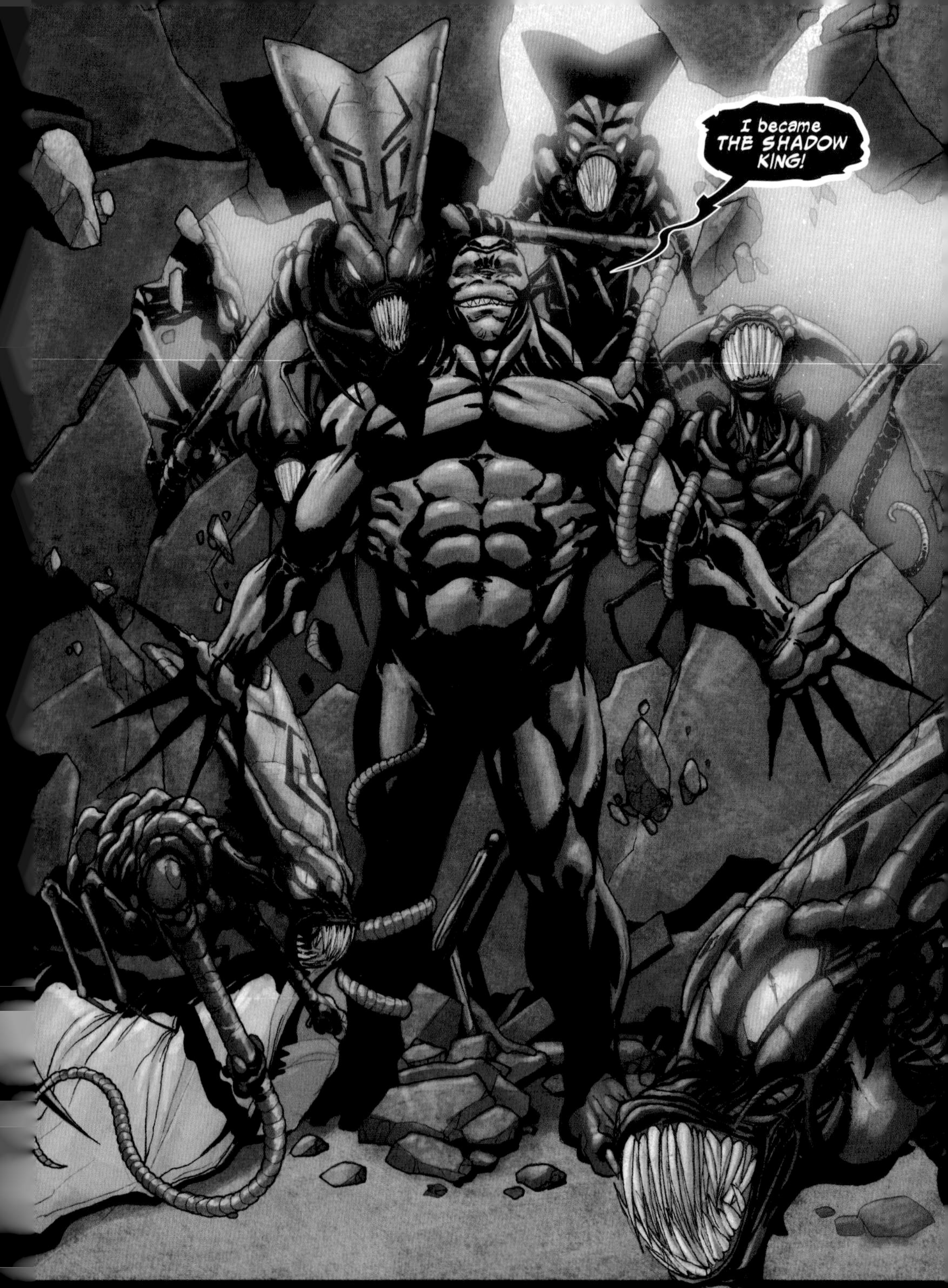
I became THE SHADOW KING!

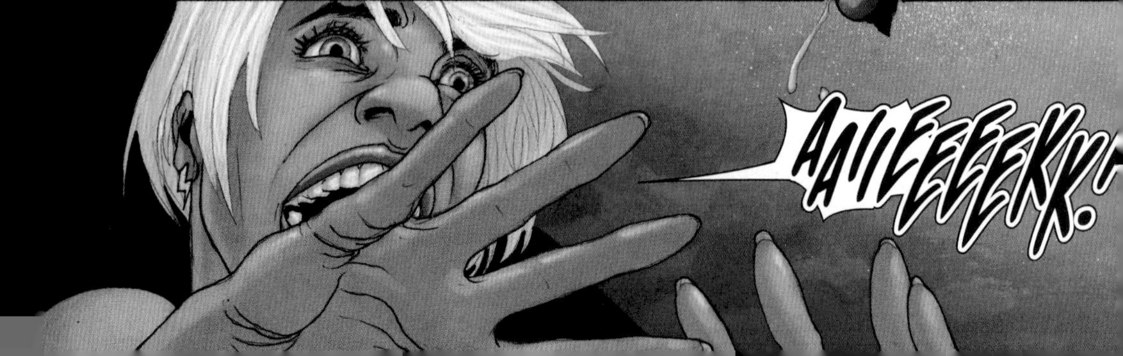
AAIIEEEEKK!

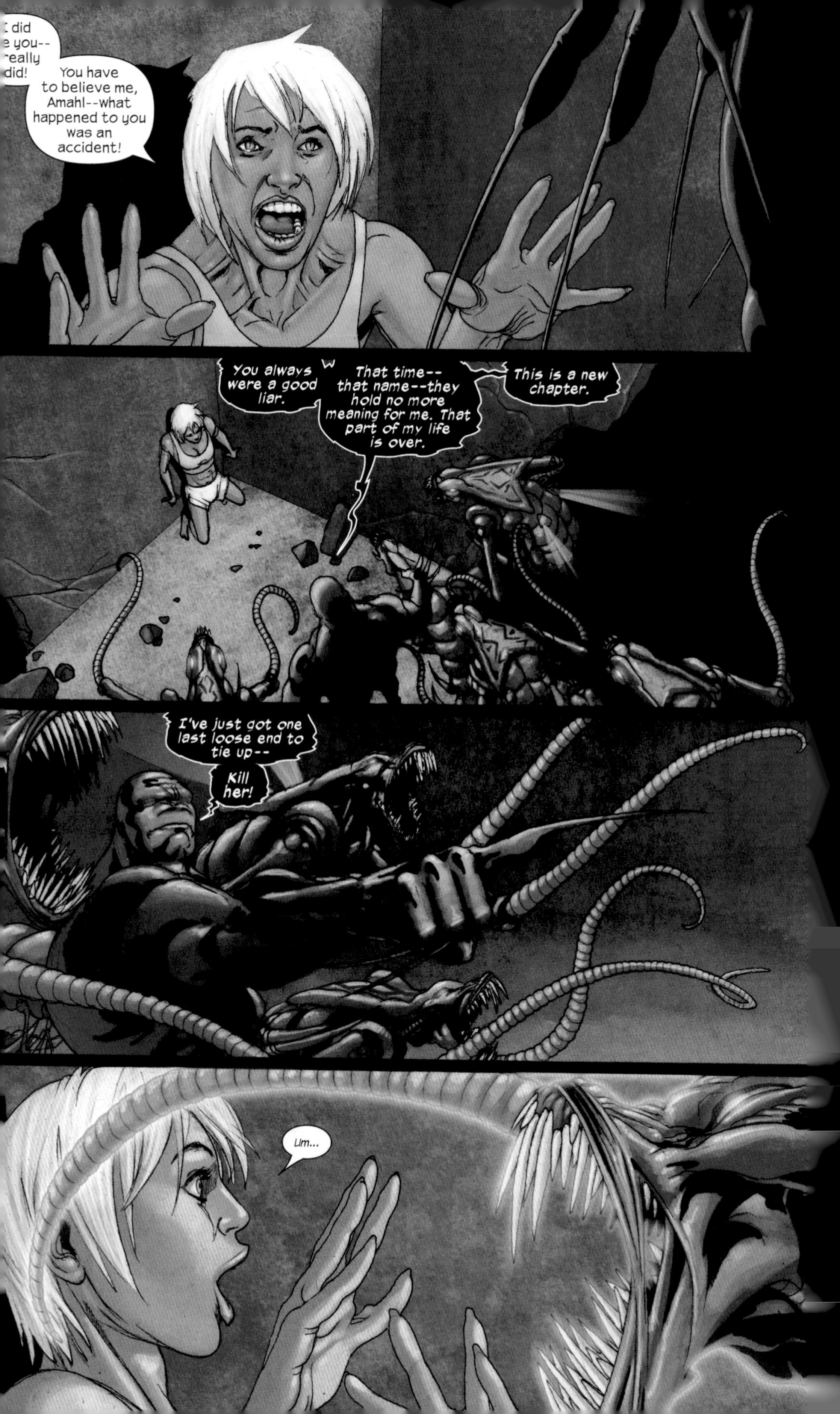
I did
e you--
really
did!
You have to believe me, Amahl--what happened to you was an accident!
You always were a good liar.
That time--that name--they hold no more meaning for me. That part of my life is over.
This is a new chapter.
I've just got one last loose end to tie up--
Kill her!
Um...

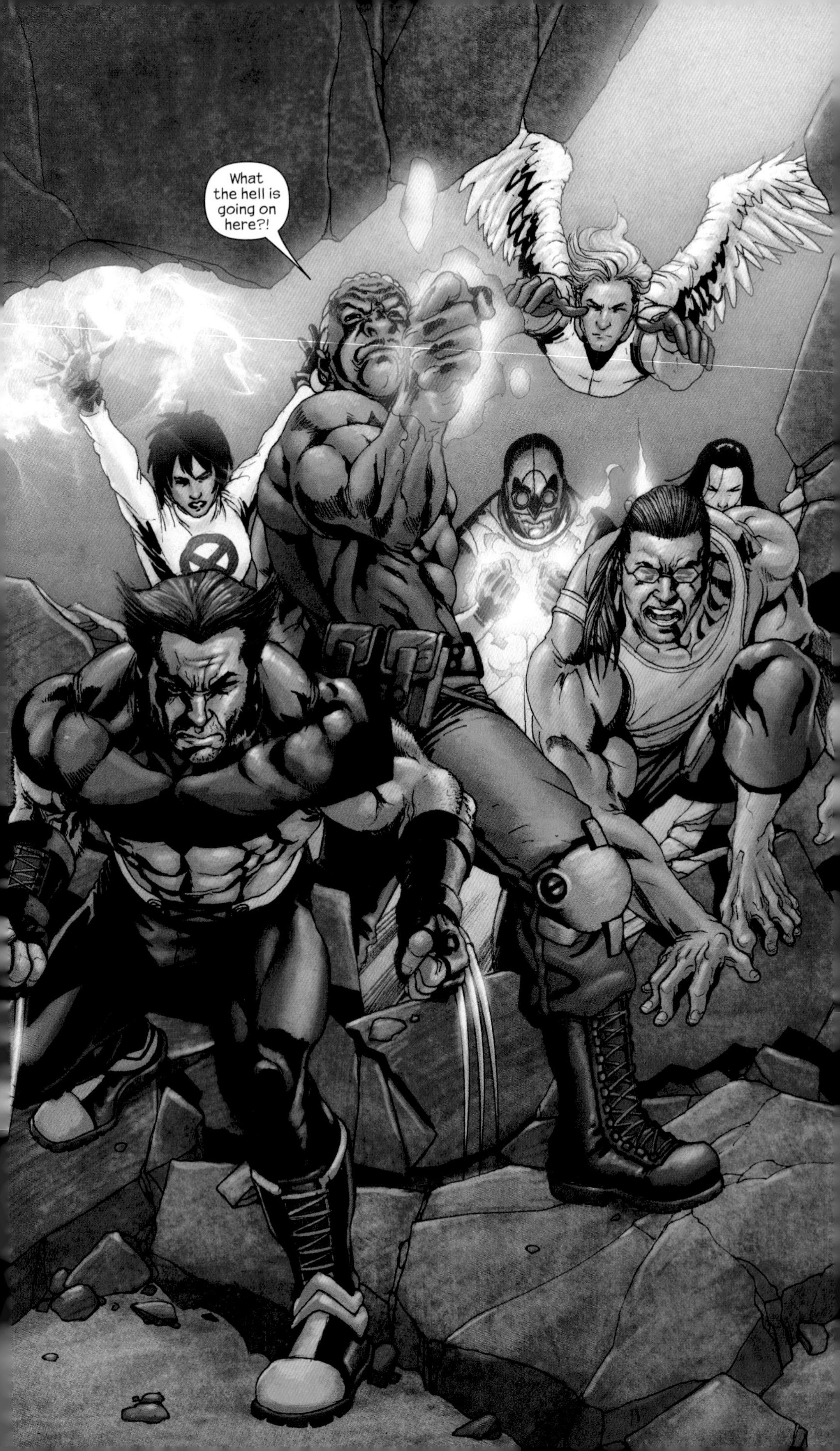
What the hell is going on here?!

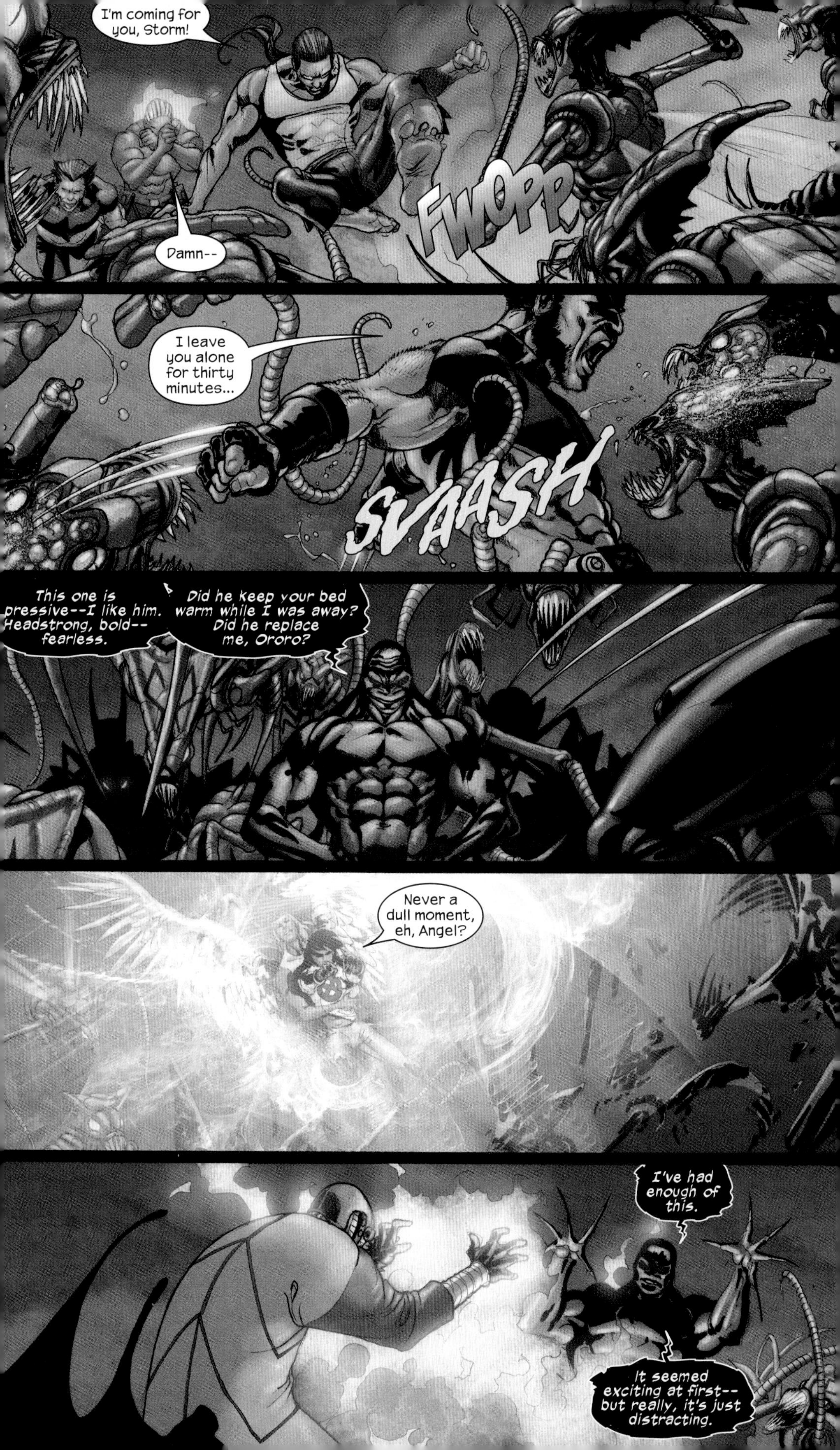

I'm coming for you, Storm!
Damn--
FWOPP
I leave you alone for thirty minutes...
SVAASH
This one is pressive--I like him. Headstrong, bold--fearless.
Did he keep your bed warm while I was away? Did he replace me, Ororo?
Never a dull moment, eh, Angel?
I've had enough of this.
It seemed exciting at first--but really, it's just distracting.

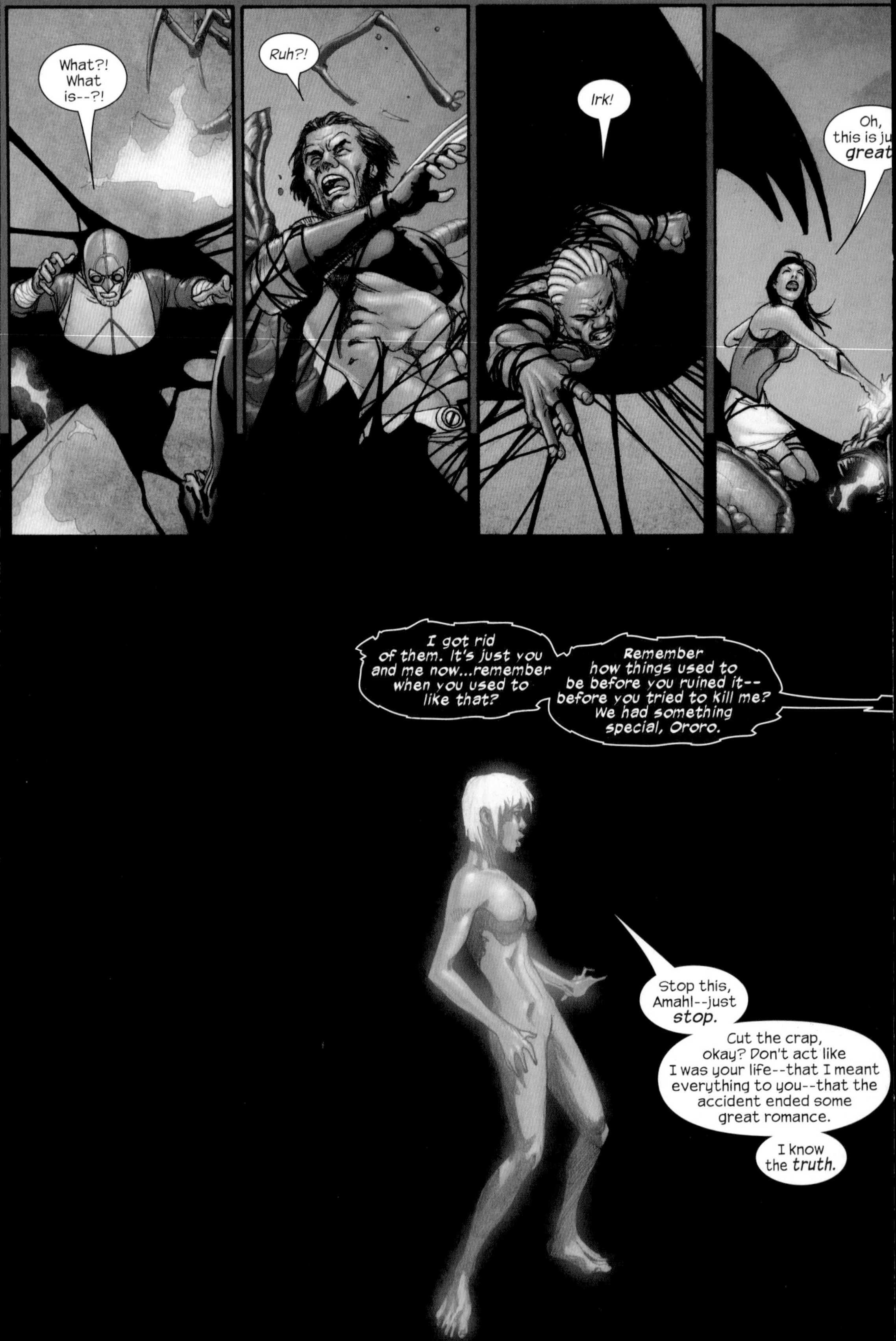
What?! What is--?!
Ruh?!
Irk!
Oh, this is ju great
I got rid of them. It's just you and me now...remember when you used to like that?
Remember how things used to be before you ruined it--before you tried to kill me? We had something special, Ororo.
Stop this, Amahl--just stop.
Cut the crap, okay? Don't act like I was your life--that I meant everything to you--that the accident ended some great romance.
I know the truth.

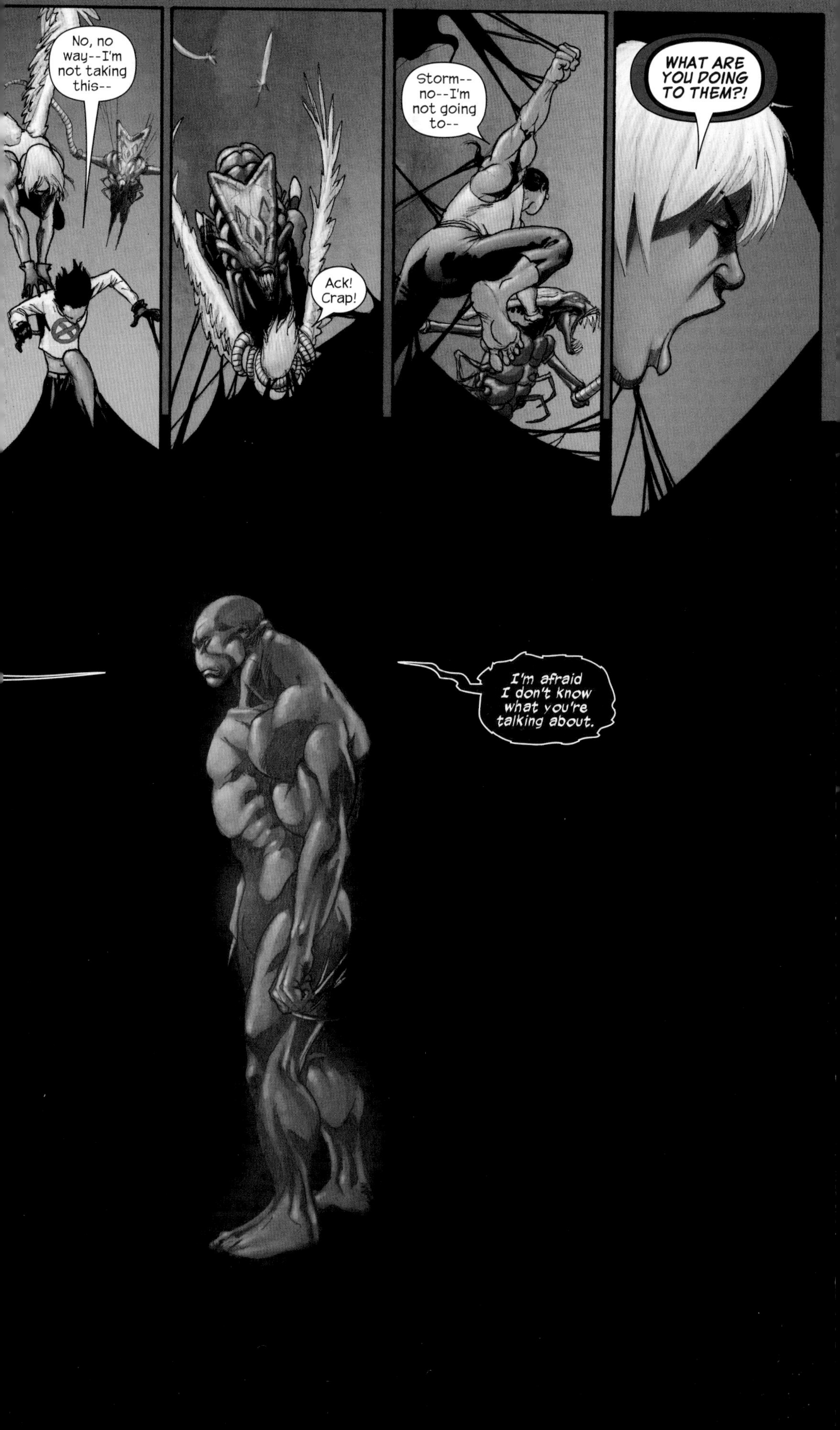

No, no way--I'm not taking this--
Ack! Crap!
Storm-- no--I'm not going to--
WHAT ARE YOU DOING TO THEM?!
I'm afraid I don't know what you're talking about.

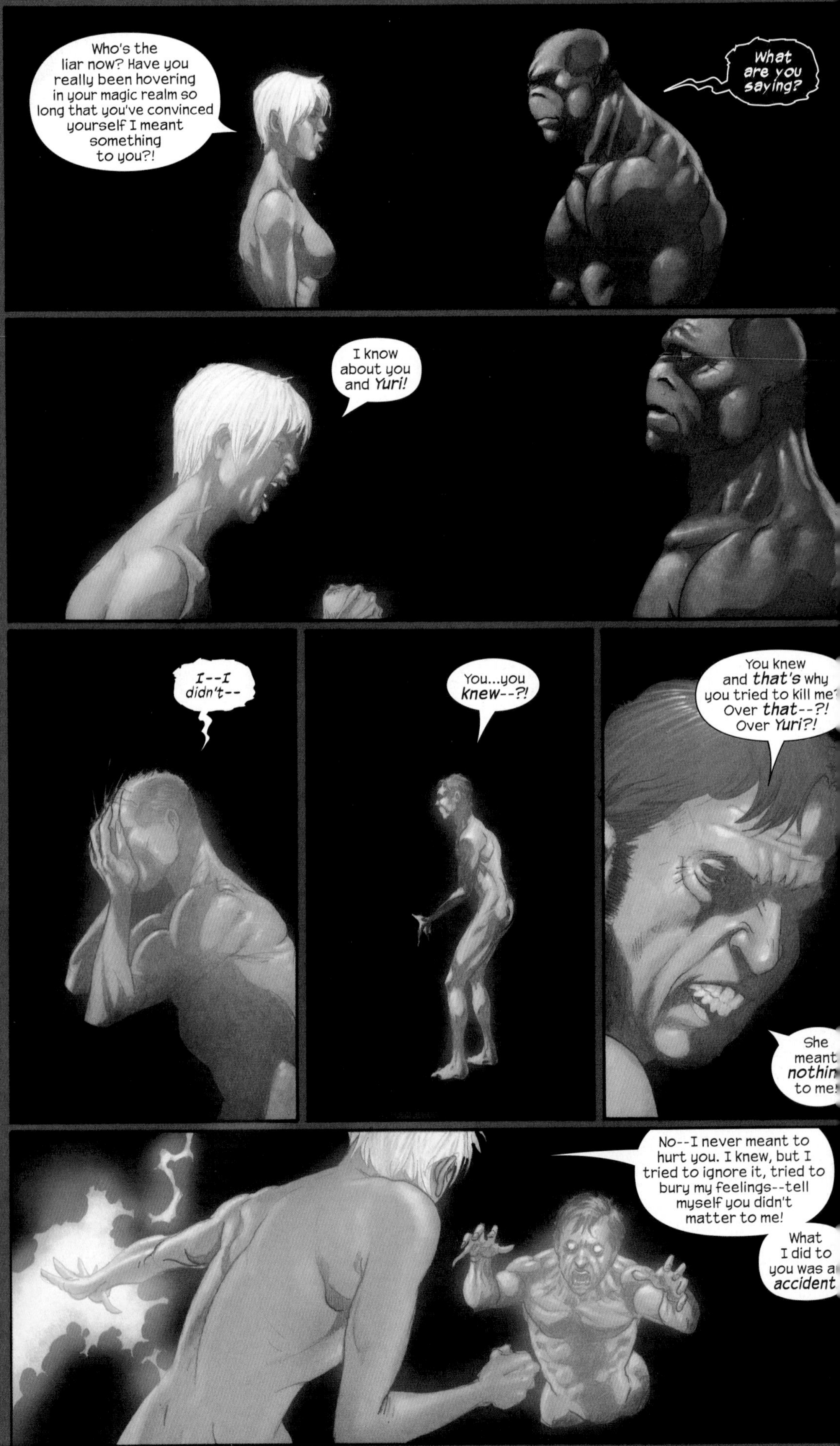
Who's the liar now? Have you really been hovering in your magic realm so long that you've convinced yourself I meant something to you?!
What are you saying?
I know about you and Yuri!
I--I didn't--
You...you knew--?!
You knew and that's why you tried to kill me? Over that--?! Over Yuri?!
She meant nothin to me!
No--I never meant to hurt you. I knew, but I tried to ignore it, tried to bury my feelings--tell myself you didn't matter to me!
What I did to you was a accident

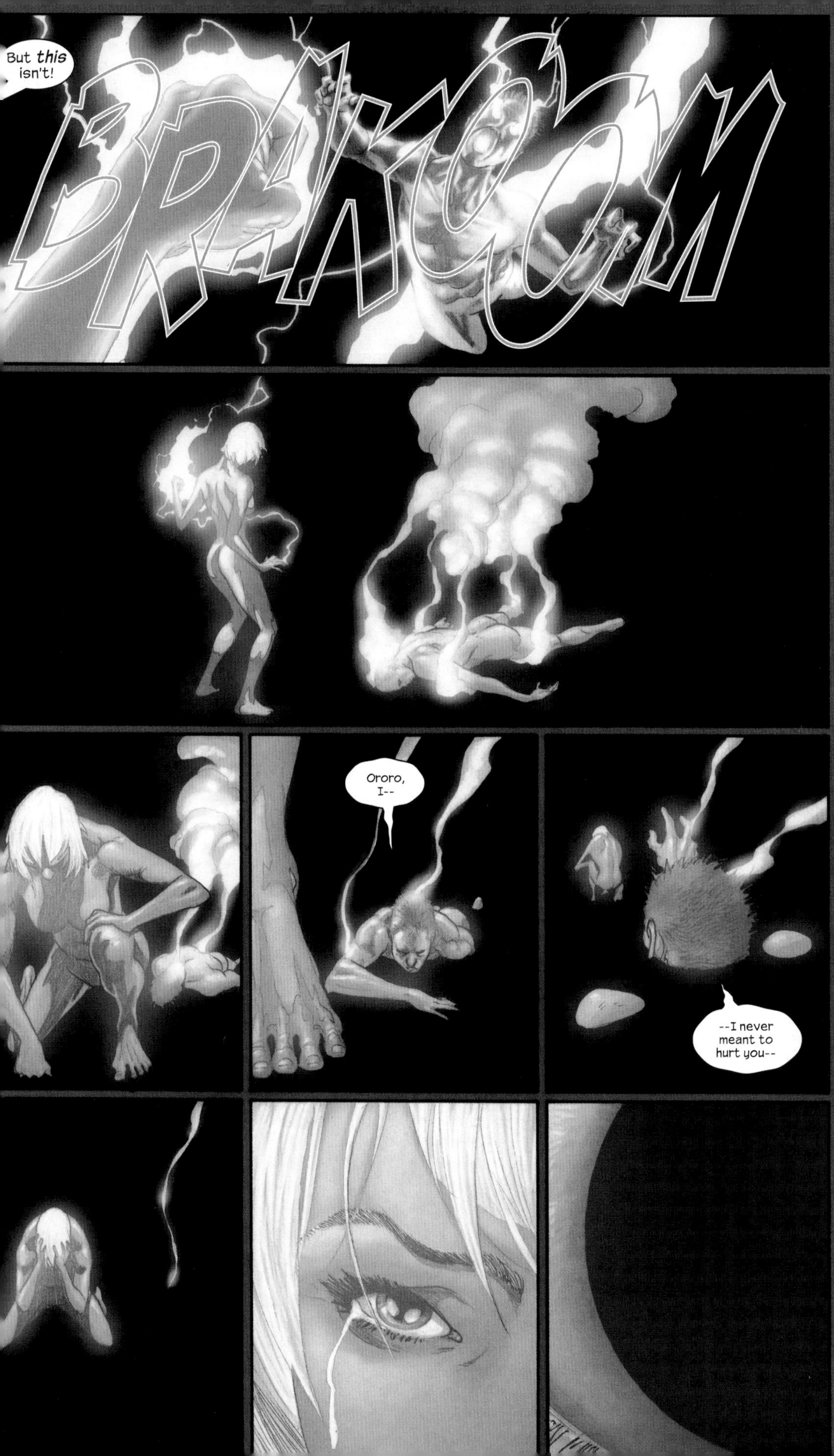
But *this* isn't!
BRAKOOM
Ororo, I--
--I never meant to hurt you--

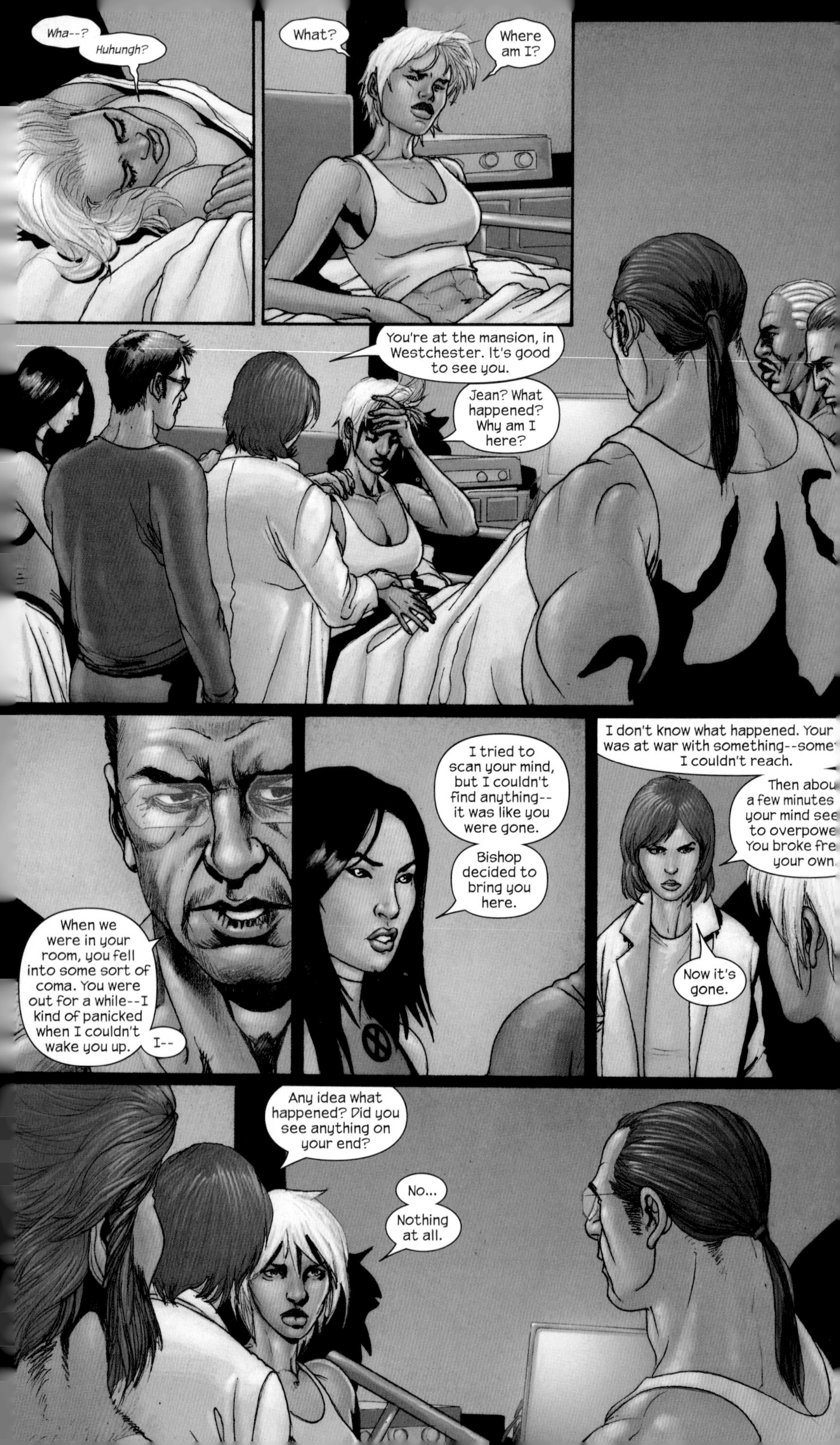

Wha--?
Huhungh?
What?
Where am I?
You're at the mansion, in Westchester. It's good to see you.
Jean? What happened? Why am I here?
When we were in your room, you fell into some sort of coma. You were out for a while--I kind of panicked when I couldn't wake you up.
I--
I tried to scan your mind, but I couldn't find anything--it was like you were gone.
Bishop decided to bring you here.
Now it's gone.
Any idea what happened? Did you see anything on your end?
No...
Nothing at all.

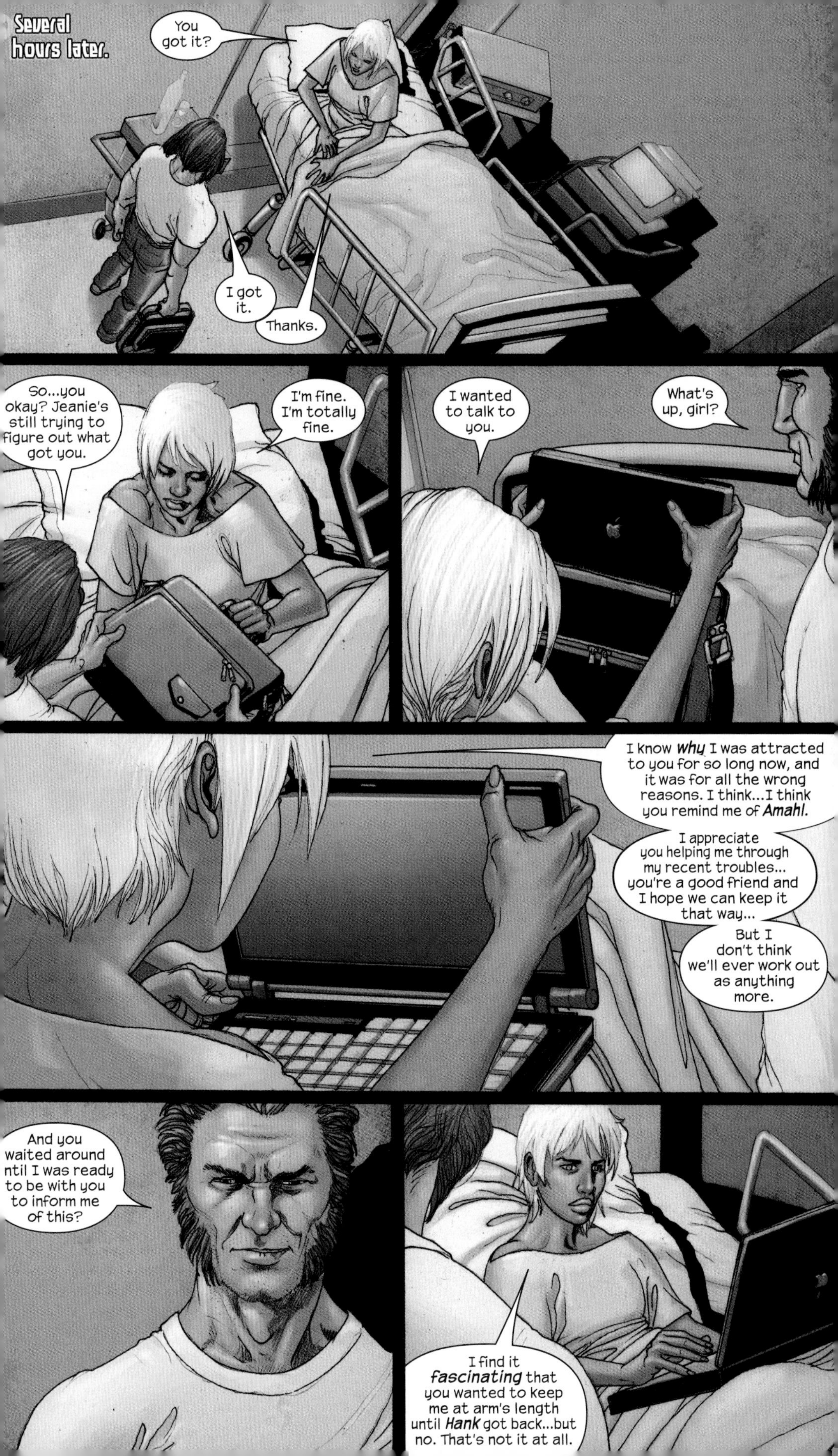
Several hours later.
You got it?
I got it.
Thanks.
So...you okay? Jeanie's still trying to figure out what got you.
I'm fine. I'm totally fine.
I wanted to talk to you.
What's up, girl?
I know *why* I was attracted to you for so long now, and it was for all the wrong reasons. I think...I think you remind me of *Amahl.*
I appreciate you helping me through my recent troubles... you're a good friend and I hope we can keep it that way...
But I don't think we'll ever work out as anything more.
And you waited around ntil I was ready to be with you to inform me of this?
I find it *fascinating* that you wanted to keep me at arm's length until *Hank* got back...but no. That's not it at all.

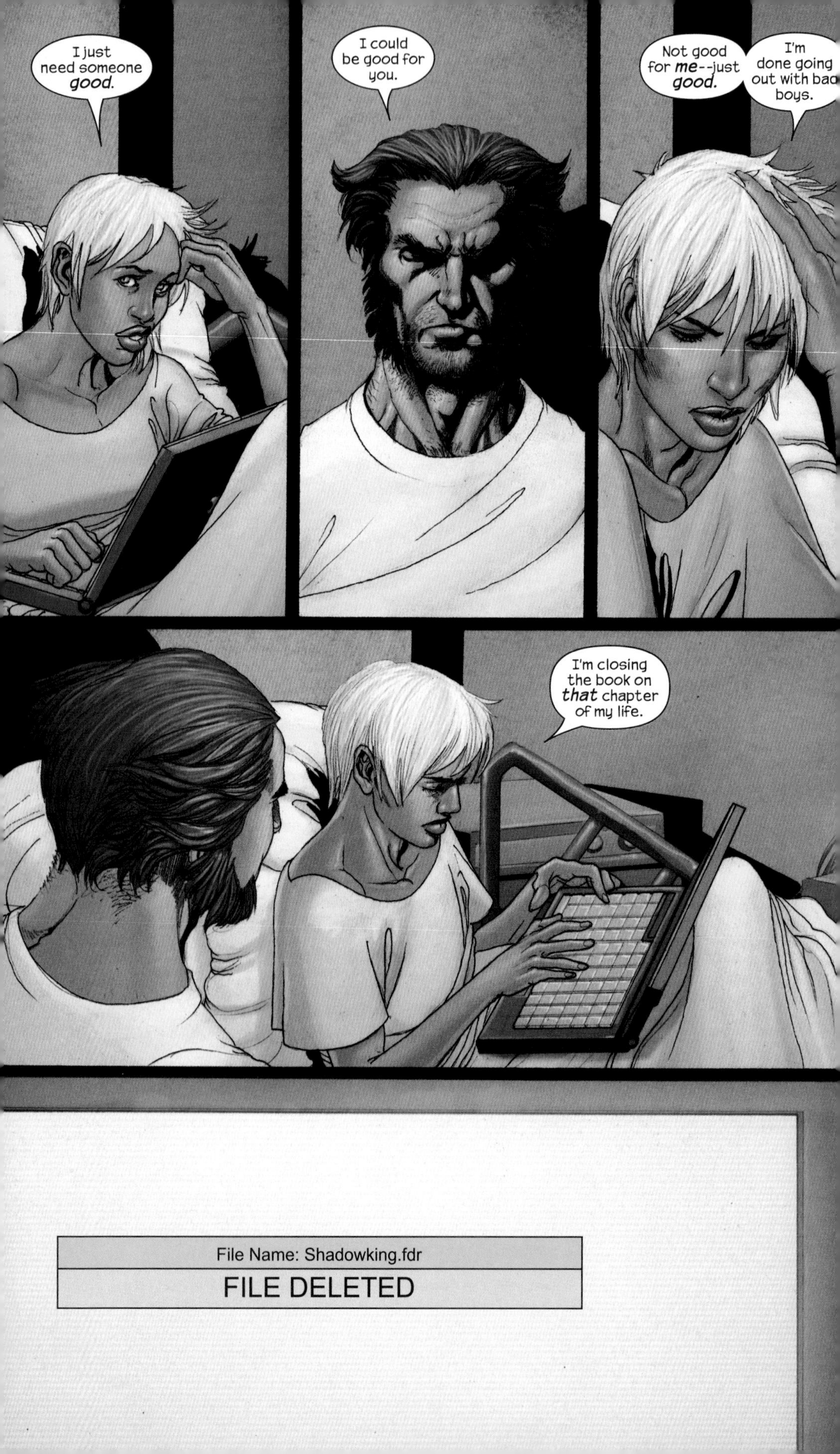
I just need someone *good*.
I could be good for you.
Not good for *me*--just *good*.
I'm done going out with bad boys.
I'm closing the book on *that* chapter of my life.
File Name: Shadowking.fdr
FILE DELETED

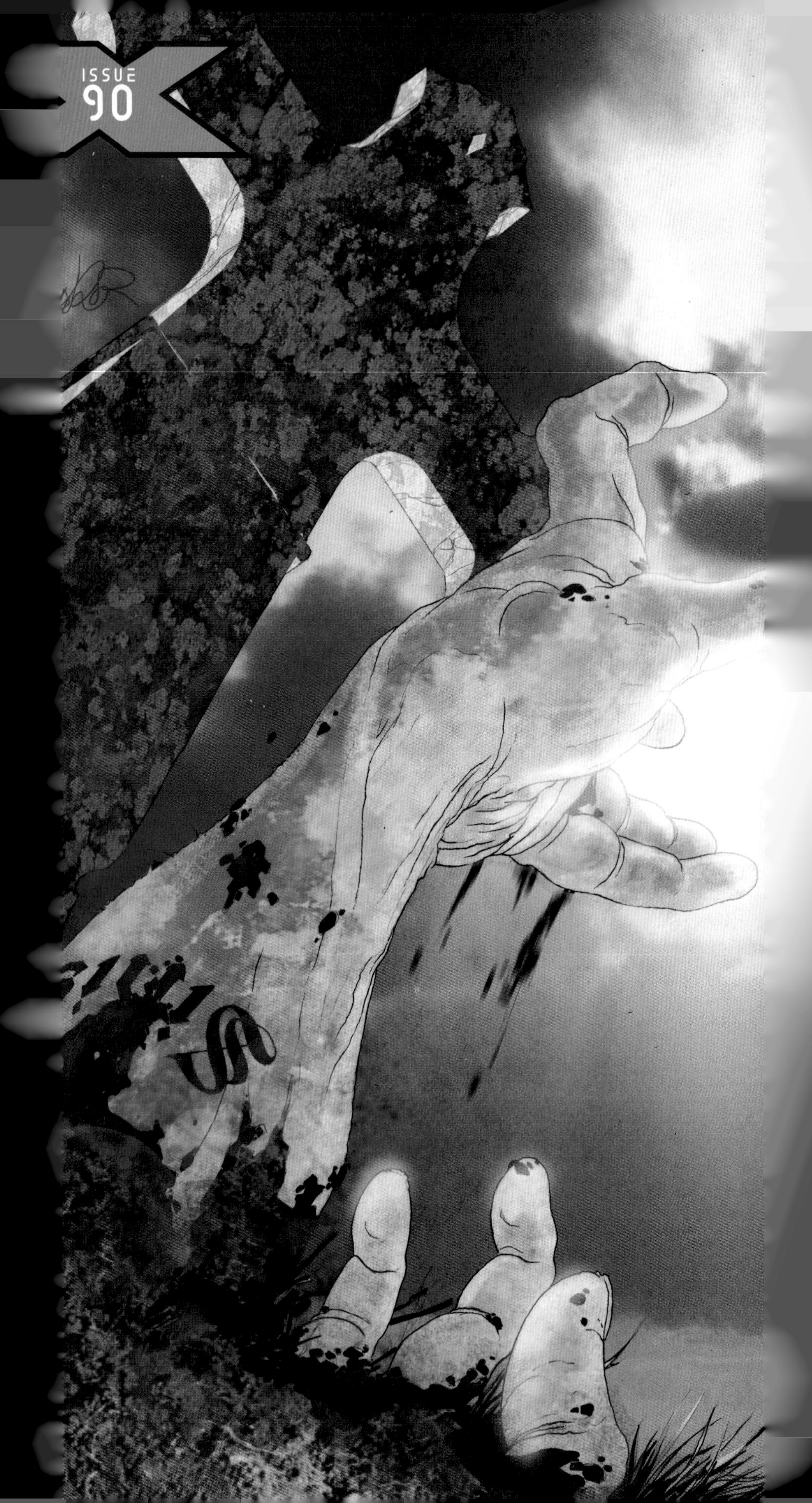
ISSUE
90

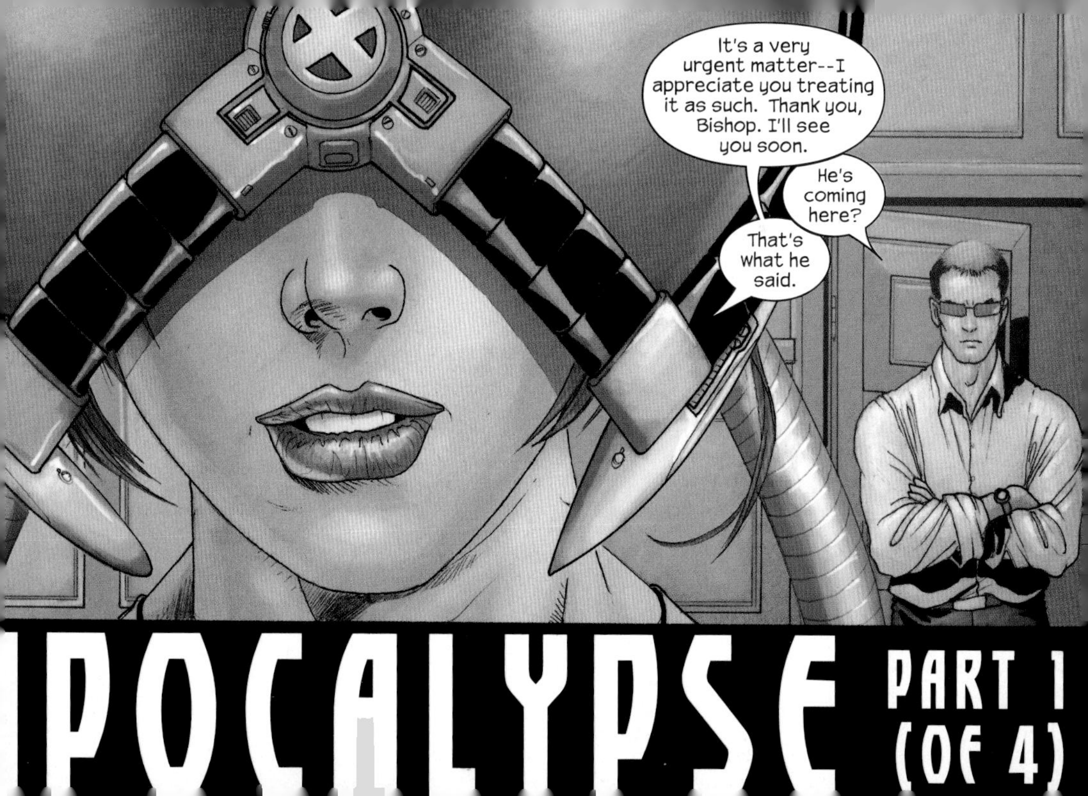
It's a very urgent matter--I appreciate you treating it as such. Thank you, Bishop. I'll see you soon.
He's coming here?
That's what he said.
POCALYPSE PART 1 (OF 4)

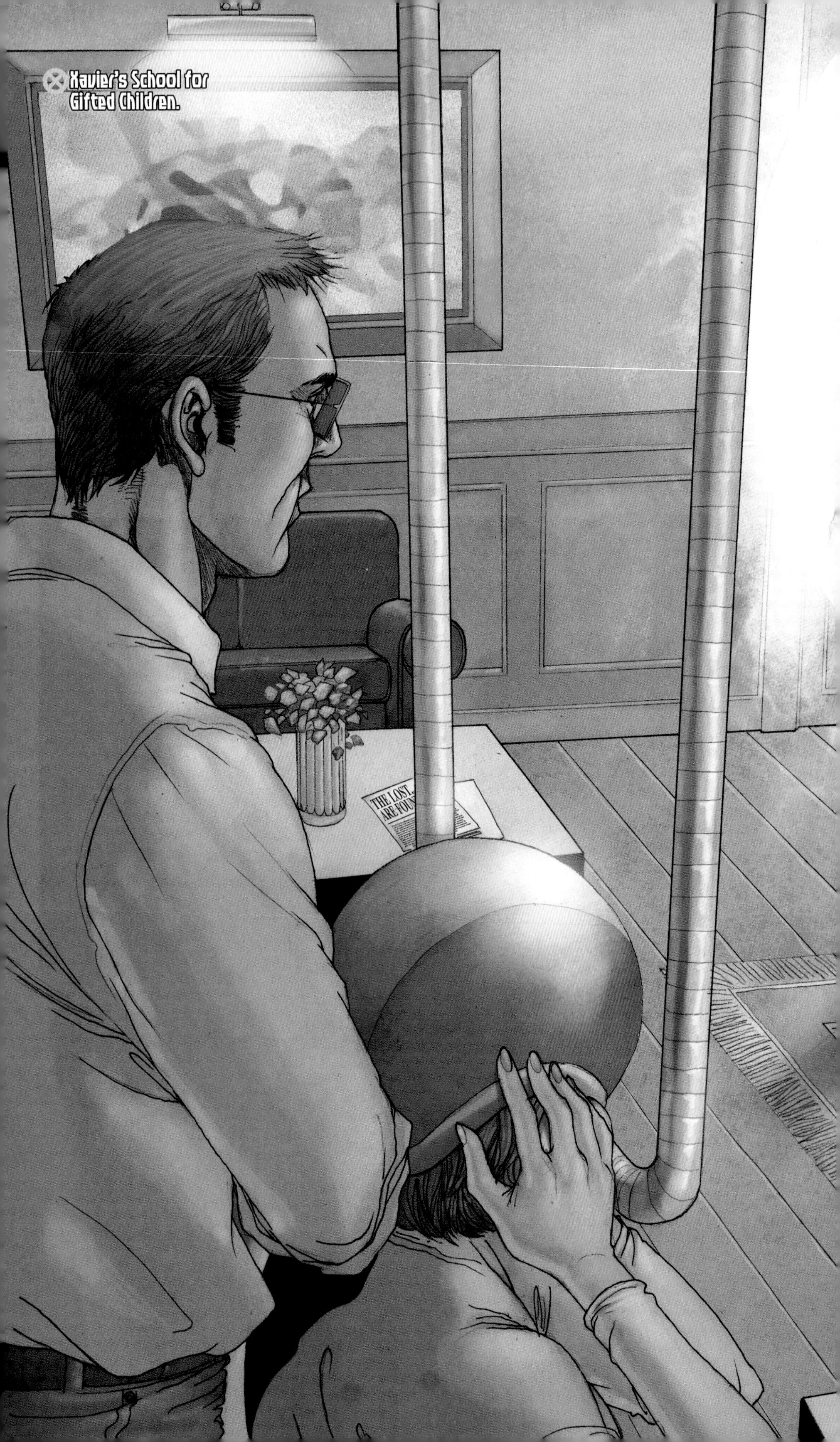
Xavier's School for Gifted Children.
THE LOST... ARE FOUND

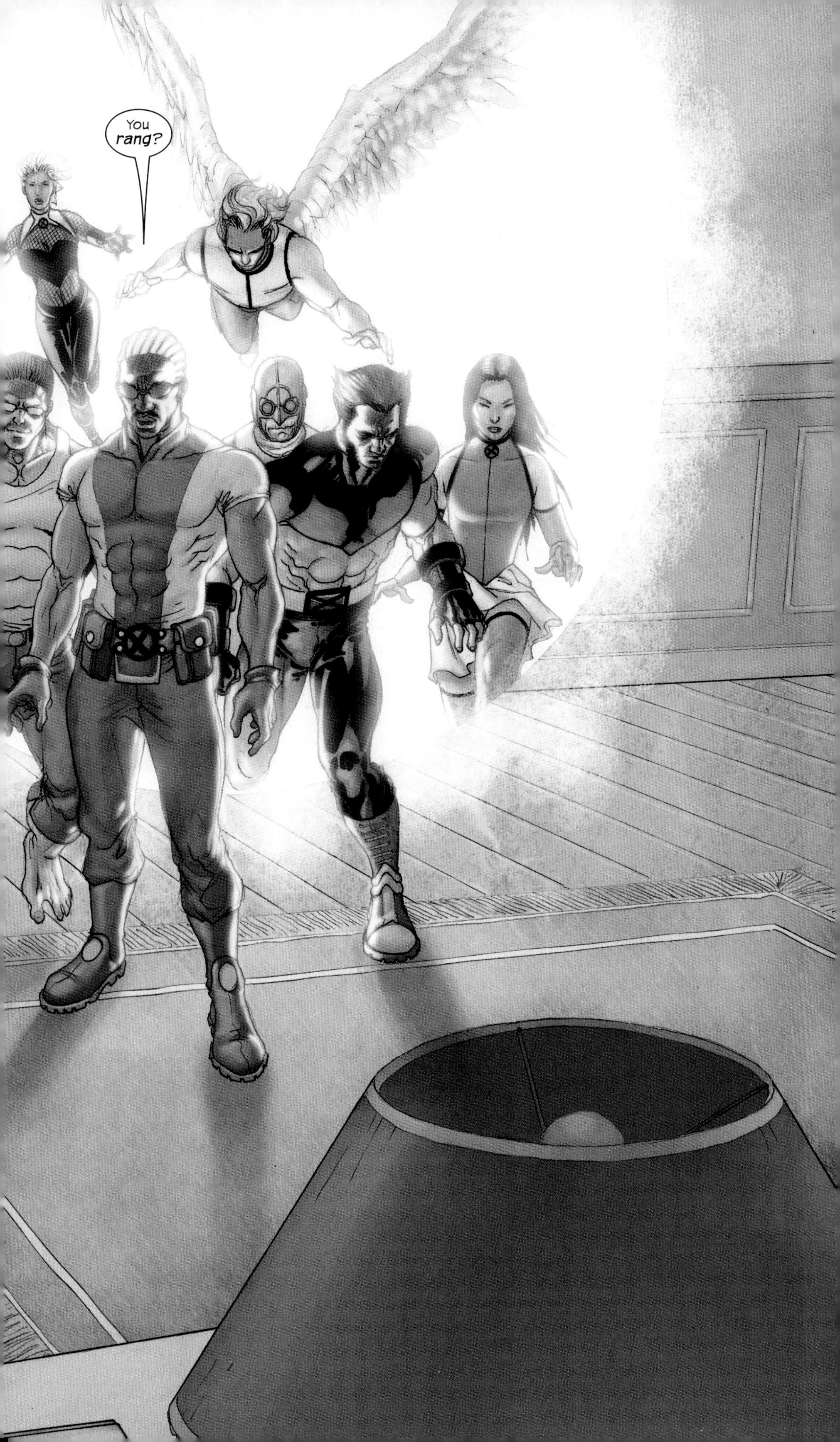
You rang?

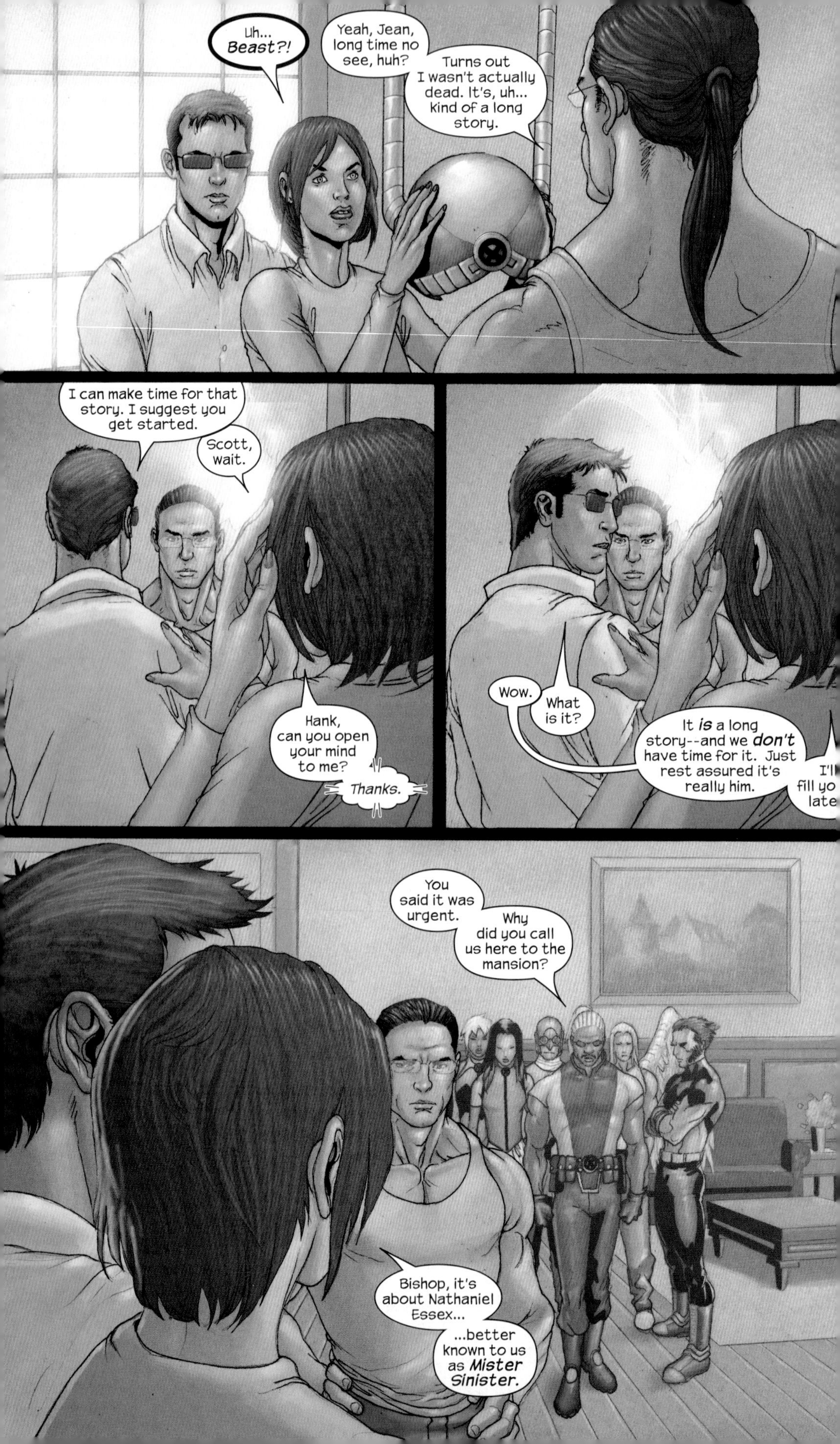
Uh... *Beast?!*
Yeah, Jean, long time no see, huh?
Turns out I wasn't actually dead. It's, uh... kind of a long story.
I can make time for that story. I suggest you get started.
Scott, wait.
Hank, can you open your mind to me?
Thanks.
Wow.
What is it?
It *is* a long story--and we *don't* have time for it. Just rest assured it's really him.
You said it was urgent.
Why did you call us here to the mansion?
Bishop, it's about Nathaniel Essex...
...better known to us as *Mister Sinister.*

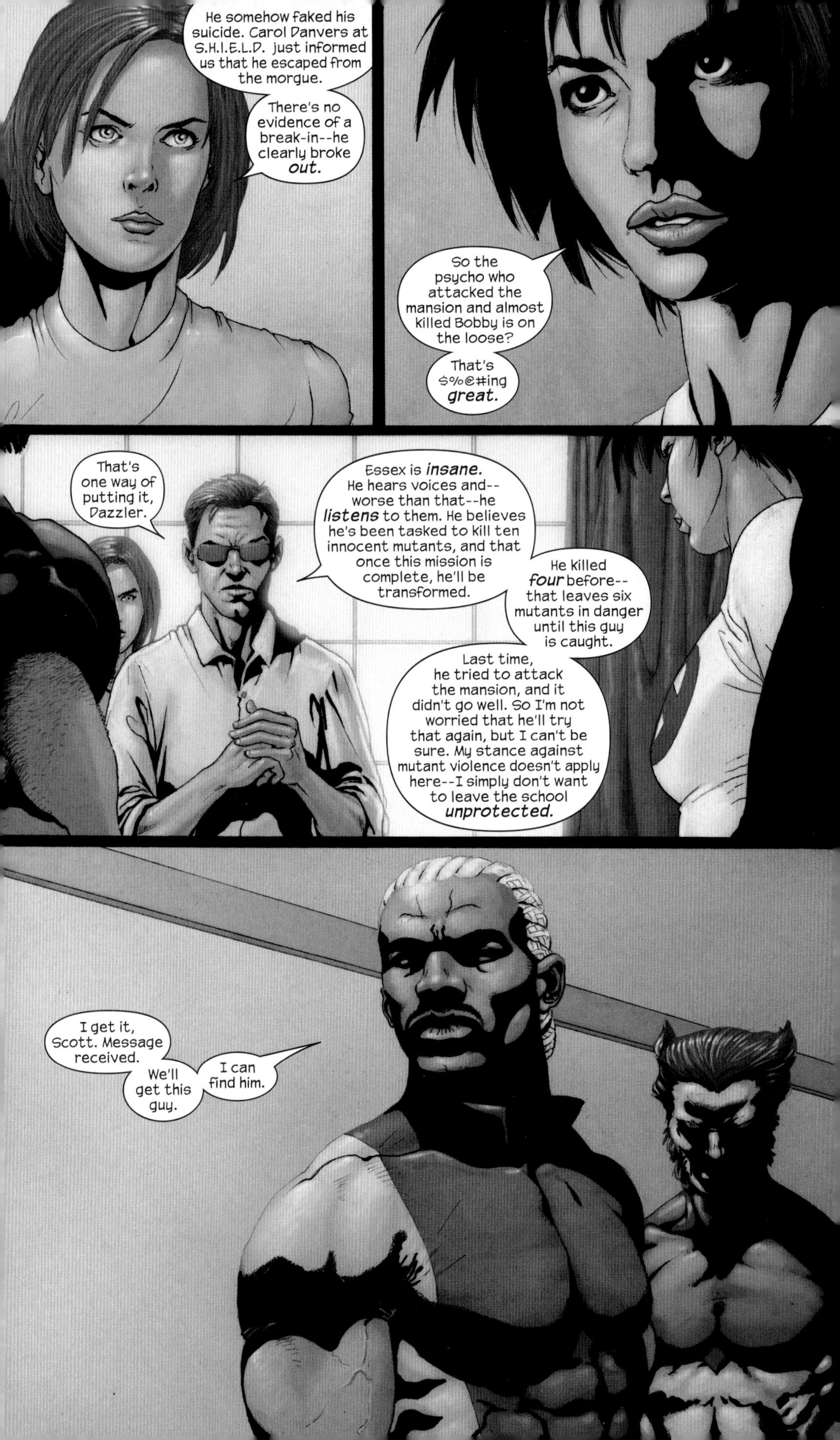
He somehow faked his suicide. Carol Danvers at S.H.I.E.L.D. just informed us that he escaped from the morgue.
There's no evidence of a break-in--he clearly broke out.
So the psycho who attacked the mansion and almost killed Bobby is on the loose?
That's $%@#ing great.
That's one way of putting it, Dazzler.
Essex is insane. He hears voices and--worse than that--he listens to them. He believes he's been tasked to kill ten innocent mutants, and that once this mission is complete, he'll be transformed.
He killed four before--that leaves six mutants in danger until this guy is caught.
Last time, he tried to attack the mansion, and it didn't go well. So I'm not worried that he'll try that again, but I can't be sure. My stance against mutant violence doesn't apply here--I simply don't want to leave the school unprotected.
I get it, Scott. Message received.
We'll get this guy.
I can find him.

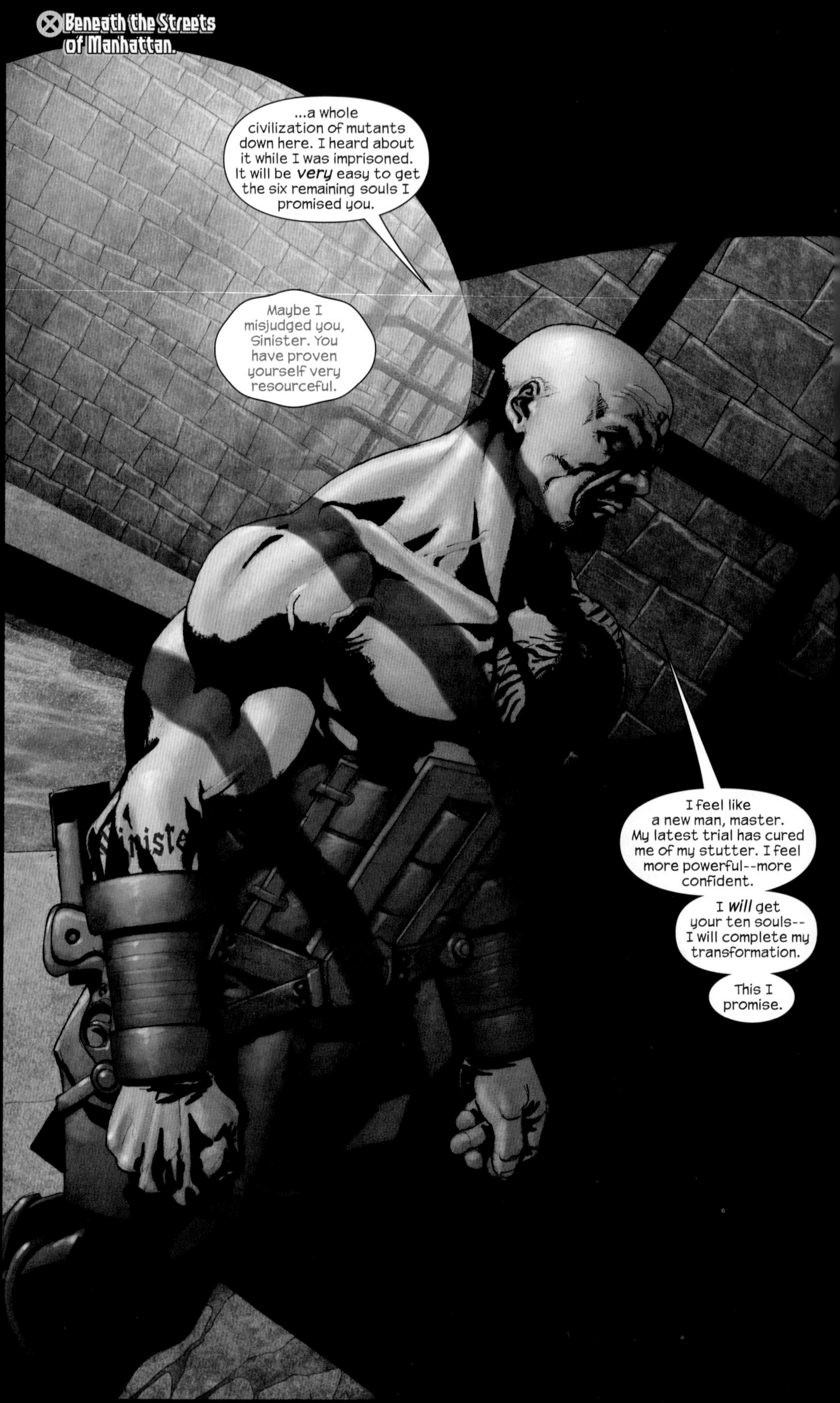
Beneath the Streets of Manhattan.
...a whole civilization of mutants down here. I heard about it while I was imprisoned. It will be *very* easy to get the six remaining souls I promised you.
Maybe I misjudged you, Sinister. You have proven yourself very resourceful.
I feel like a new man, master. My latest trial has cured me of my stutter. I feel more powerful--more confident.
I *will* get your ten souls-- I will complete my transformation.
This I promise.

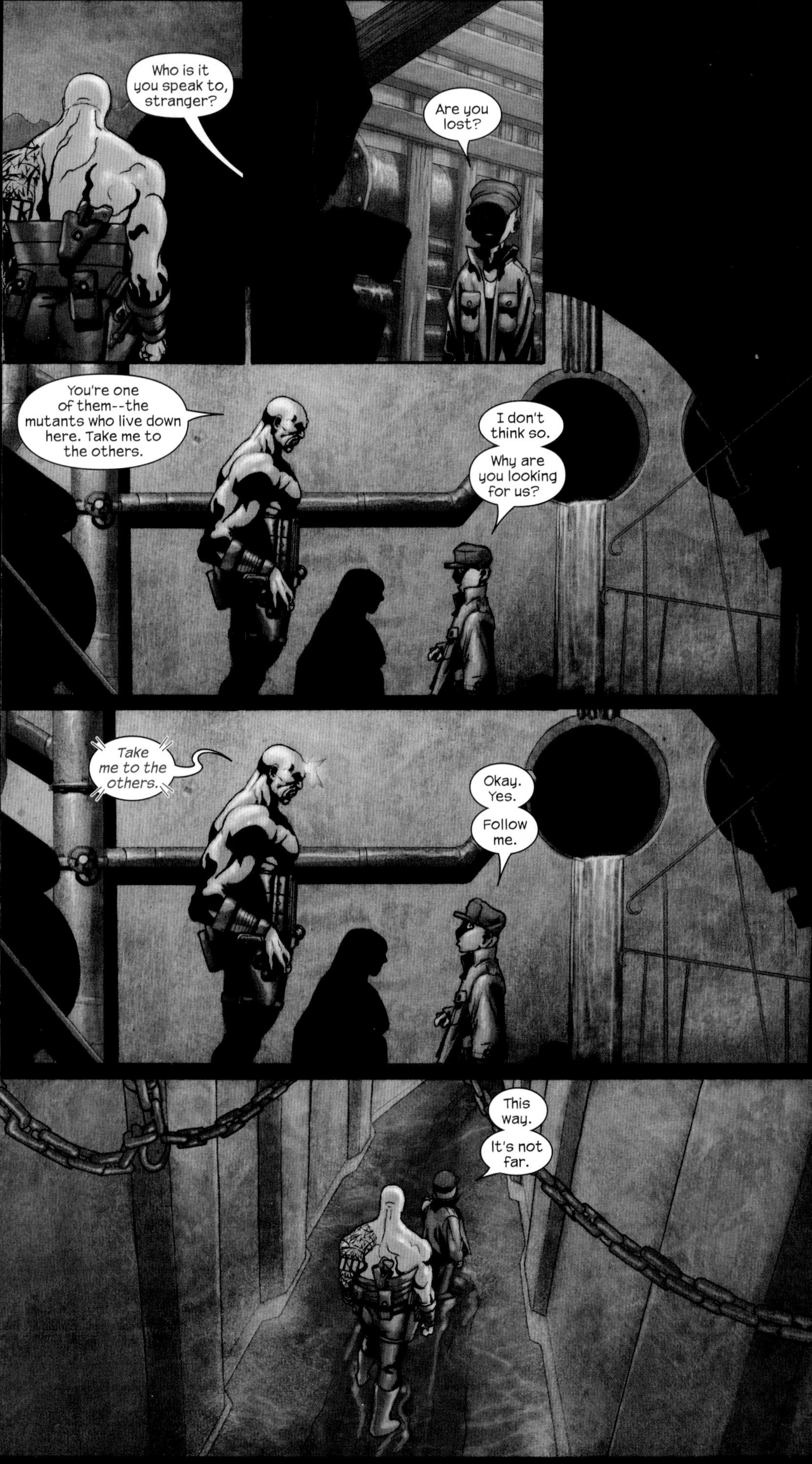
Who is it you speak to, stranger?
Are you lost?
You're one of them--the mutants who live down here. Take me to the others.
I don't think so.
Why are you looking for us?
Take me to the others.
Okay. Yes.
Follow me.
This way.
It's not far.

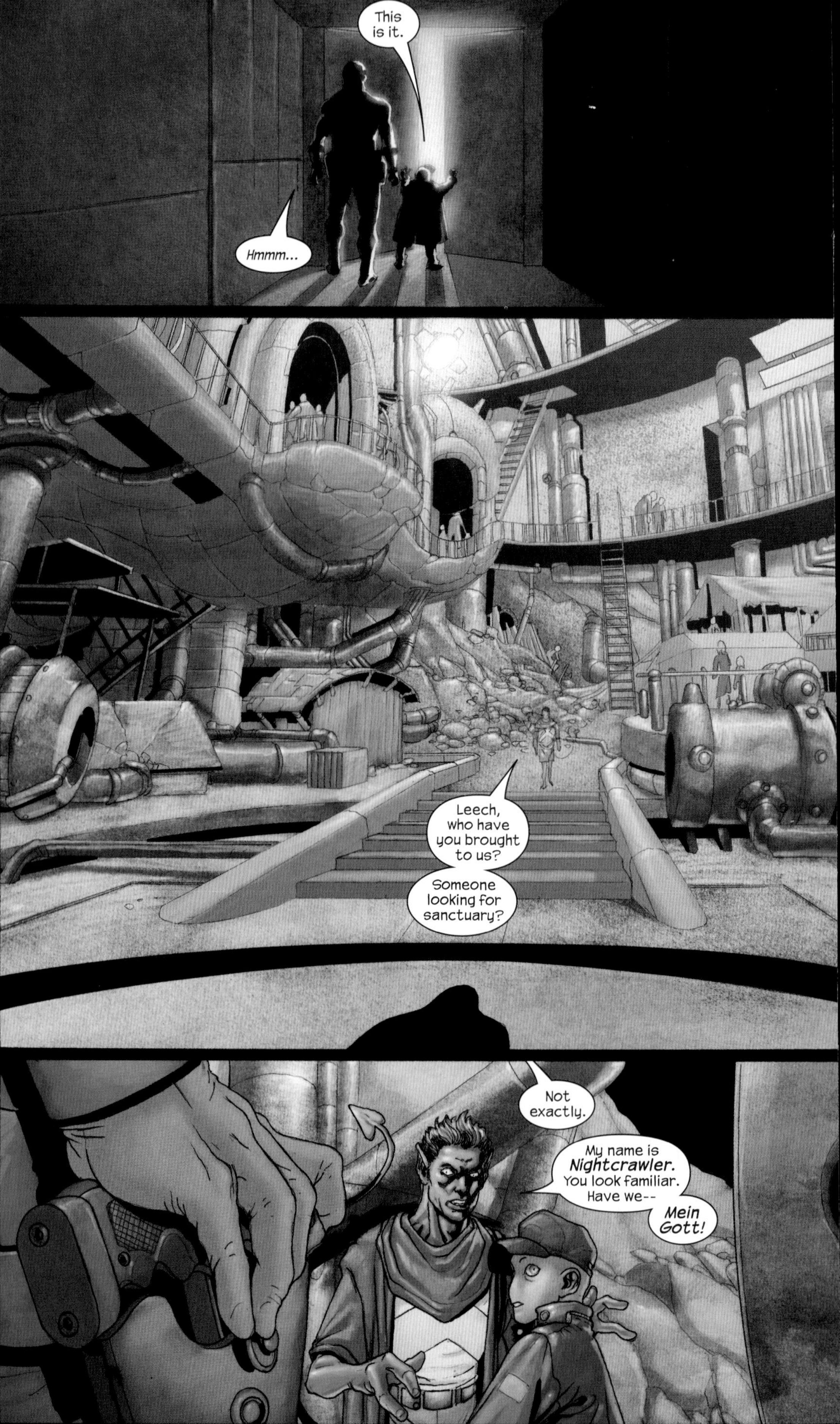
This is it.
Hmmm...
Leech, who have you brought to us?
Someone looking for sanctuary?
Not exactly.
My name is *Nightcrawler.* You look familiar. Have we--
Mein Gott!

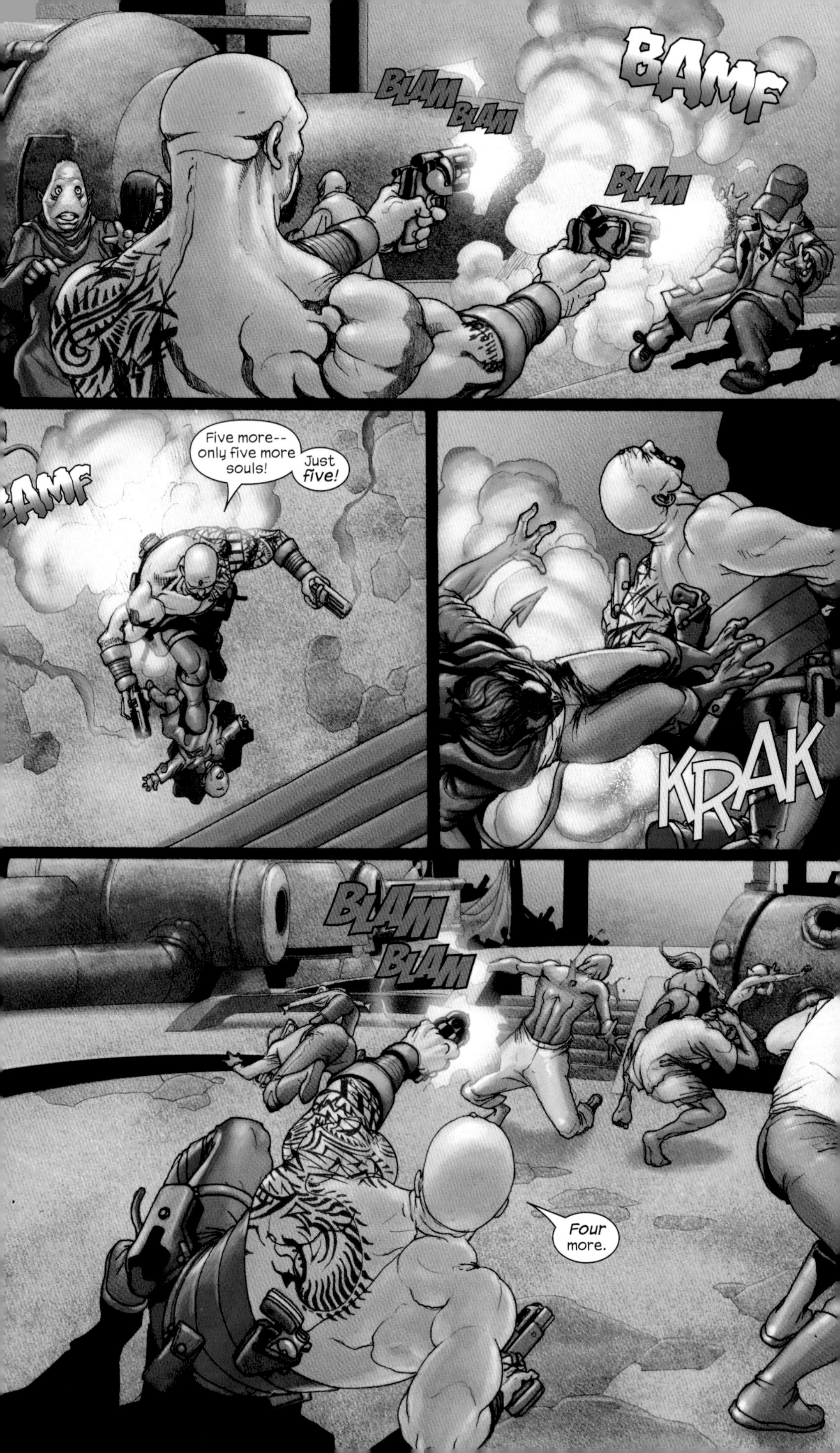
BLAM BLAM
BAMF
BLAM
BAMF
Five more-- only five more souls!
Just five!
KRAK
BLAM BLAM
Four more.

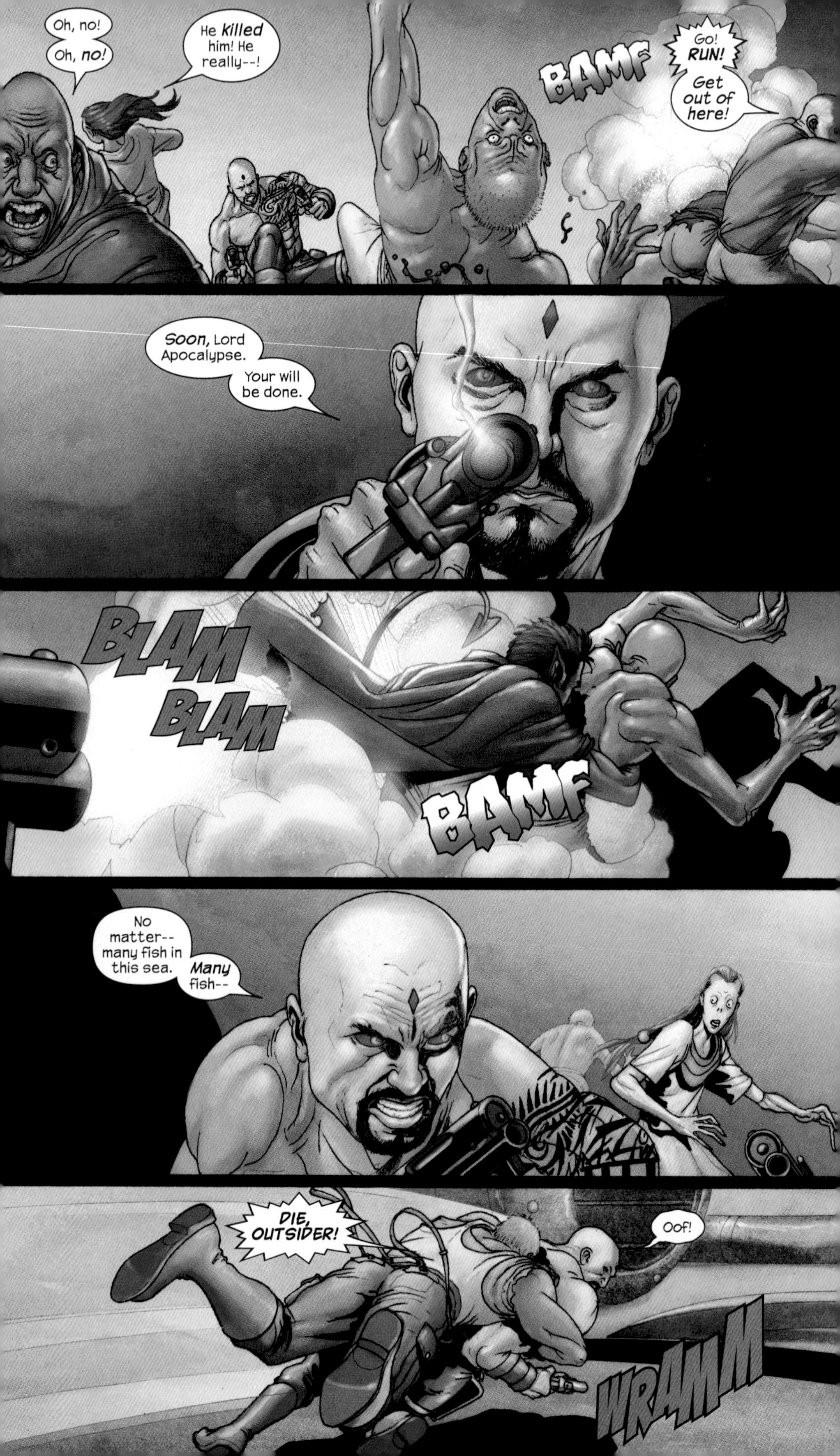
Oh, no!
Oh, no!
He killed him! He really--!
BAMF
Go! RUN!
Get out of here!
Soon, Lord Apocalypse.
Your will be done.
BLAM
BLAM
BAMF
No matter-- many fish in this sea.
Many fish--
DIE, OUTSIDER!
Oof!
WRAMM

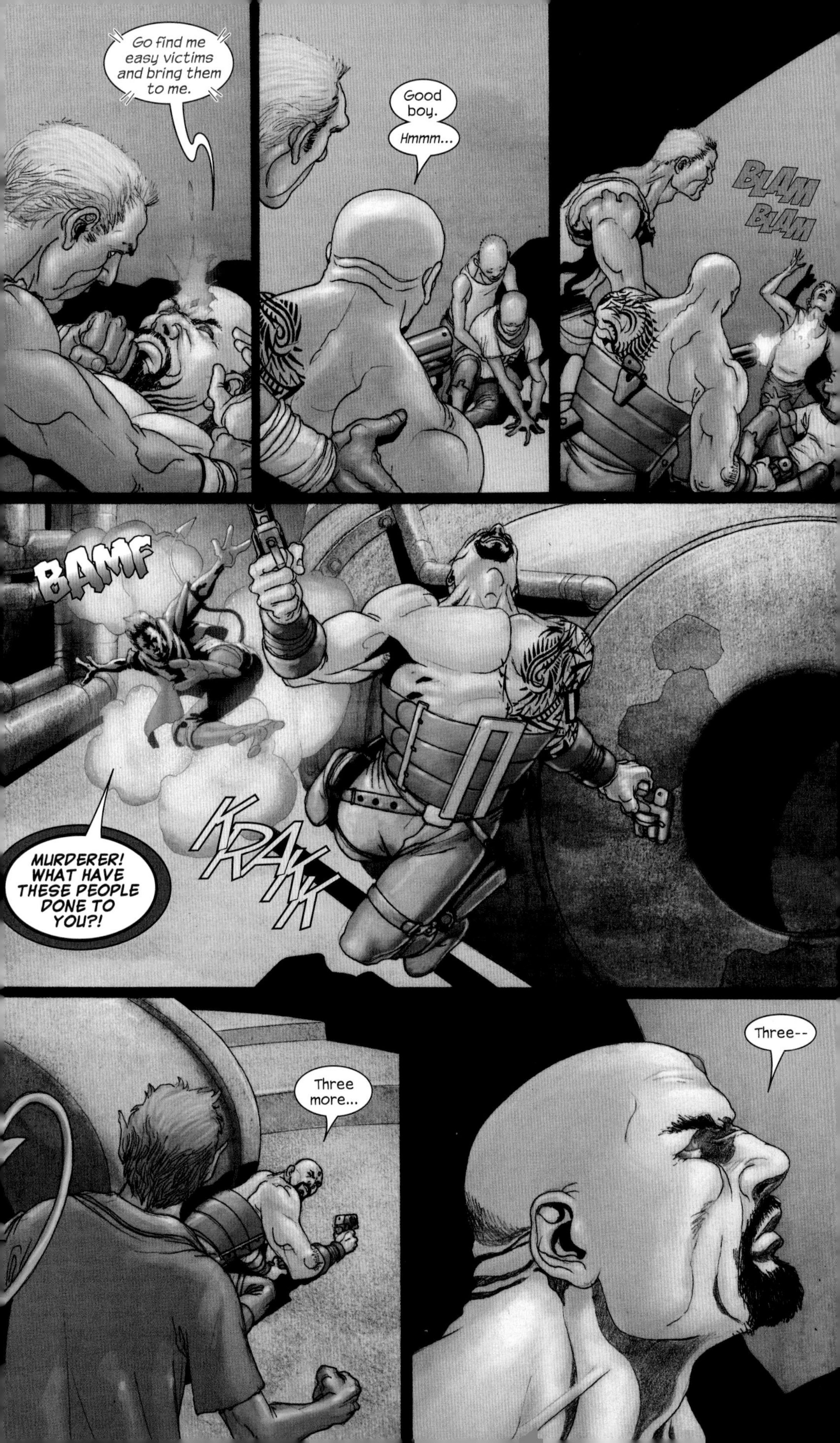
Go find me easy victims and bring them to me.
Good boy.
Hmmm...
BLAM
BLAM
BAMF
MURDERER! WHAT HAVE THESE PEOPLE DONE TO YOU?!
KRAKK
Three more...
Three--

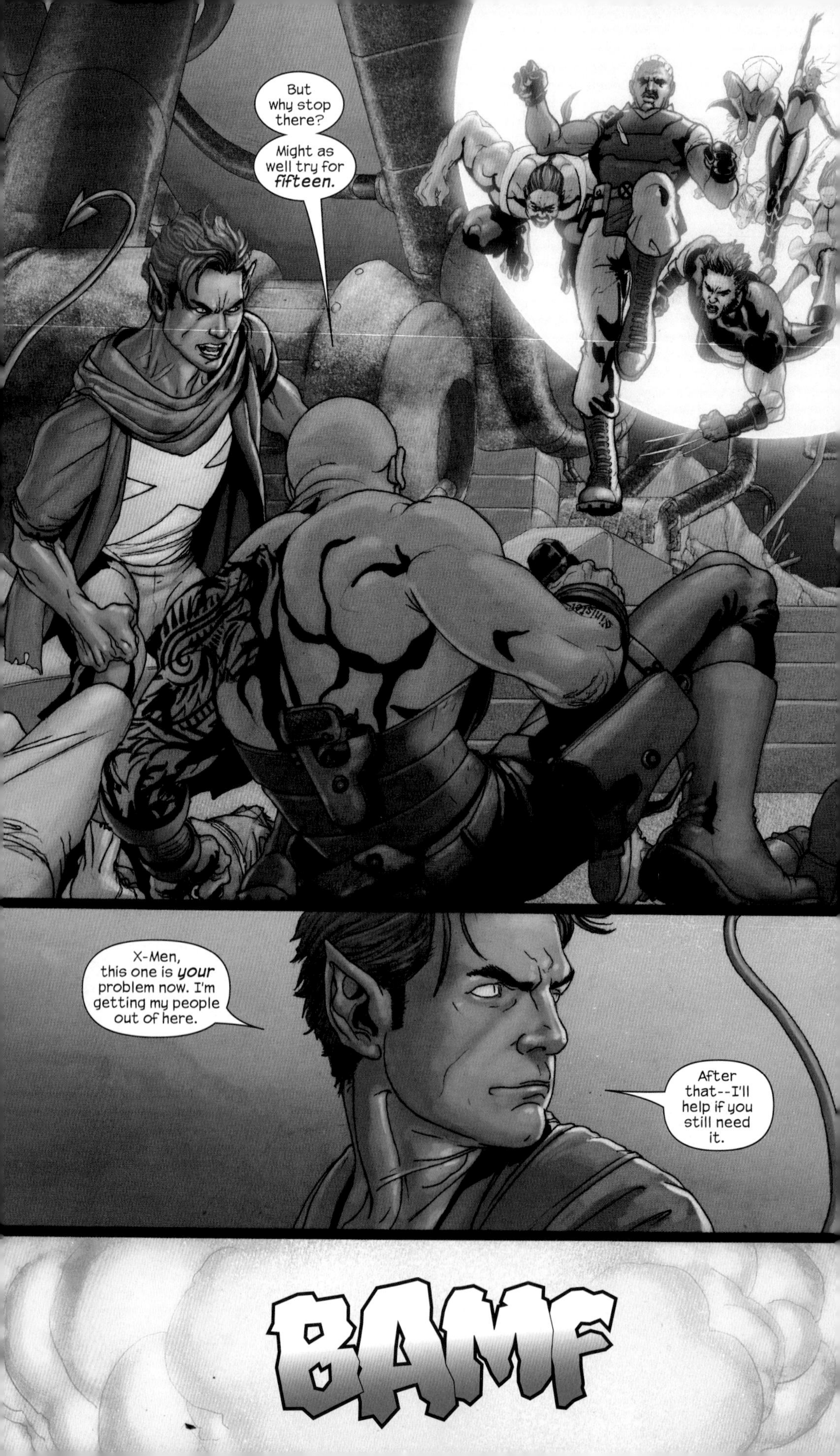
But why stop there?
Might as well try for *fifteen.*
X-Men, this one is *your* problem now. I'm getting my people out of here.
After that--I'll help if you still need it.
BAMF

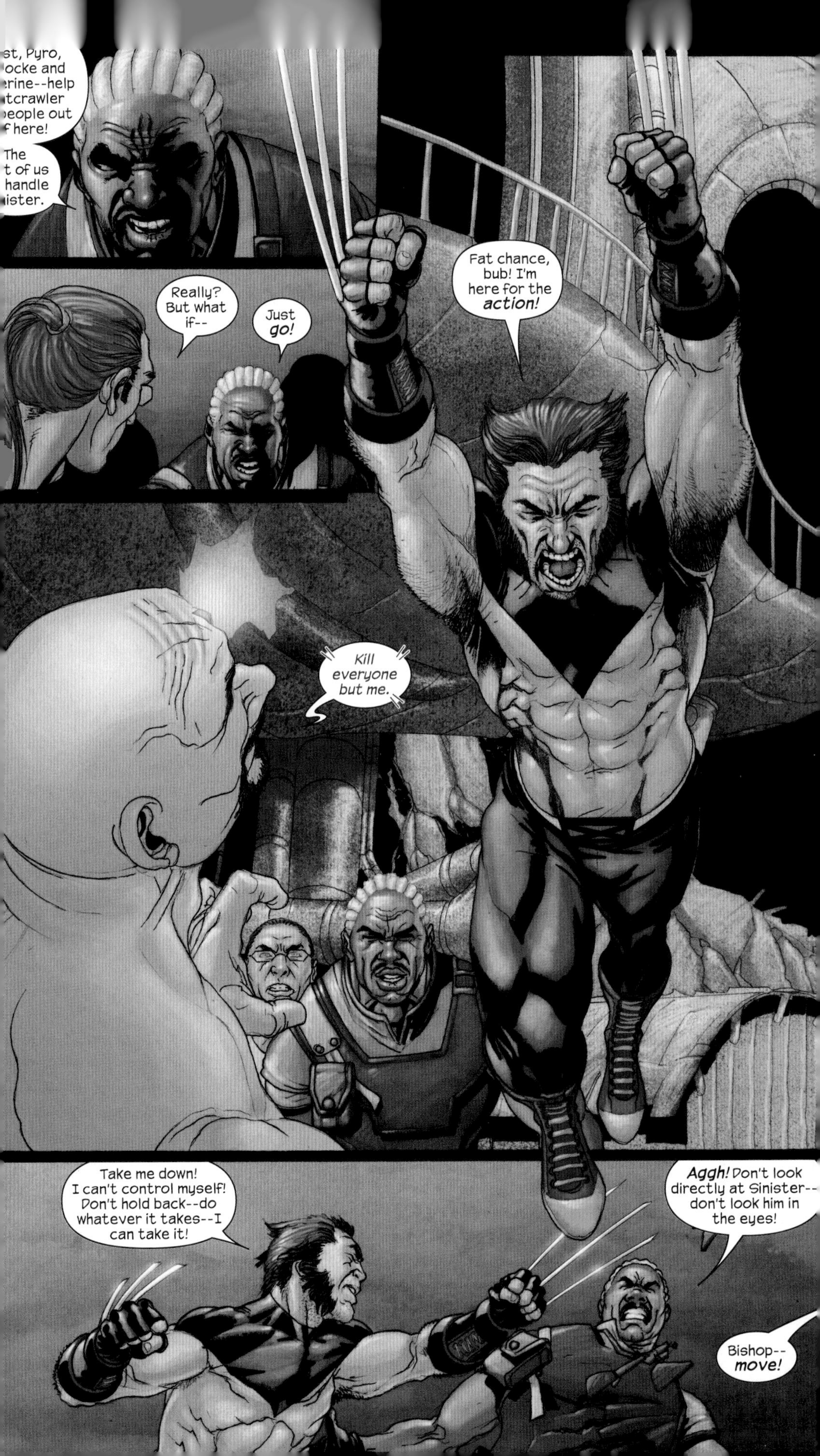
st, Pyro,
ocke and
erine--help
tcrawler
people out
f here!
The
t of us
handle
ister.
Really? But what if--
Just go!
Fat chance, bub! I'm here for the action!
Kill everyone but me.
Take me down! I can't control myself! Don't hold back--do whatever it takes--I can take it!
Aggh! Don't look directly at Sinister--don't look him in the eyes!
Bishop--move!

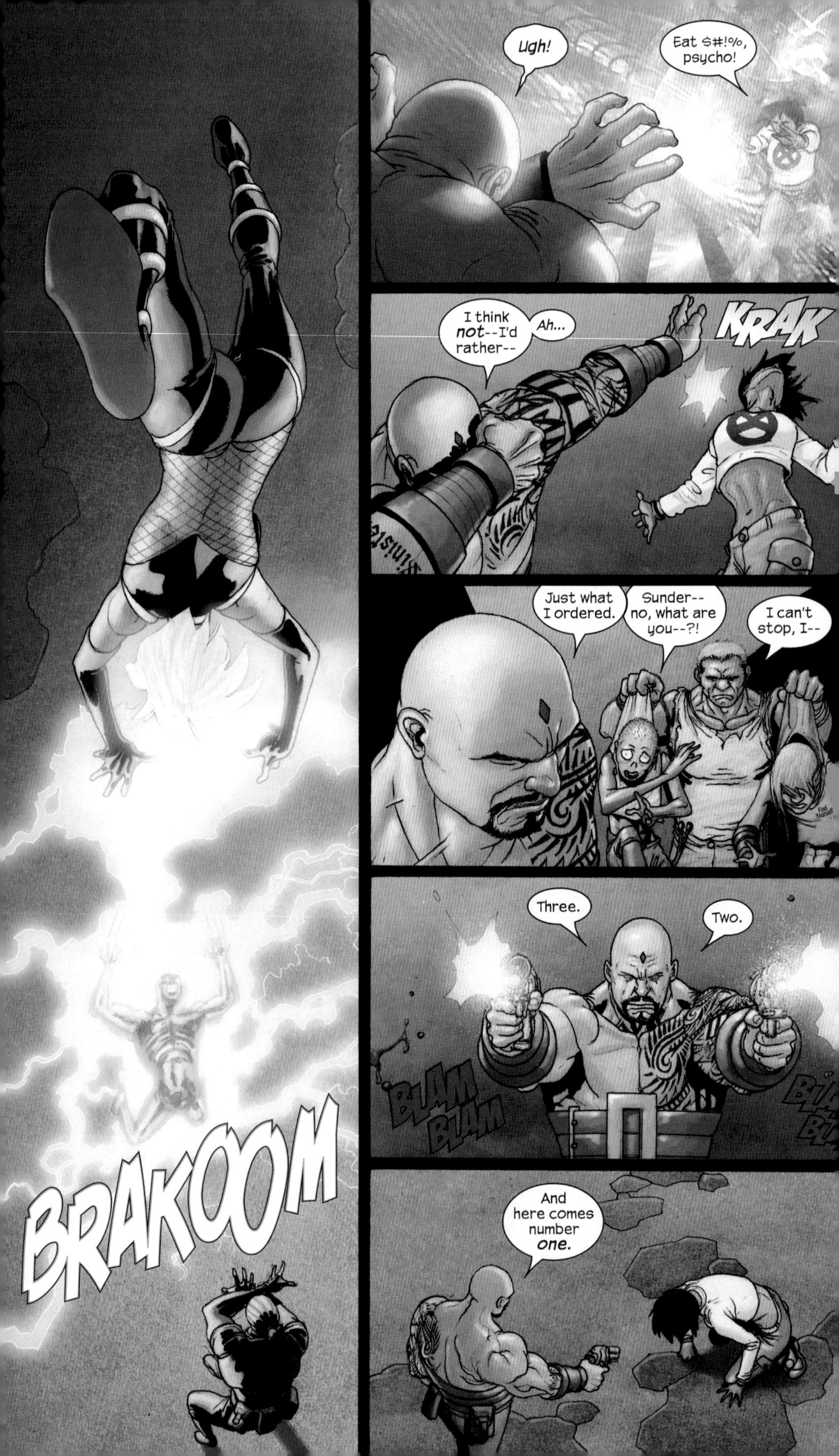

BRAKOOM
Ugh!
Eat $#!%, psycho!
I think not--I'd rather--
Ah...
KRAK
Just what I ordered.
Sunder--no, what are you--?!
I can't stop, I--
Three.
Two.
BLAM BLAM
And here comes number one.

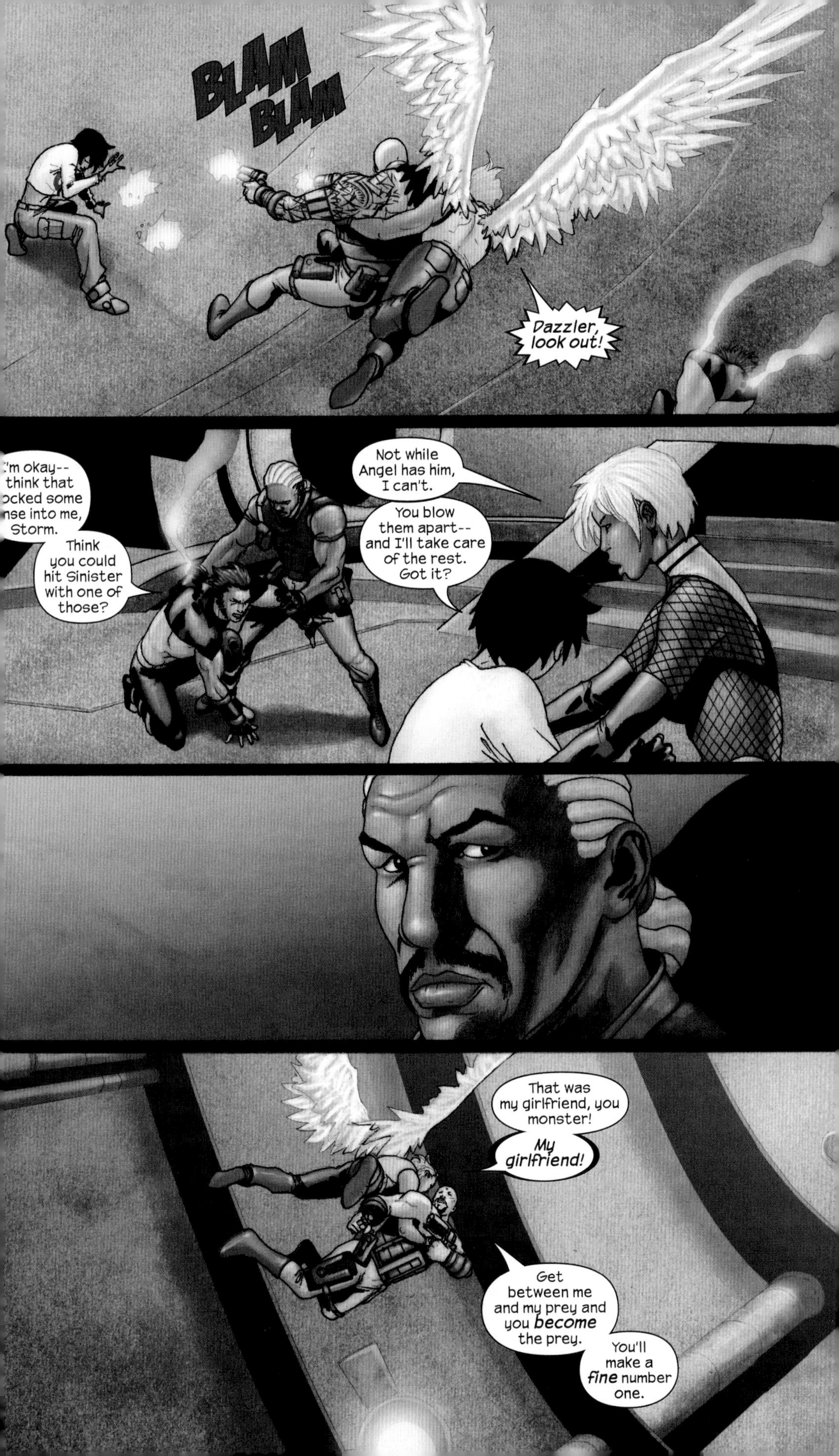

BLAM BLAM
Dazzler, look out!
'm okay-- think that ocked some nse into me, Storm.
Think you could hit Sinister with one of those?
Not while Angel has him, I can't.
You blow them apart-- and I'll take care of the rest. Got it?
That was my girlfriend, you monster!
My girlfriend!
Get between me and my prey and you become the prey.
You'll make a fine number one.

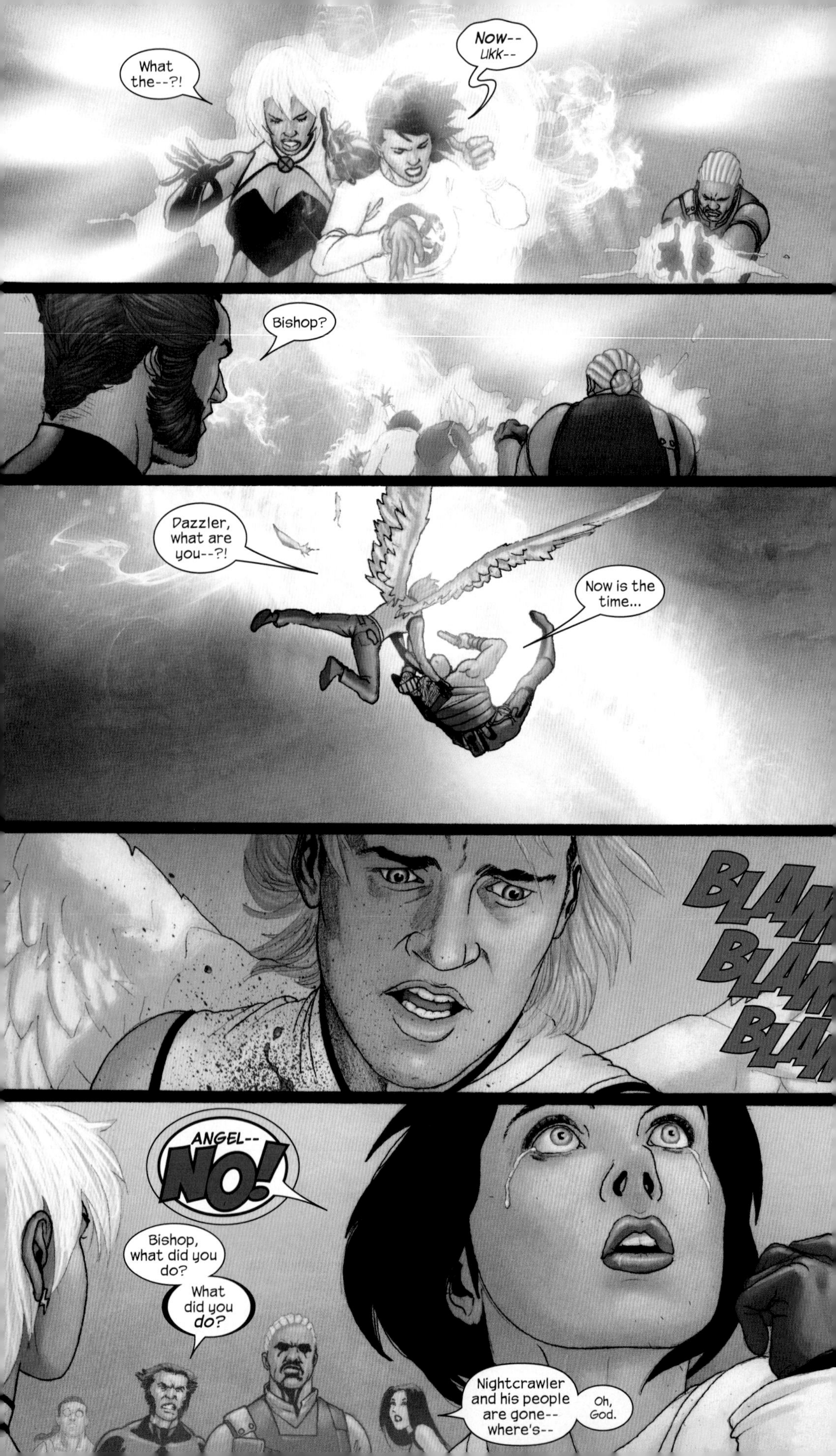
What the--?!
NOW-- UKK--
Bishop?
Dazzler, what are you--?!
Now is the time...
BLAM BLAM BLAM
ANGEL-- NO!
Bishop, what did you do?
What did you do?
Nightcrawler and his people are gone-- where's--
Oh, God.

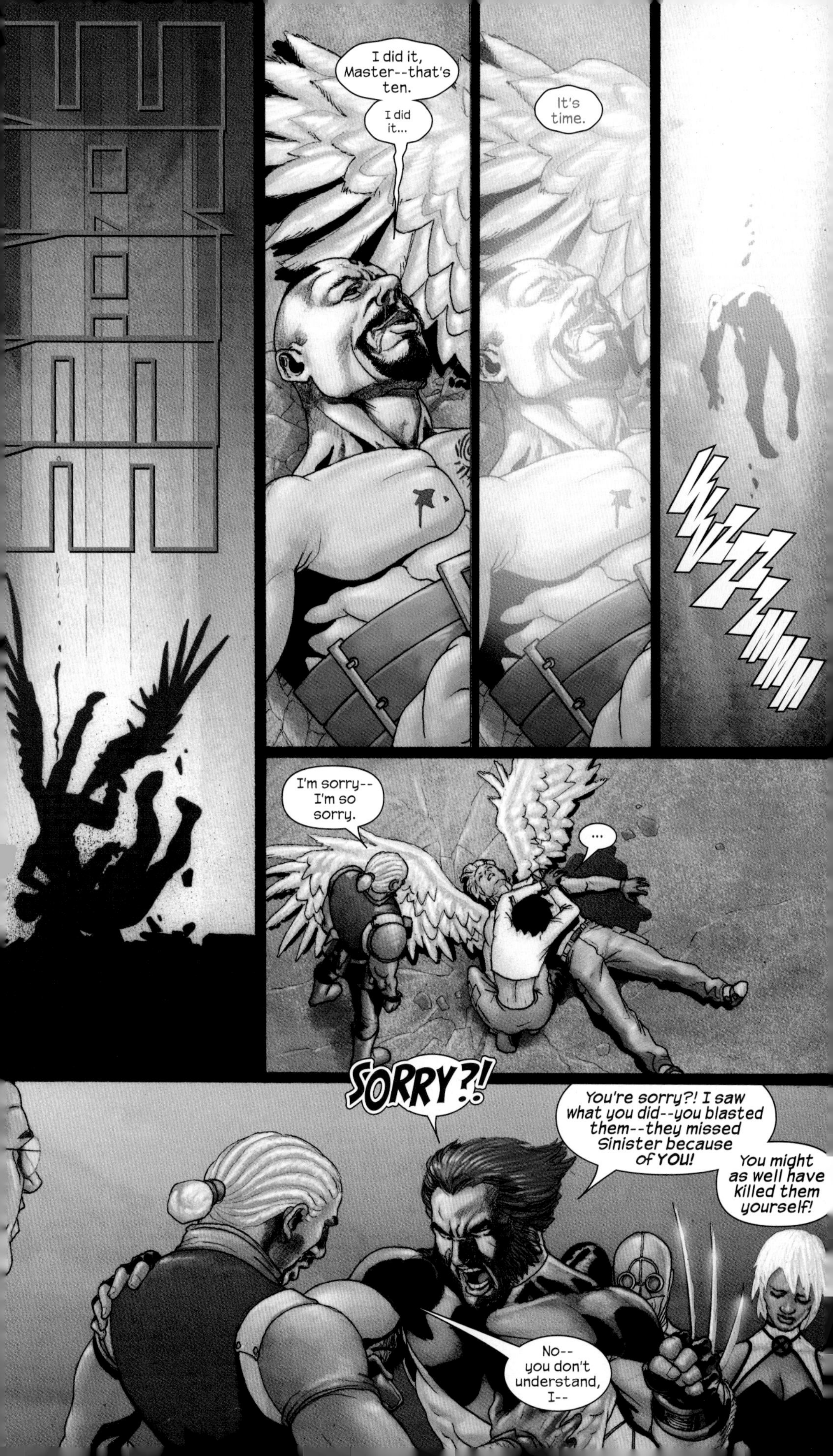

I did it, Master--that's ten.
I did it...
It's time.
VVZZMMMM
I'm sorry-- I'm so sorry.
...
SORRY?!
You're sorry?! I saw what you did--you blasted them--they missed Sinister because of YOU!
You might as well have killed them yourself!
No-- you don't understand, I--

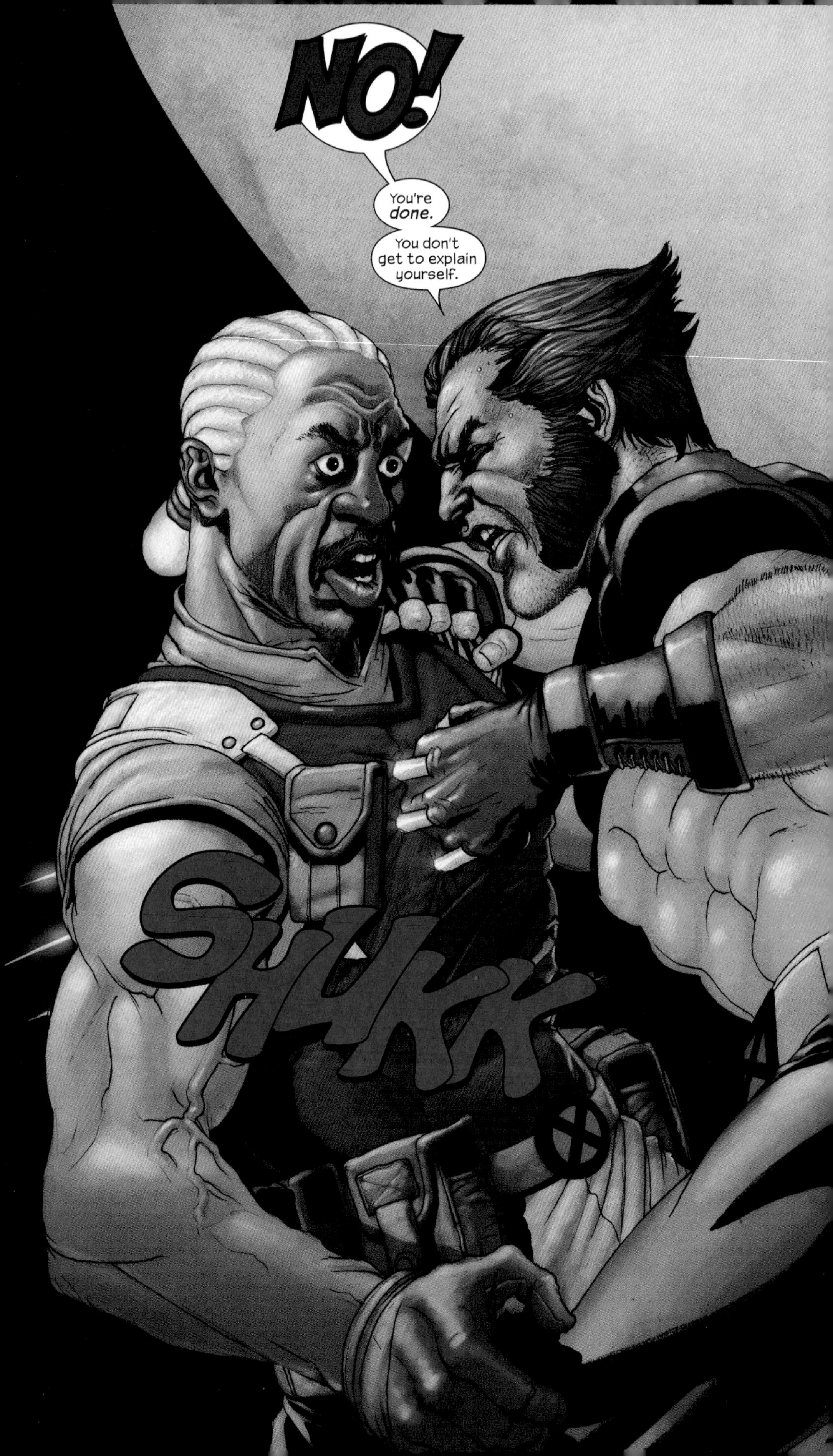
NO!
You're *done.*
You don't get to explain yourself.
SHKK

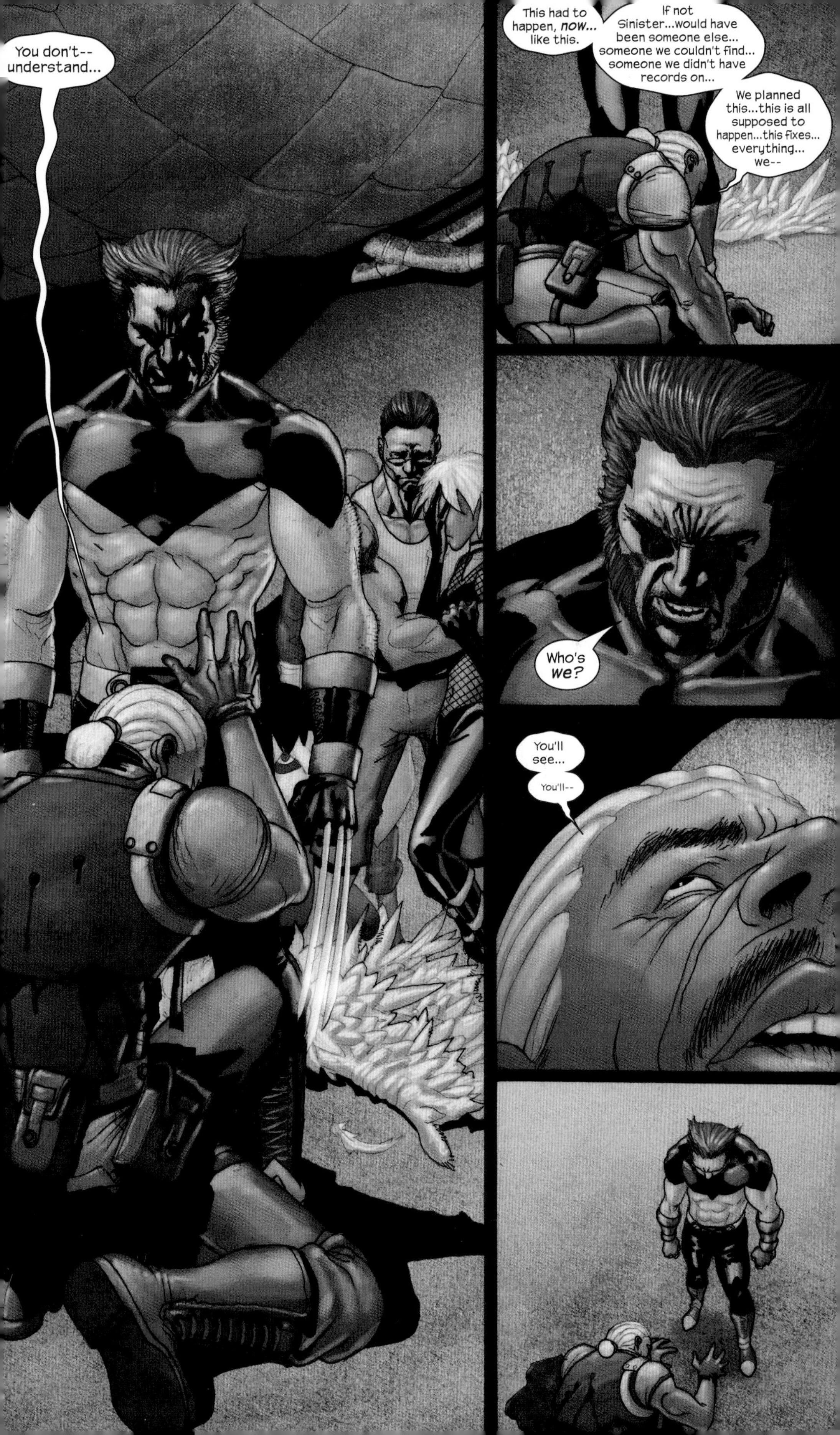
You don't--
understand...
This had to happen, *now...* like this.
If not Sinister...would have been someone else... someone we couldn't find... someone we didn't have records on...
We planned this...this is all supposed to happen...this fixes... everything... we--
Who's *we?*
You'll see...
You'll--

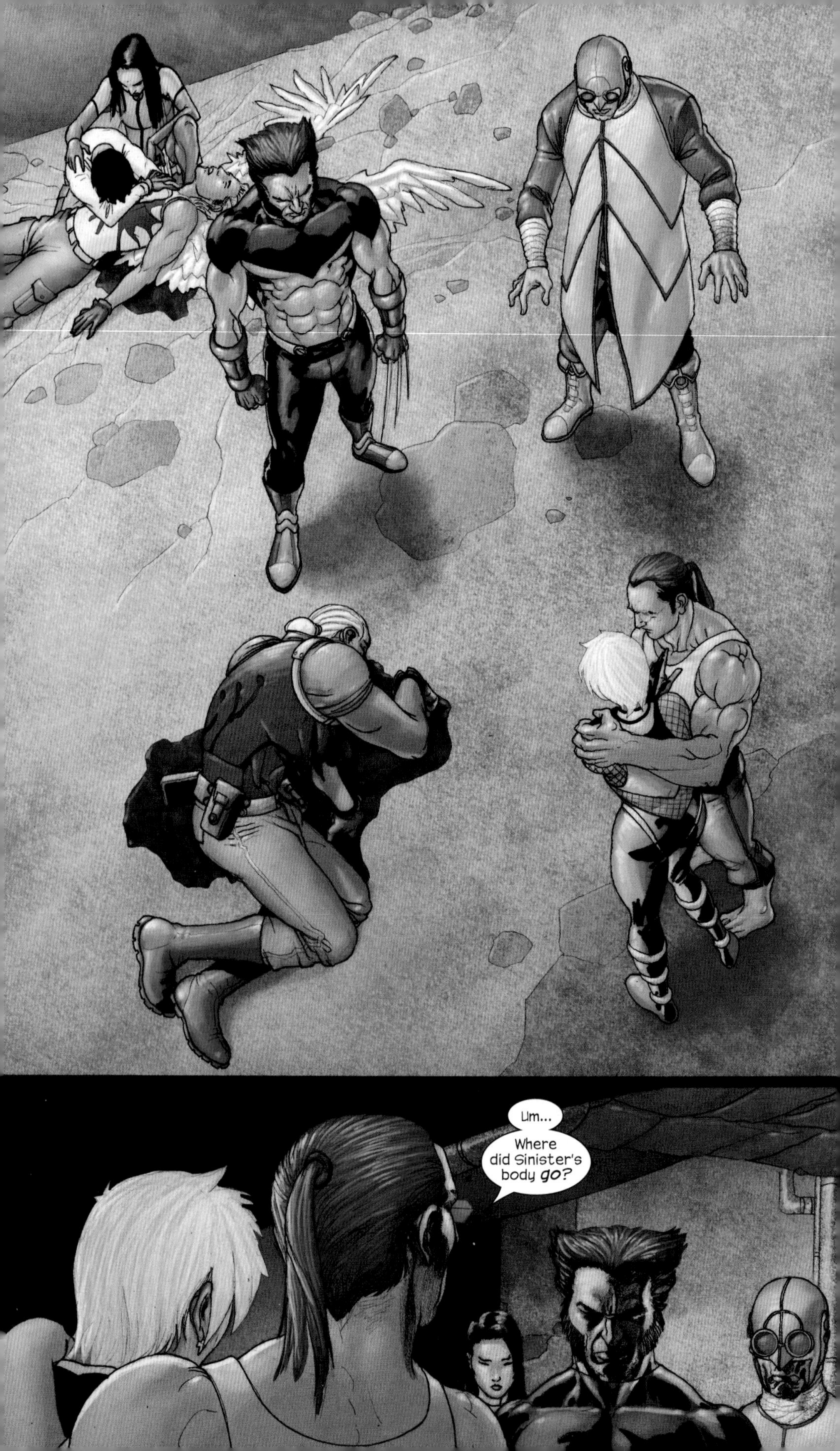
Um...
Where did Sinister's body go?

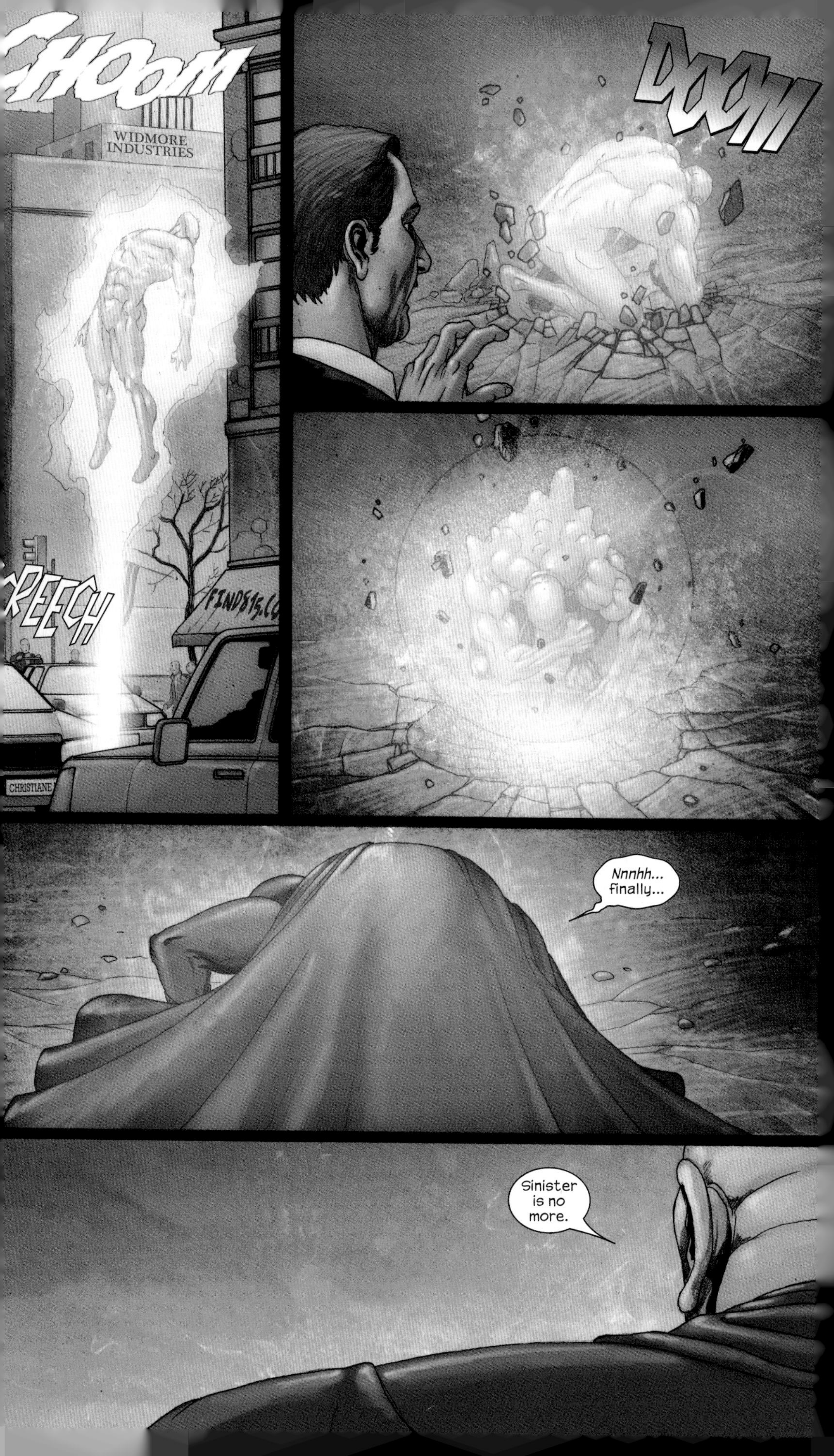
CHOOM
WIDMORE INDUSTRIES
SCREECH
FINDS15.CO
CHRISTIANE
DOOM
Nnnhh... finally...
Sinister is no more.

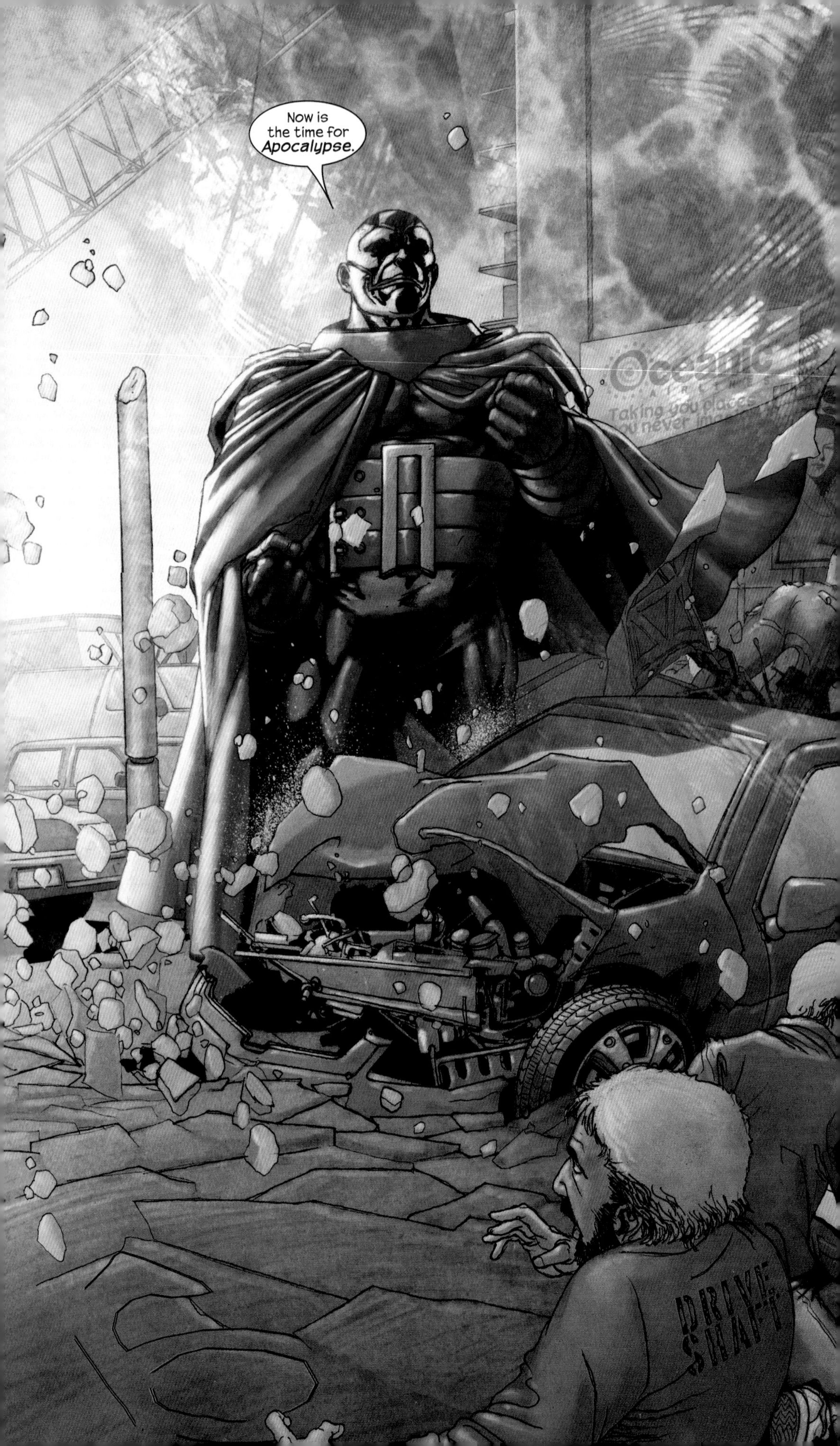
Now is the time for *Apocalypse*.

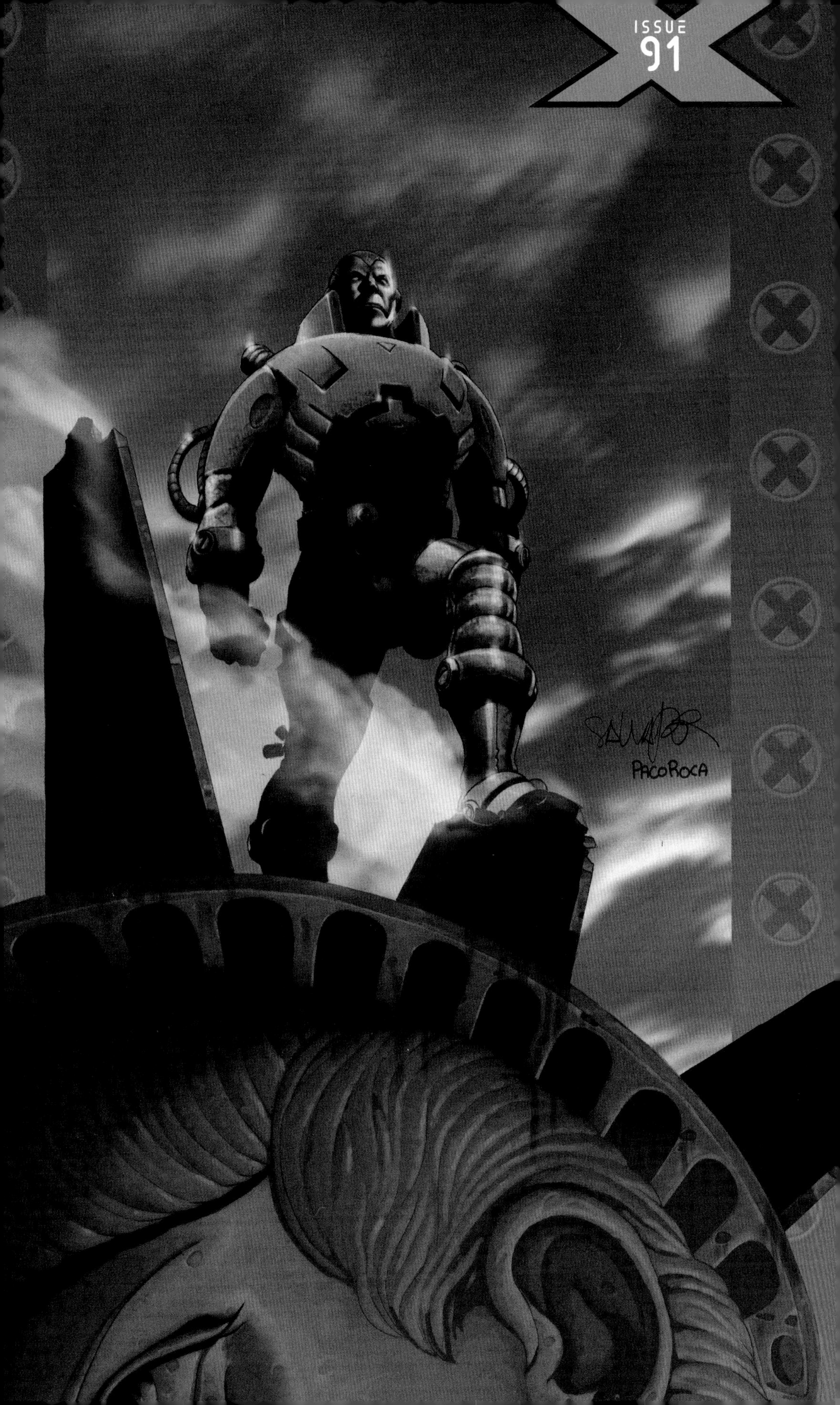
ISSUE
91
SALVADOR
PACO ROCA

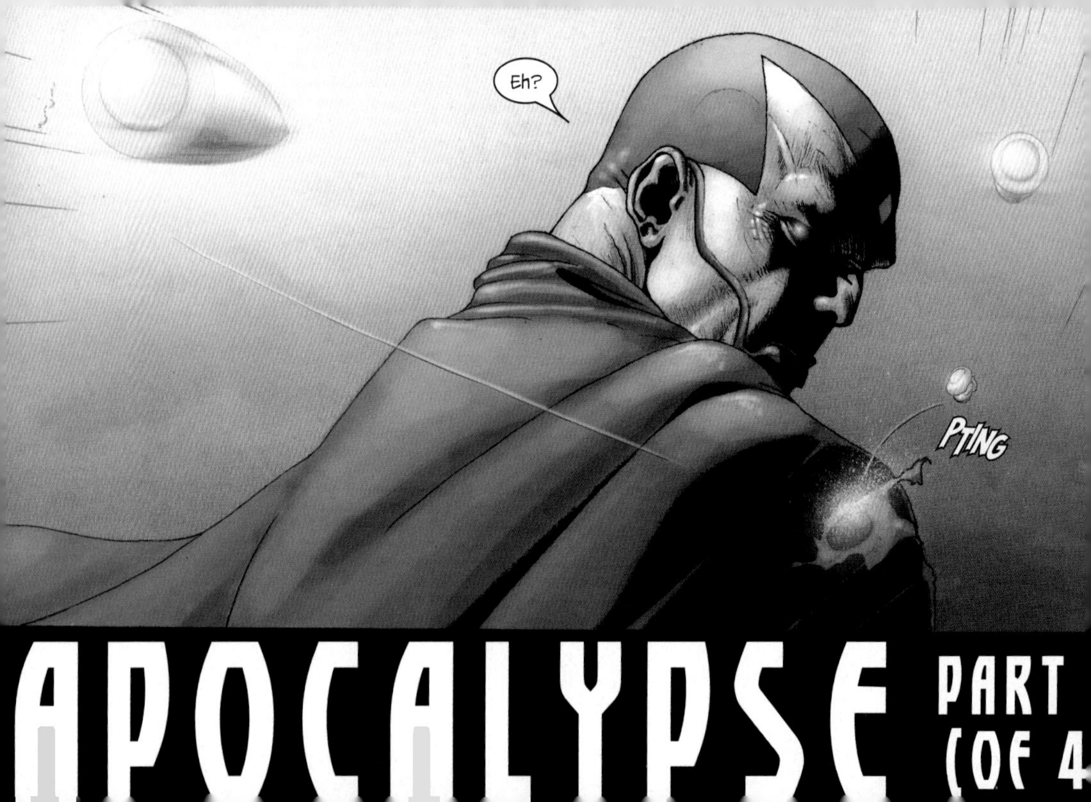
Eh?
PTING
APOCALYPSE
PART
(OF 4

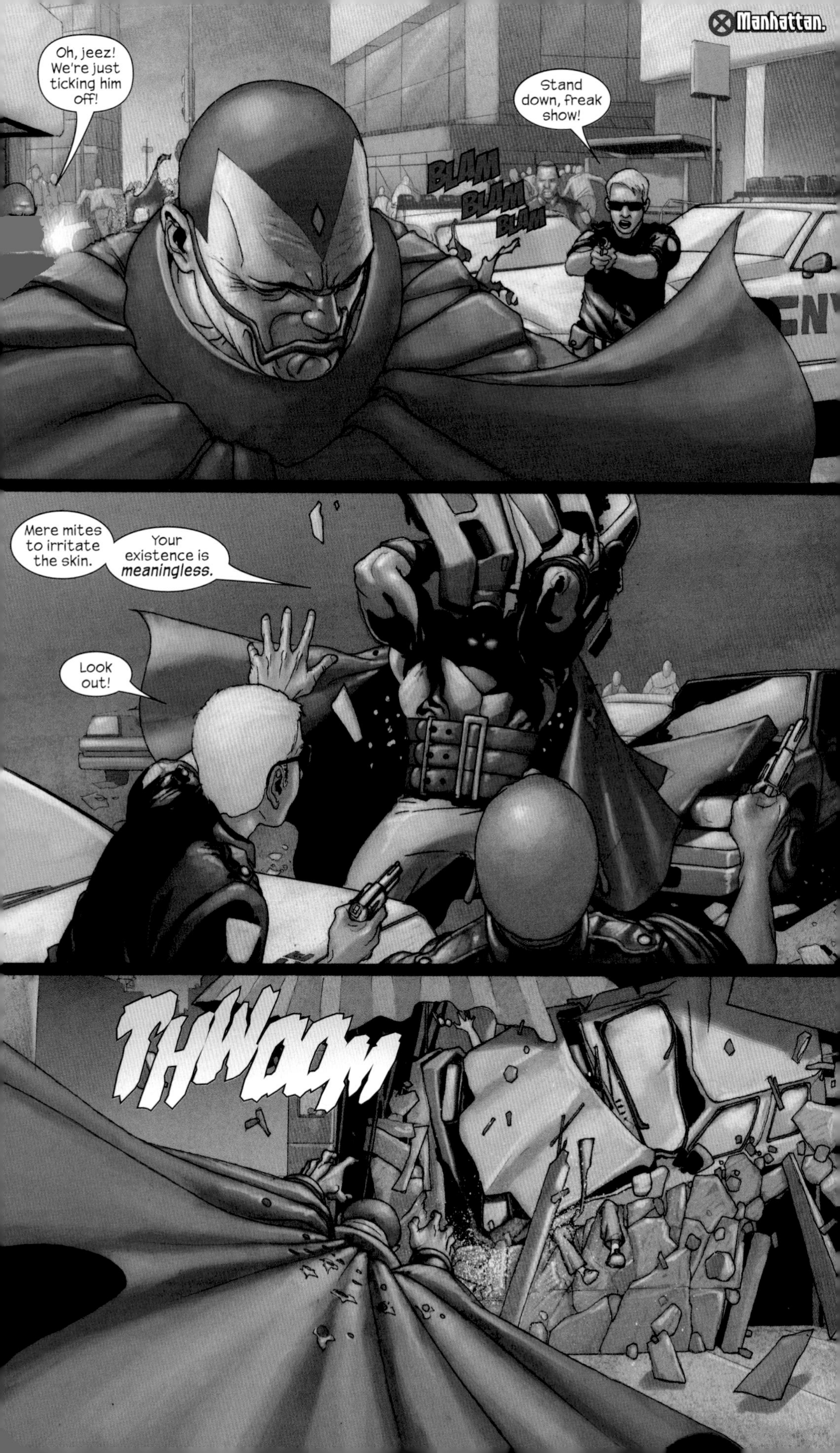
Manhattan.
Oh, jeez! We're just ticking him off!
Stand down, freak show!
BLAM BLAM BLAM
Mere mites to irritate the skin.
Your existence is *meaningless.*
Look out!
THWOOM

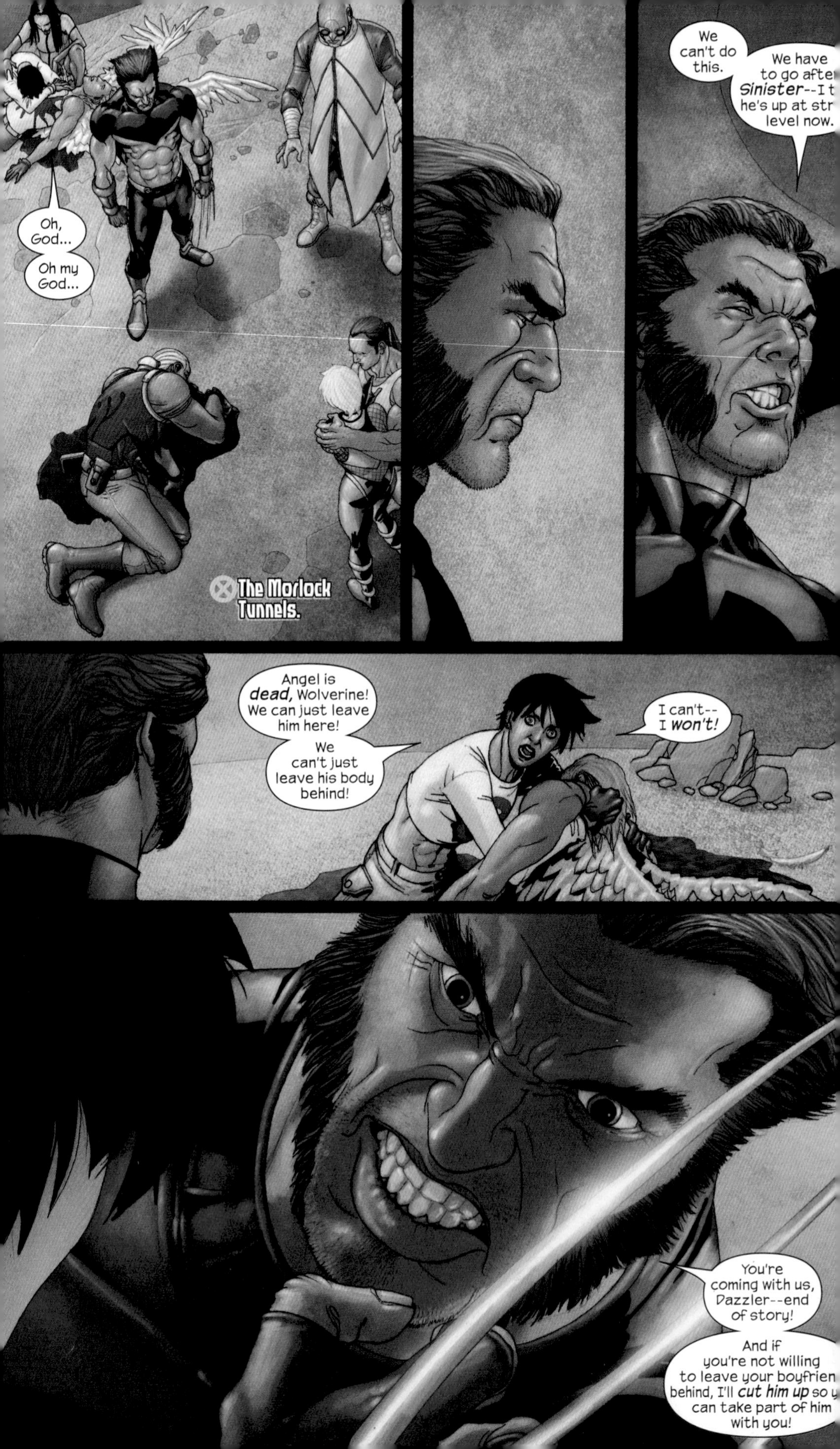

Oh, God...
Oh my God...
The Morlock Tunnels.
We can't do this.
We have to go afte Sinister--I t he's up at str level now.
Angel is dead, Wolverine! We can just leave him here!
We can't just leave his body behind!
I can't-- I won't!
You're coming with us, Dazzler--end of story!
And if you're not willing to leave your boyfrien behind, I'll cut him up so can take part of him with you!

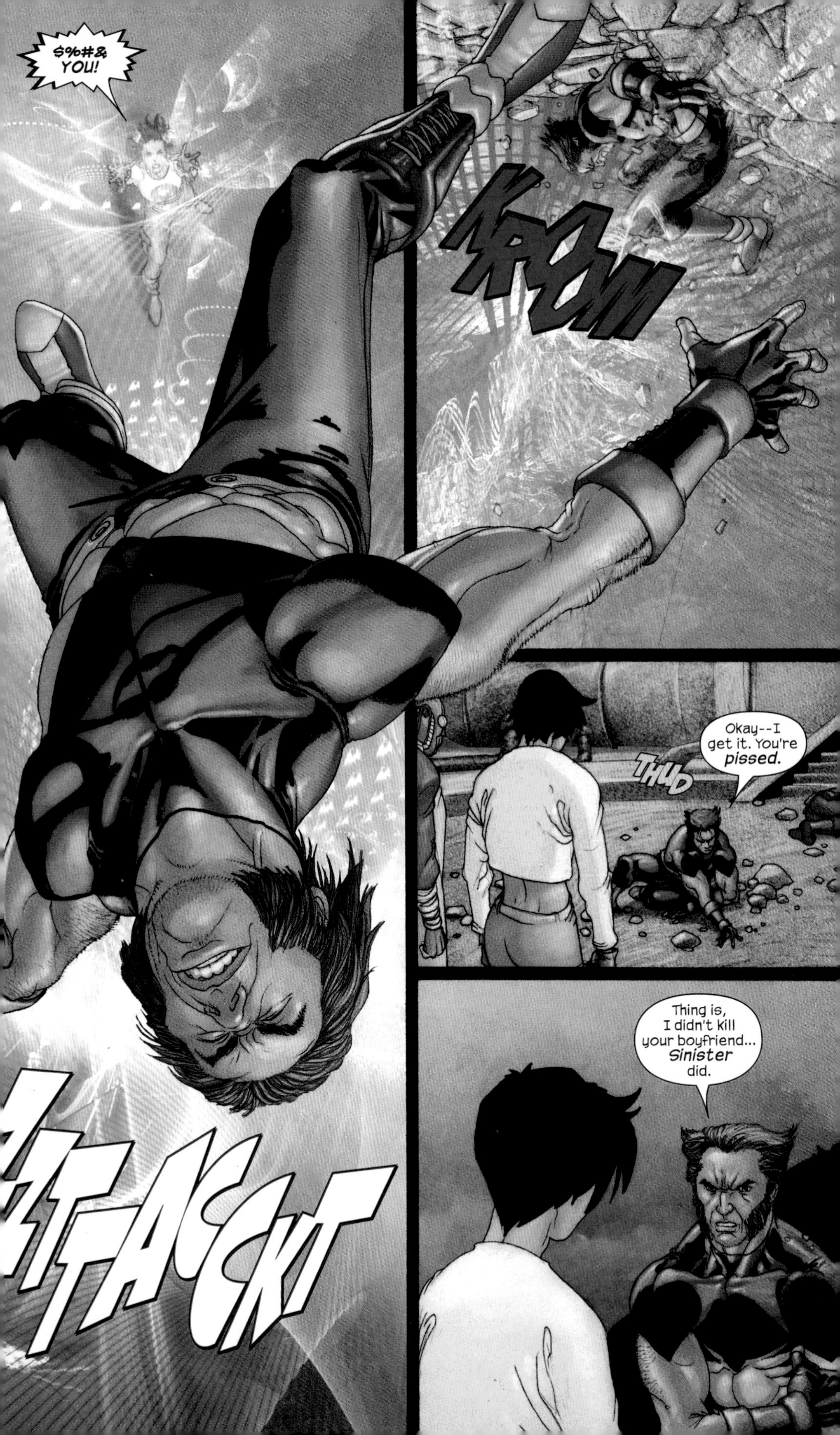
$%#& YOU!
KROOM
ZZTTAACCKT
Okay--I get it. You're *pissed.*
THUD
Thing is, I didn't kill your boyfriend... *Sinister* did.

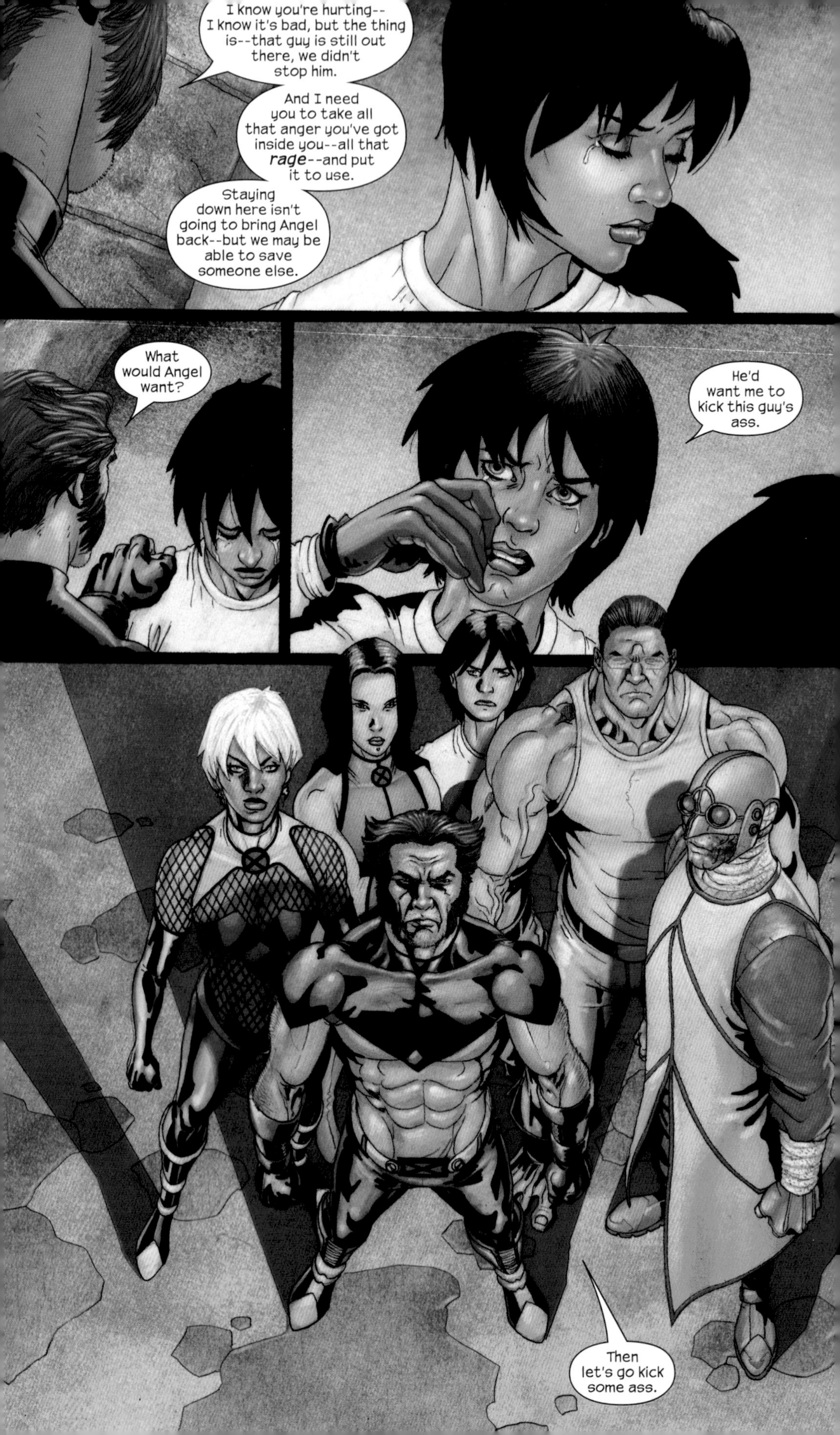
I know you're hurting-- I know it's bad, but the thing is--that guy is still out there, we didn't stop him.
And I need you to take all that anger you've got inside you--all that *rage*--and put it to use.
Staying down here isn't going to bring Angel back--but we may be able to save someone else.
What would Angel want?
He'd want me to kick this guy's ass.
Then let's go kick some ass.

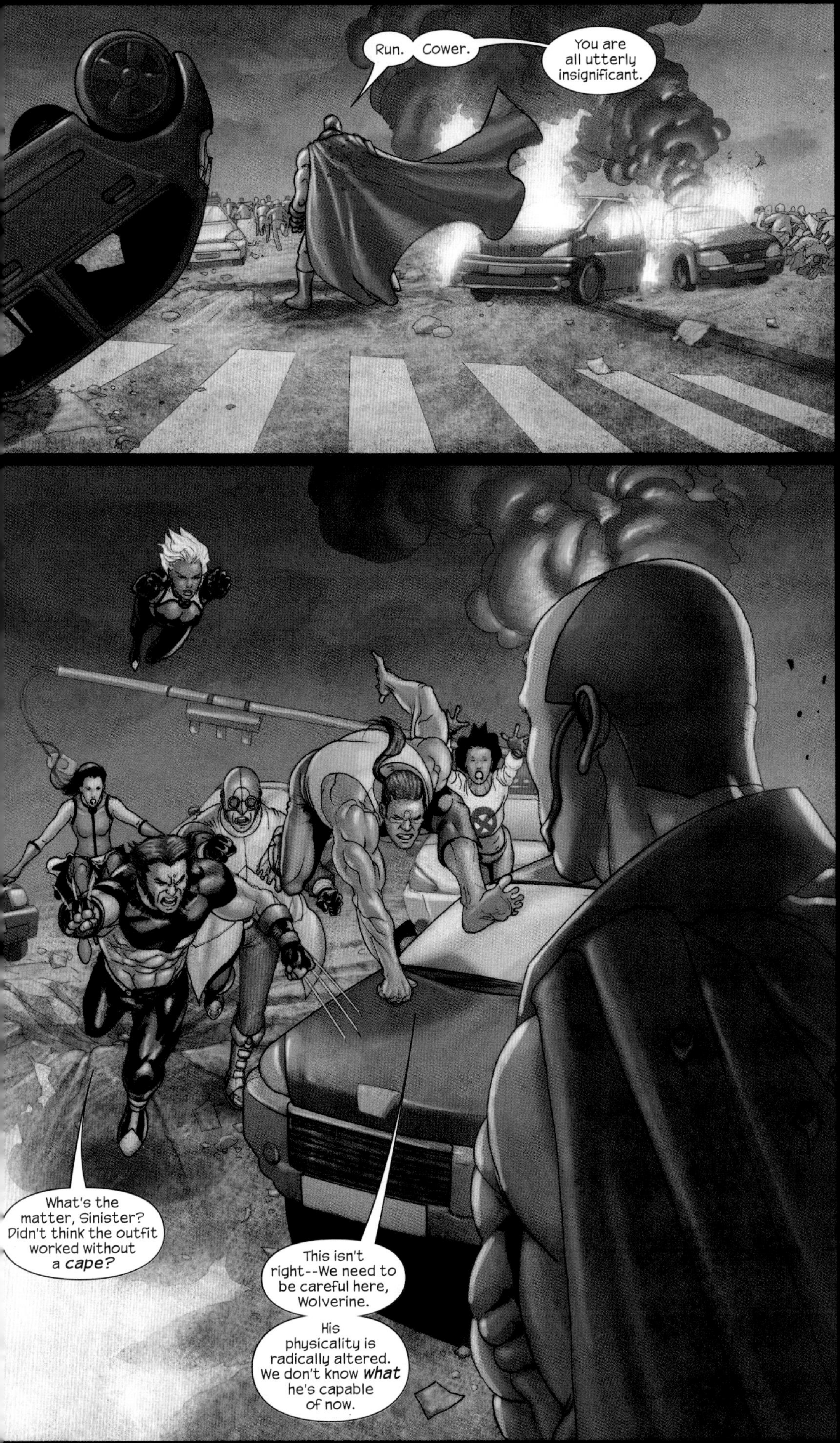
Run.
Cower.
You are all utterly insignificant.
What's the matter, Sinister? Didn't think the outfit worked without a *cape?*
This isn't right--We need to be careful here, Wolverine.
His physicality is radically altered. We don't know *what* he's capable of now.

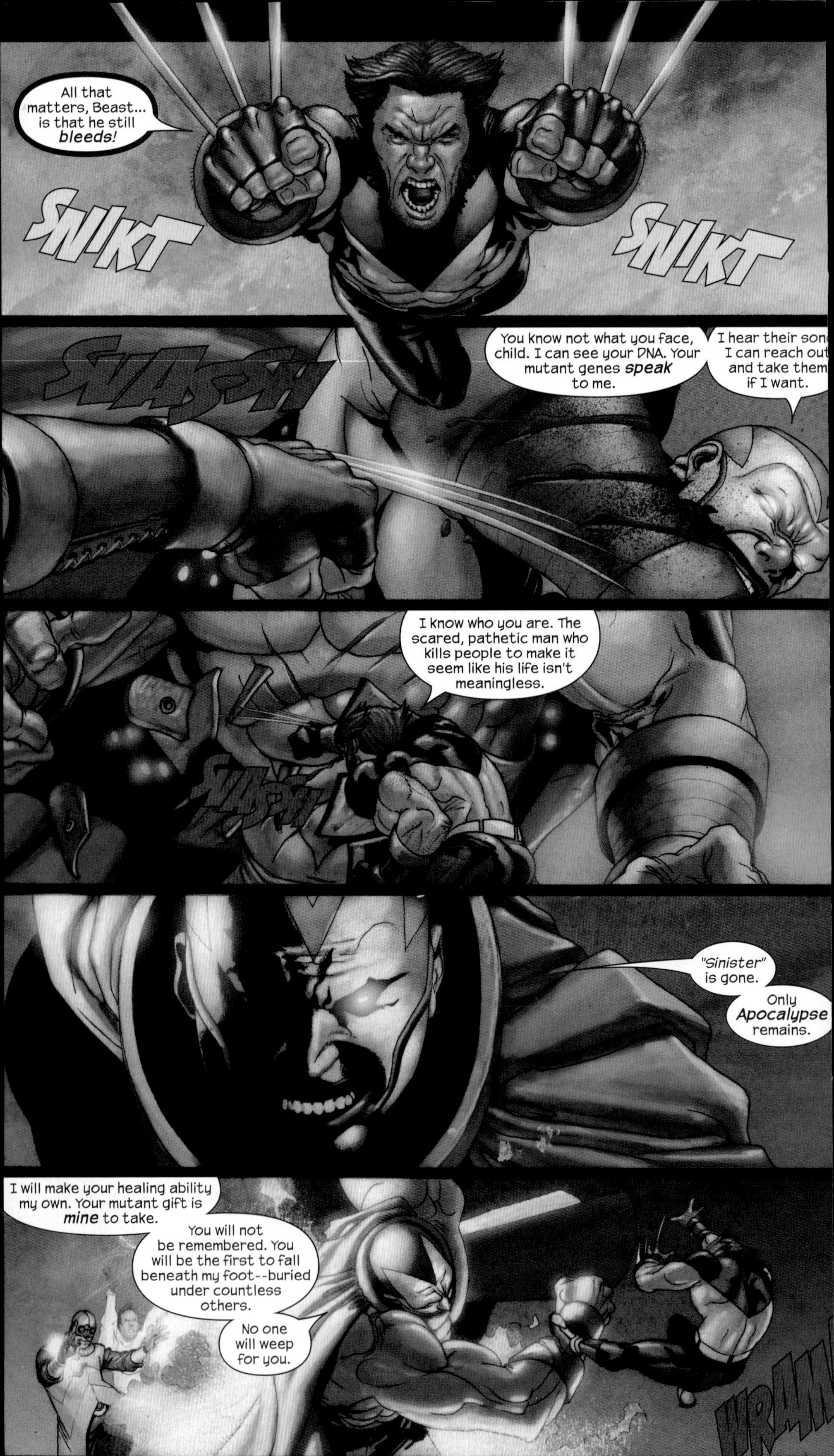

All that matters, Beast... is that he still *bleeds!*
SNIKT
SNIKT
SLASH
You know not what you face, child. I can see your DNA. Your mutant genes *speak* to me.
I hear their son I can reach out and take them if I want.
I know who you are. The scared, pathetic man who kills people to make it seem like his life isn't meaningless.
SLASH
"Sinister" is gone.
Only *Apocalypse* remains.
I will make your healing ability my own. Your mutant gift is *mine* to take.
You will not be remembered. You will be the first to fall beneath my foot--buried under countless others.
No one will weep for you.

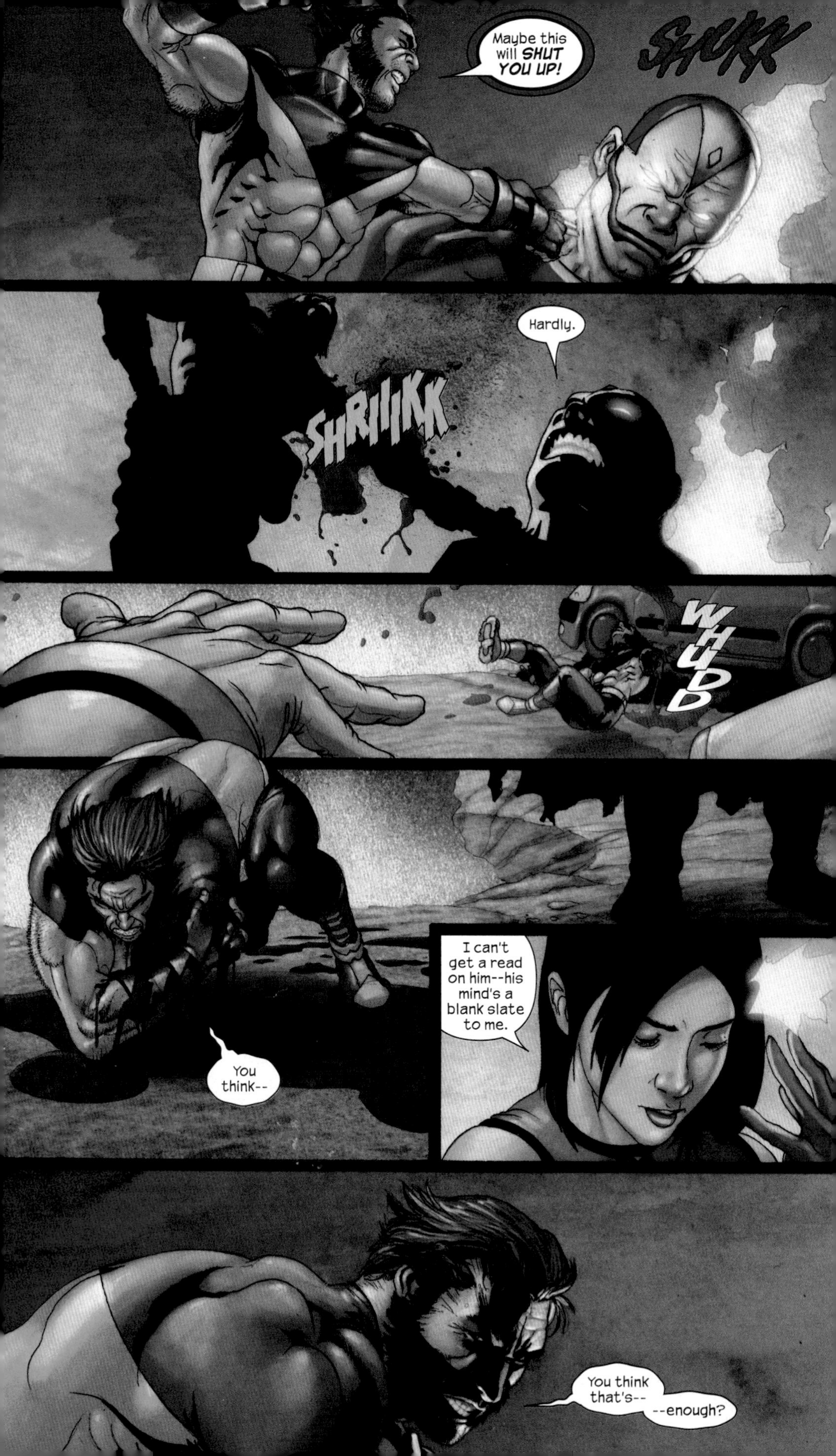
Maybe this will **SHUT YOU UP!**
SHUKK
Hardly.
SHRIIIKK
WHUDD
You think--
I can't get a read on him--his mind's a blank slate to me.
You think that's--
--enough?

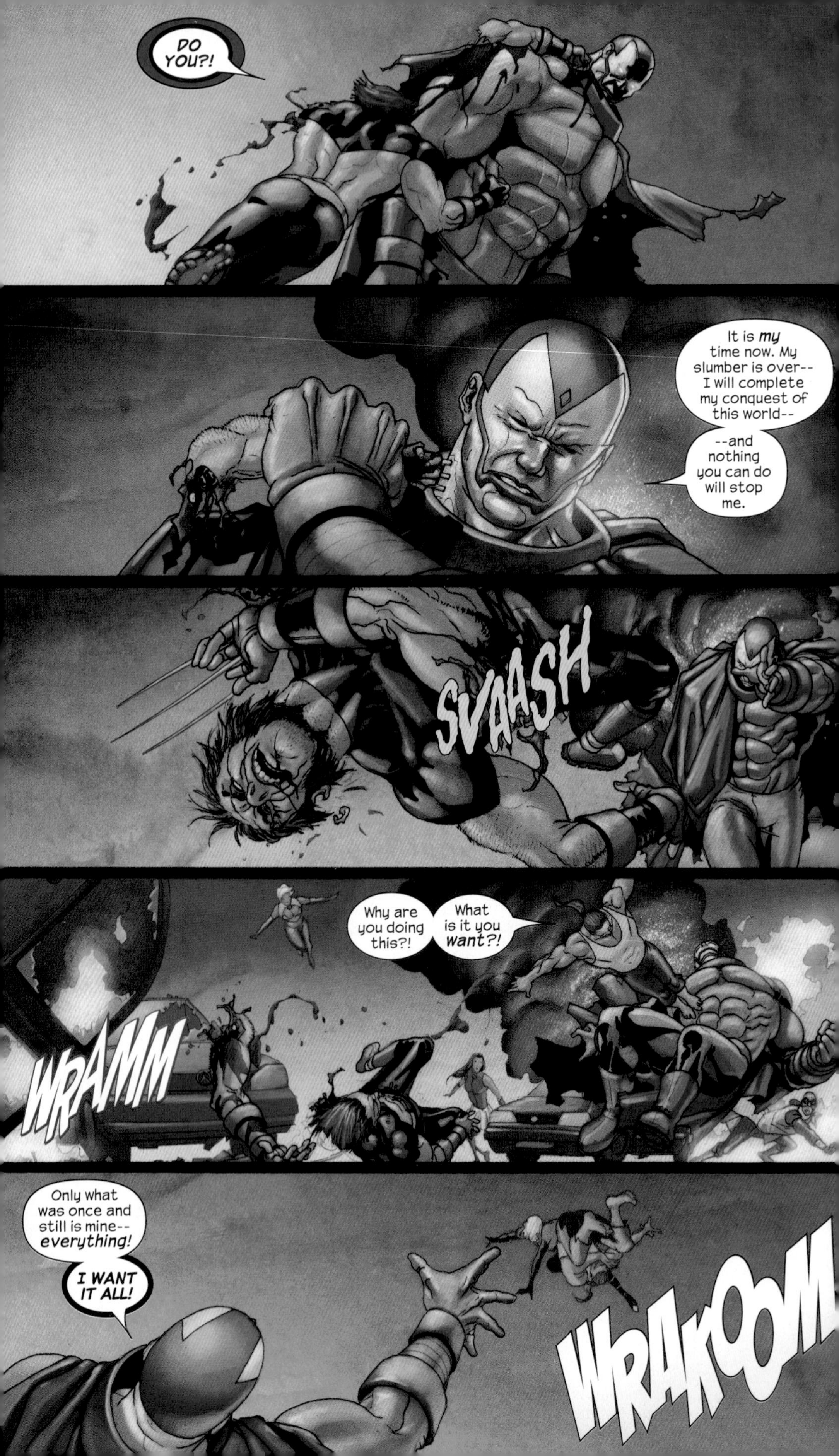
DO YOU?!
It is *my* time now. My slumber is over-- I will complete my conquest of this world--
--and nothing you can do will stop me.
SVAASH
Why are you doing this?!
What is it you *want?!*
WRAMM
Only what was once and still is mine-- *everything!*
I WANT IT ALL!
WRAKOOM

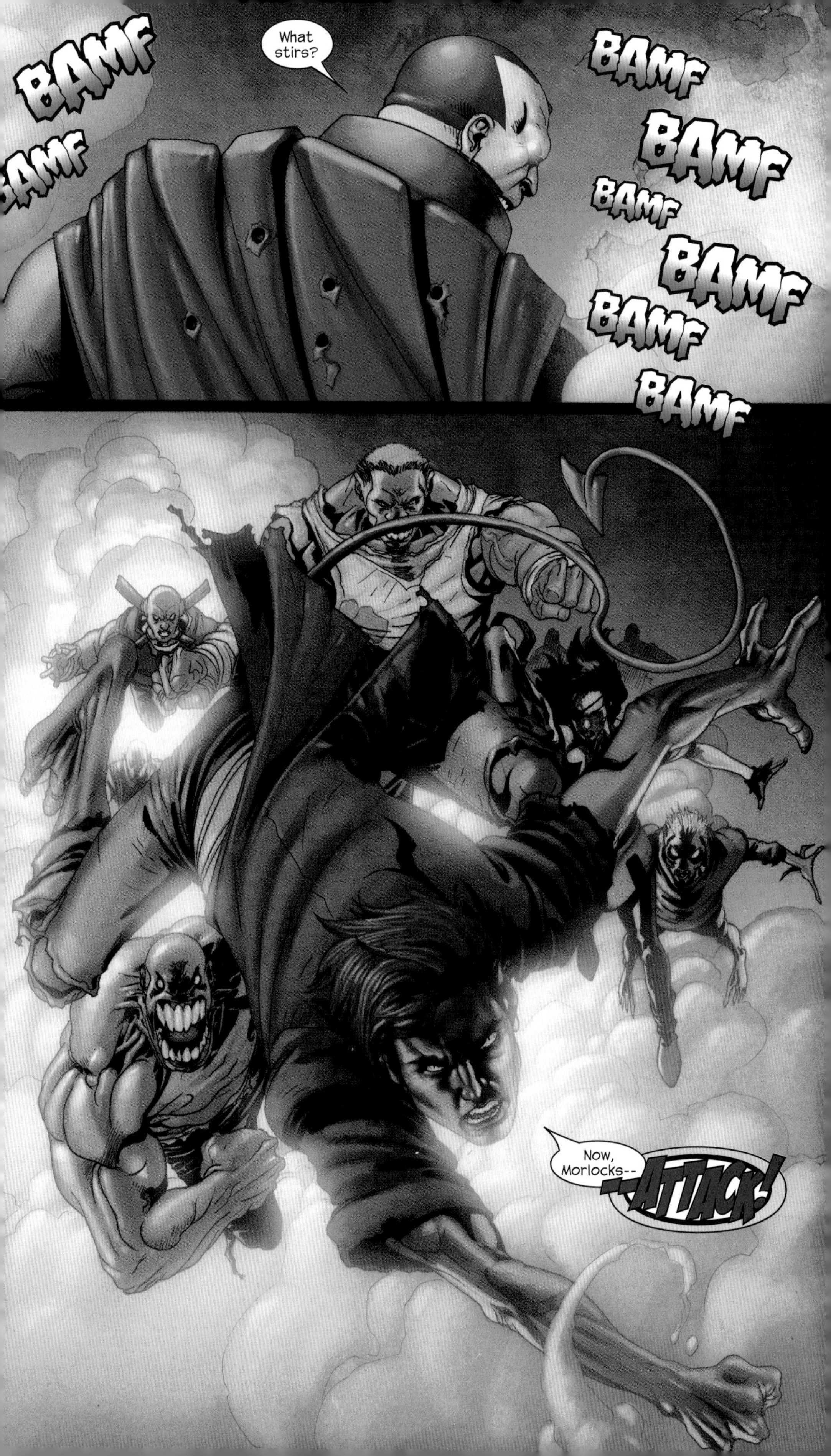

BAMF
BAMF
What stirs?
BAMF
BAMF
BAMF
BAMF
BAMF
BAMF
Now, Morlocks-- --ATTACK!

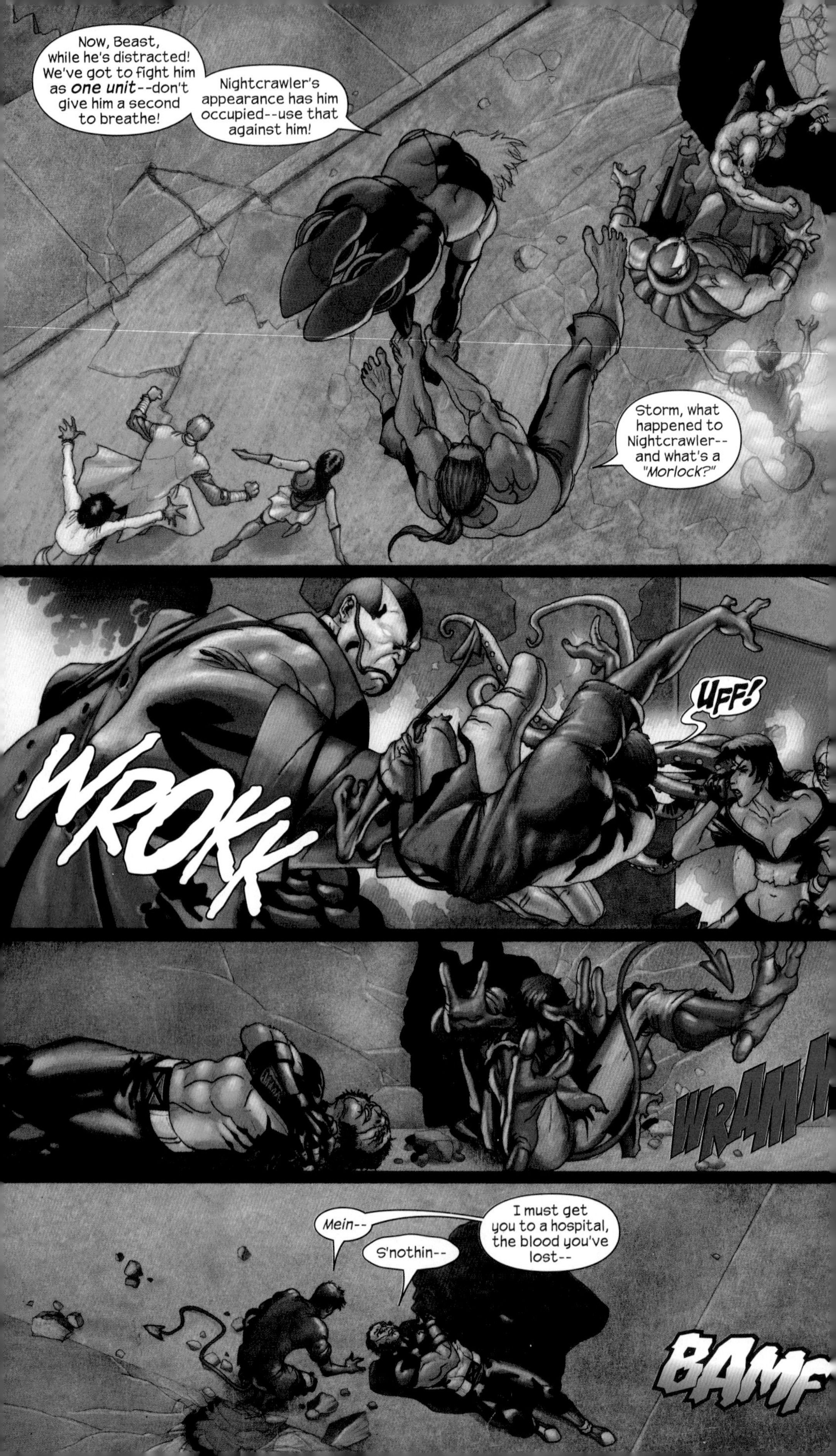

Now, Beast, while he's distracted! We've got to fight him as *one unit*--don't give him a second to breathe!
Nightcrawler's appearance has him occupied--use that against him!
Storm, what happened to Nightcrawler--and what's a *"Morlock?"*
WROKK
UFF!
WRAMM
Mein--
I must get you to a hospital, the blood you've lost--
S'nothin--
BAMF

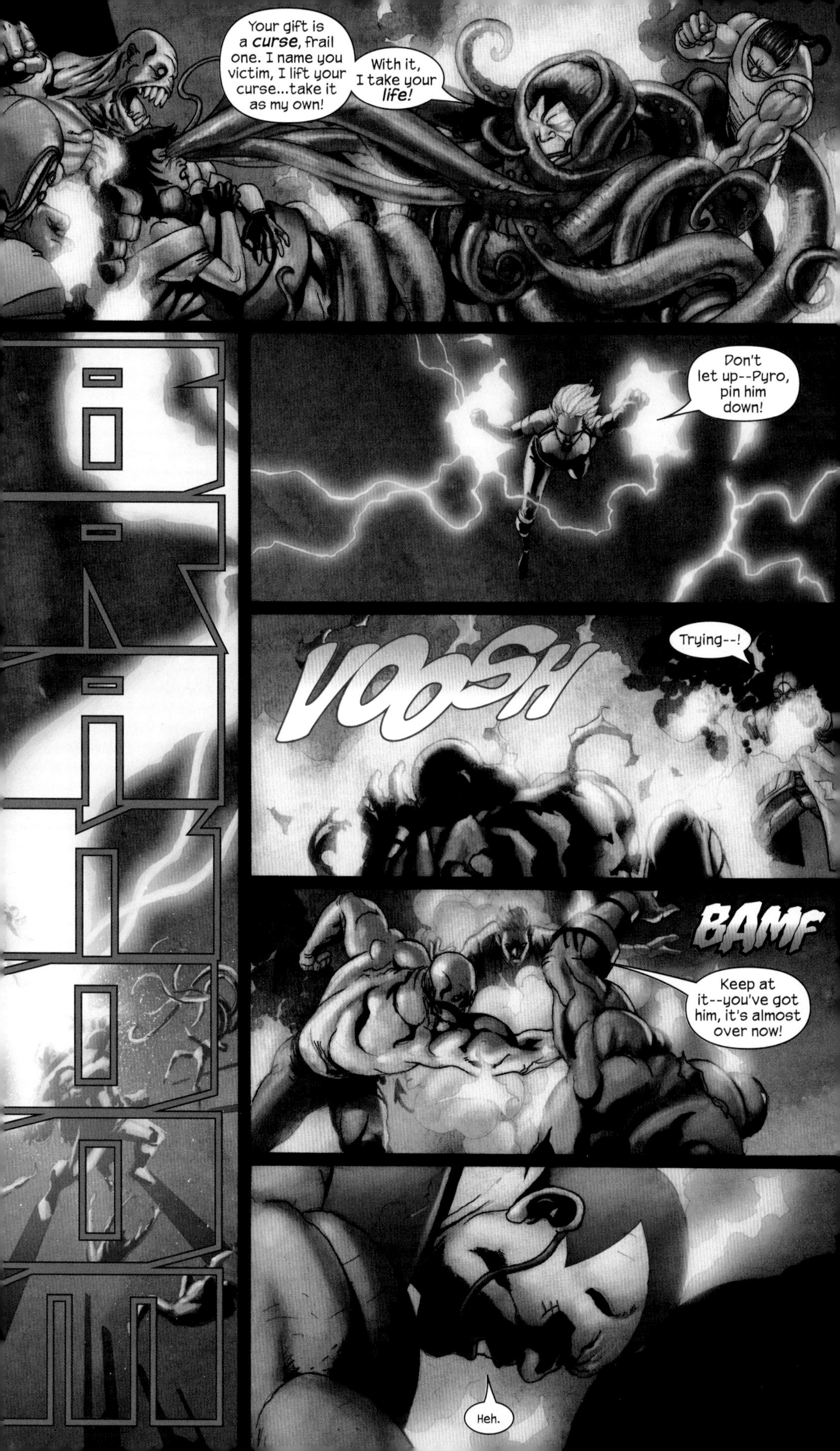
Your gift is a *curse*, frail one. I name you victim, I lift your curse...take it as my own!
With it, I take your *life!*
Don't let up--Pyro, pin him down!
VOOSH
Trying--!
BAMF
Keep at it--you've got him, it's almost over now!
Heh.

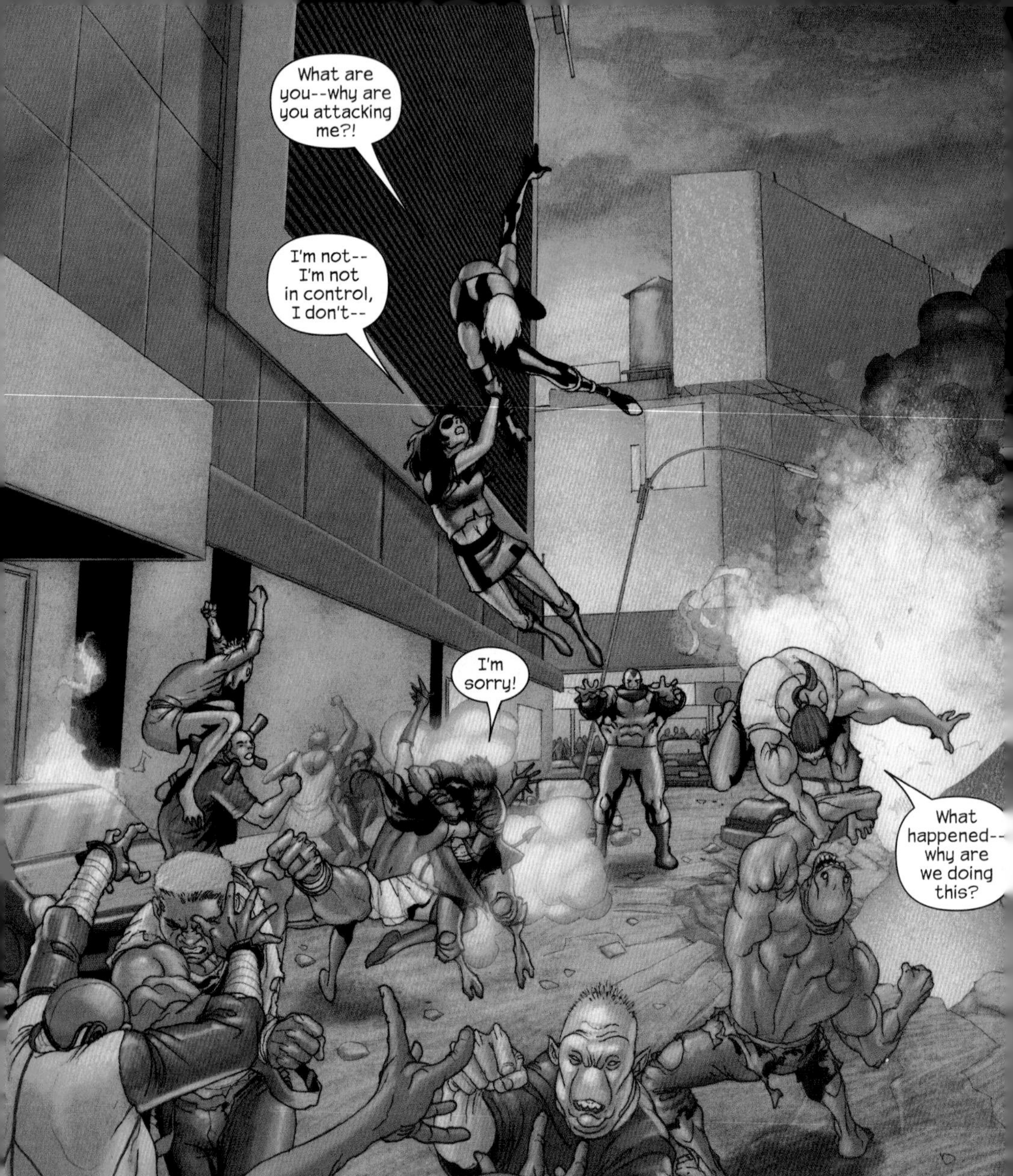
What are you--why are you attacking me?!
I'm not-- I'm not in control, I don't--
I'm sorry!
What happened--why are we doing this?
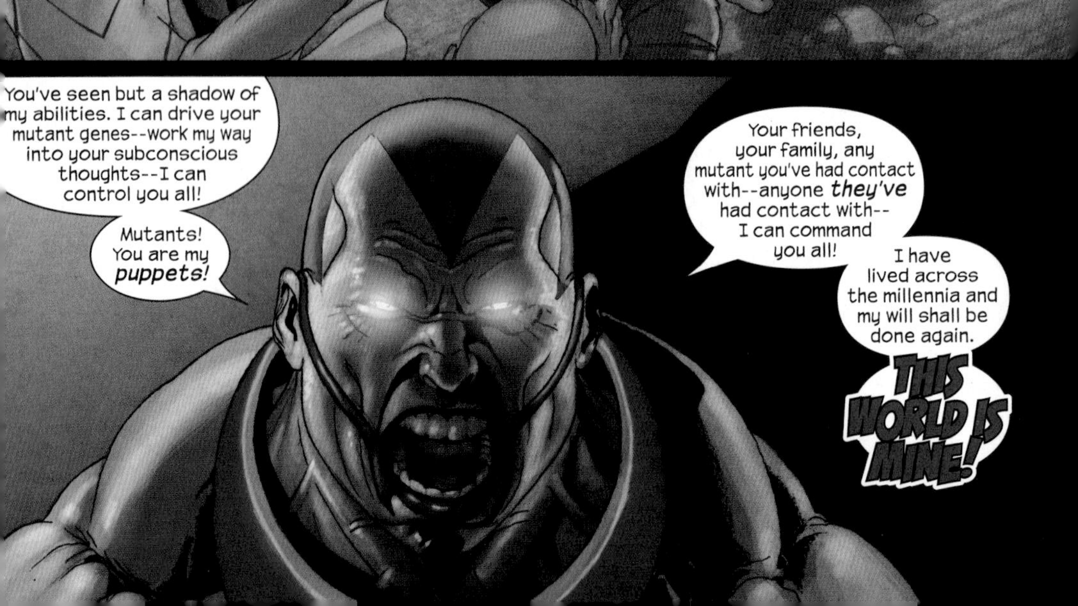
You've seen but a shadow of my abilities. I can drive your mutant genes--work my way into your subconscious thoughts--I can control you all!
Mutants! You are my *puppets!*
Your friends, your family, any mutant you've had contact with--anyone *they've* had contact with--I can command you all!
I have lived across the millennia and my will shall be done again.
THIS WORLD IS MINE!

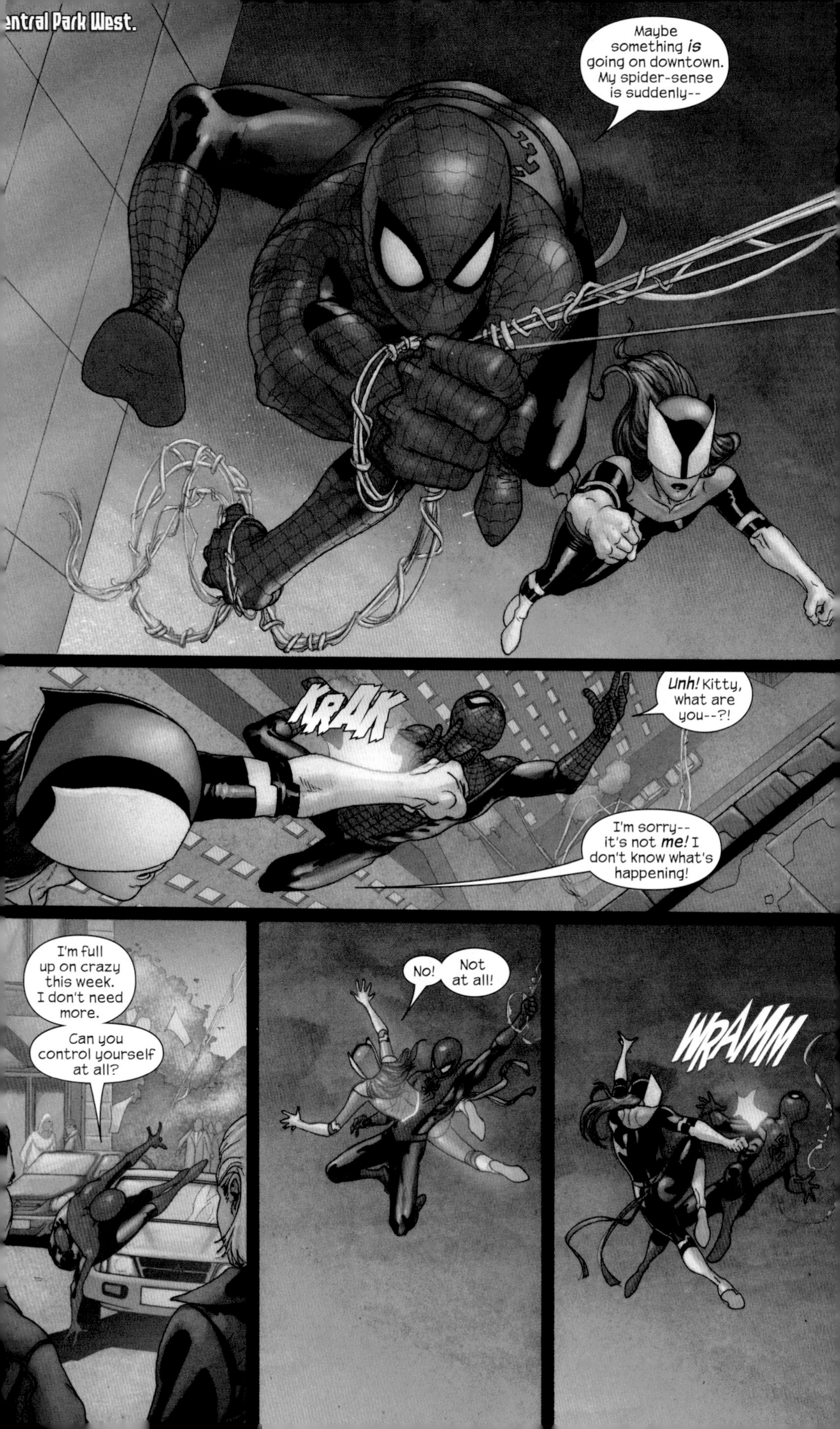
entral Park West.
Maybe something *is* going on downtown. My spider-sense is suddenly--
KRAK
Unh! Kitty, what are you--?!
I'm sorry-- it's not *me!* I don't know what's happening!
I'm full up on crazy this week. I don't need more.
Can you control yourself at all?
No!
Not at all!
WRAMM

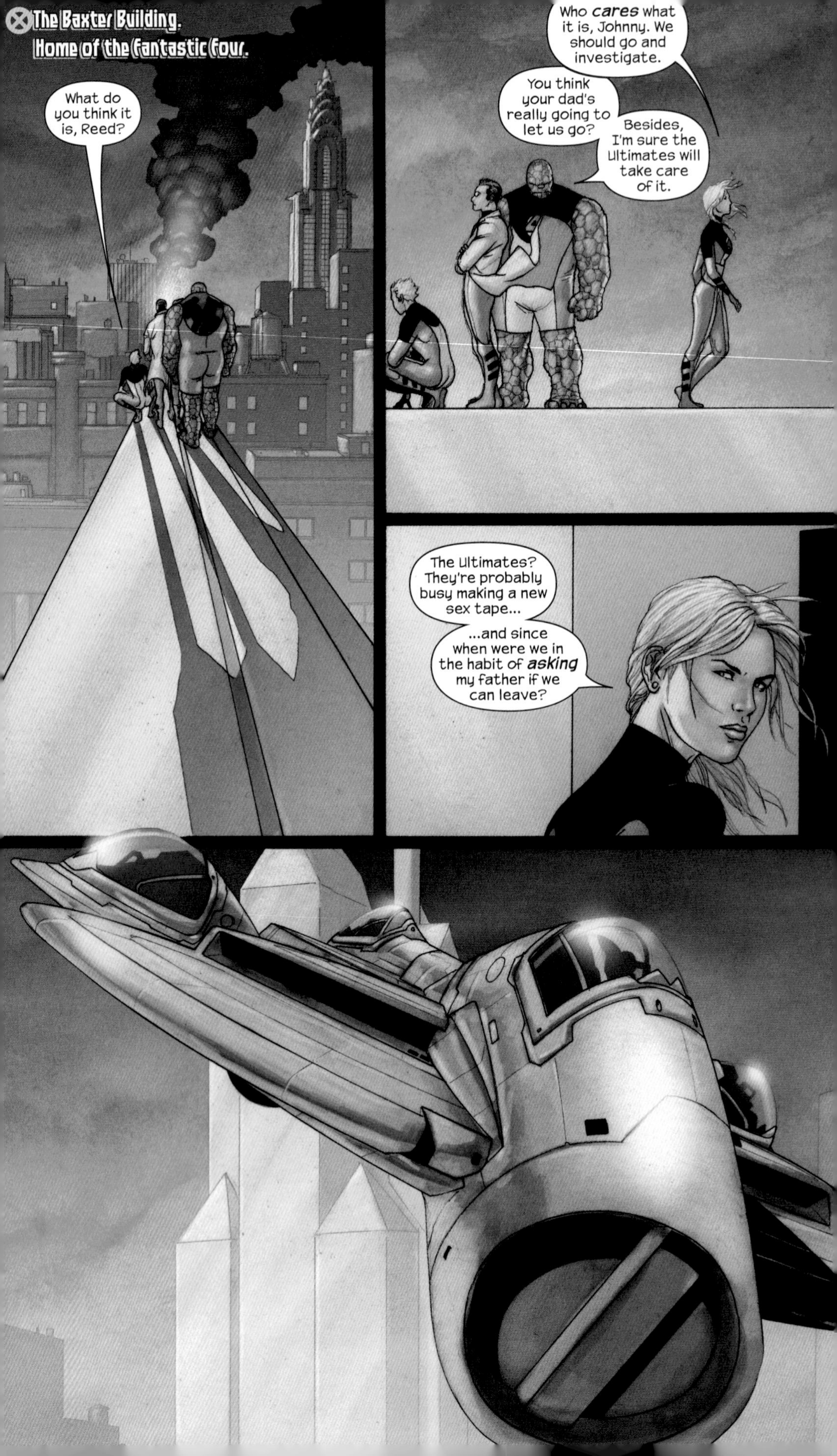
The Baxter Building.
Home of the Fantastic Four.
What do you think it is, Reed?
Who cares what it is, Johnny. We should go and investigate.
You think your dad's really going to let us go?
Besides, I'm sure the Ultimates will take care of it.
The Ultimates? They're probably busy making a new sex tape...
...and since when were we in the habit of asking my father if we can leave?

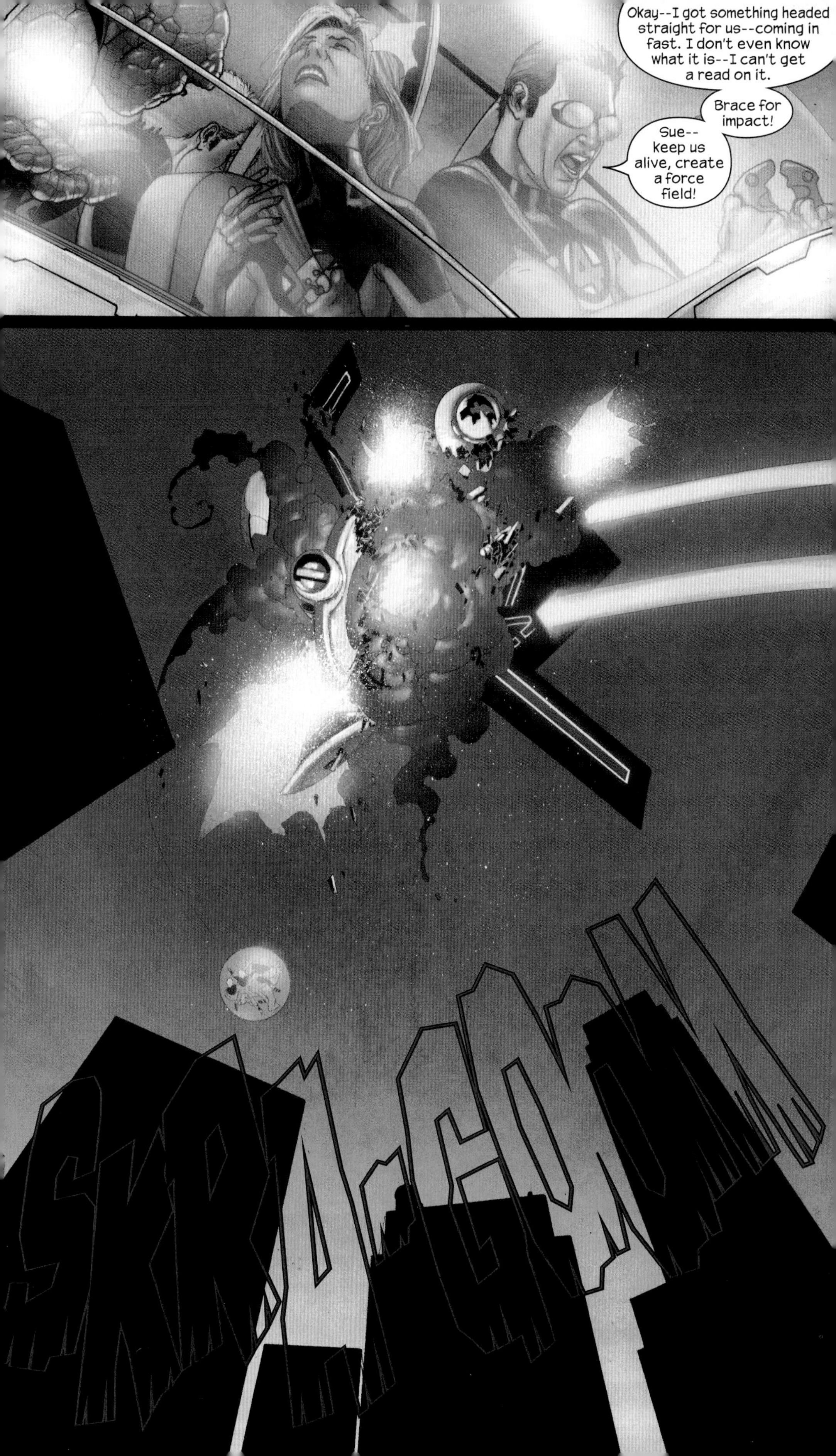
Okay--I got something headed straight for us--coming in fast. I don't even know what it is--I can't get a read on it.
Brace for impact!
Sue--keep us alive, create a force field!

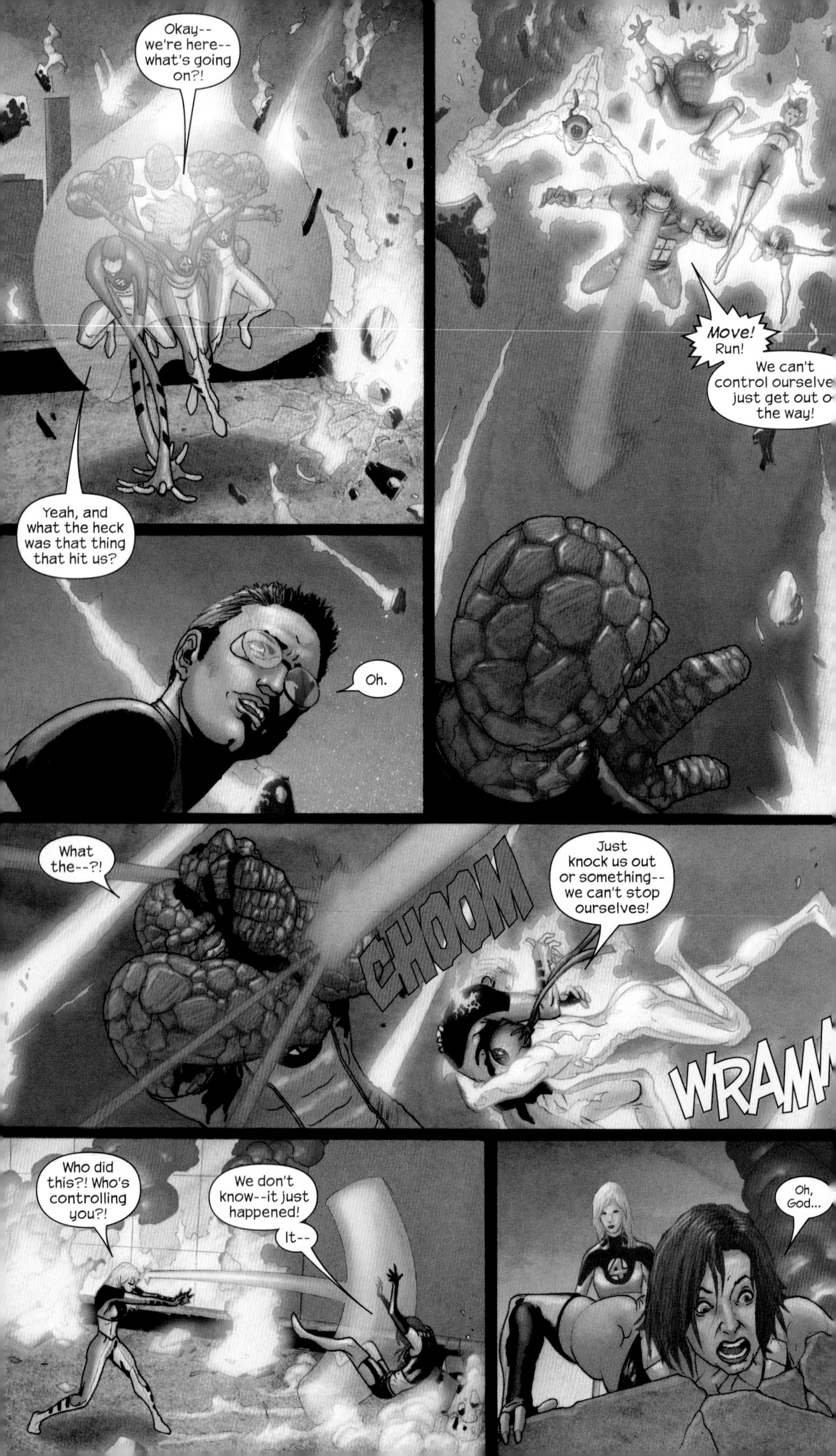

Okay-- we're here-- what's going on?!
Yeah, and what the heck was that thing that hit us?
Oh.
Move! Run!
We can't control ourselve just get out o the way!
What the--?!
Just knock us out or something-- we can't stop ourselves!
CHOOM
WRAM
Who did this?! Who's controlling you?!
We don't know--it just happened!
It--
Oh, God...

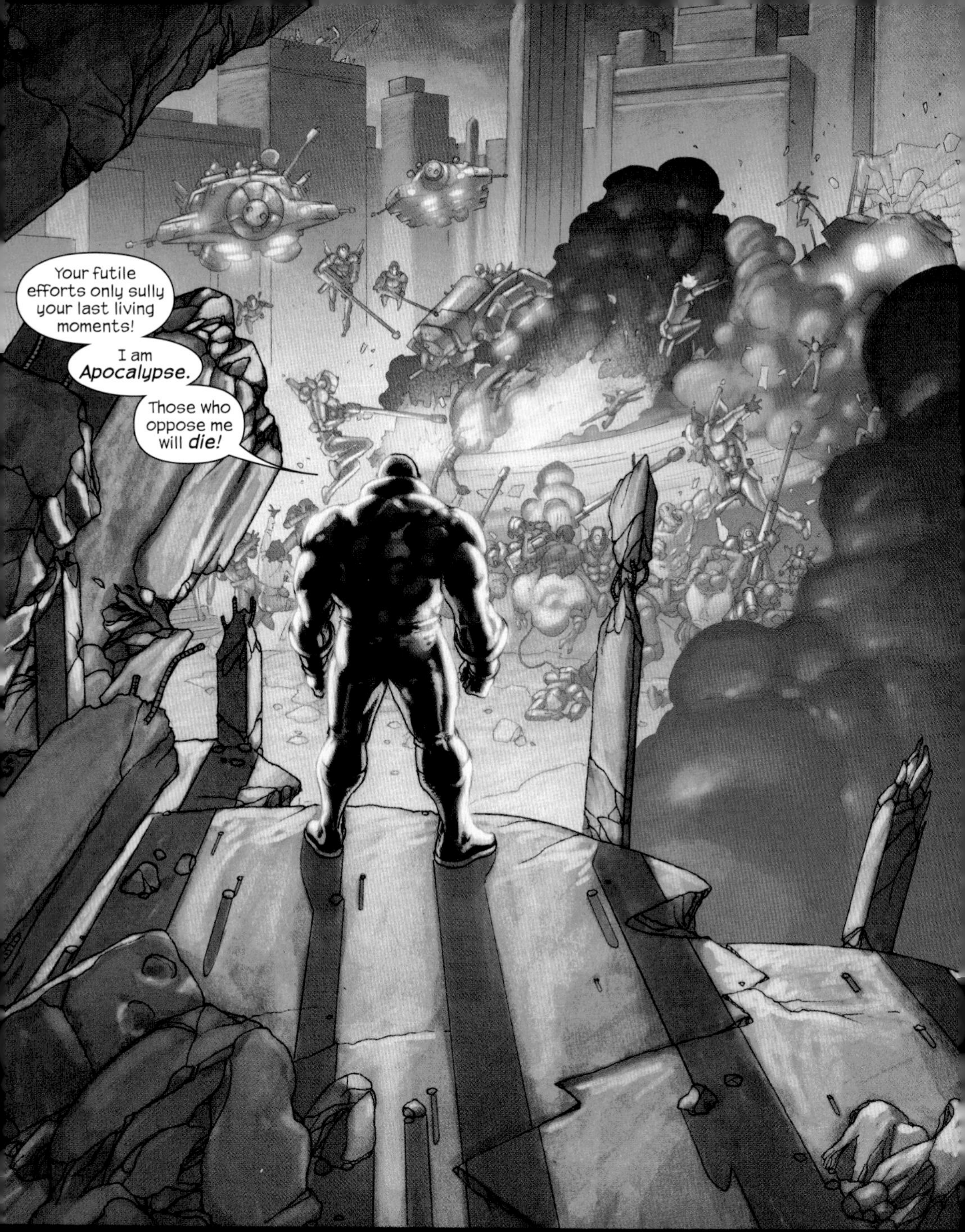
Your futile efforts only sully your last living moments!
I am *Apocalypse.*
Those who oppose me will *die!*

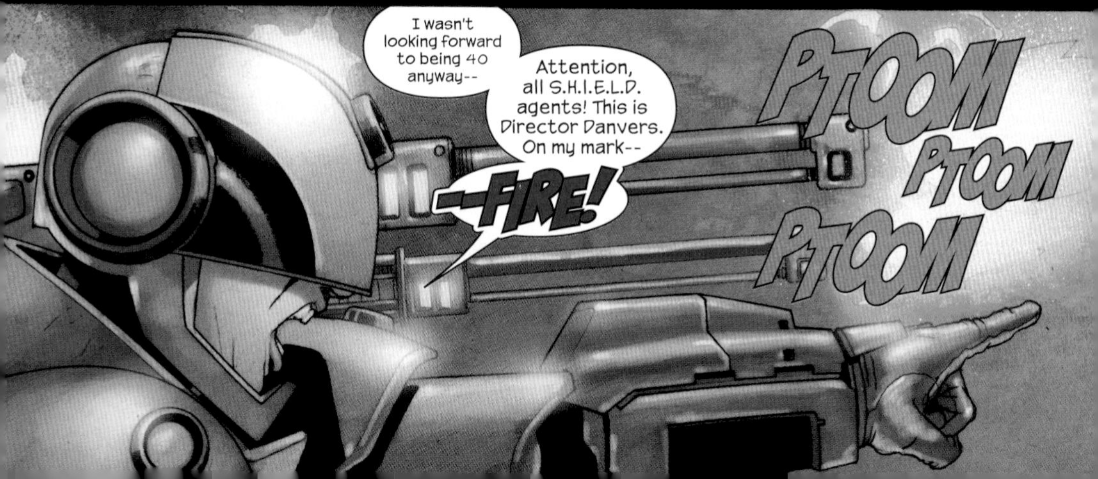
I wasn't looking forward to being 40 anyway--
Attention, all S.H.I.E.L.D. agents! This is Director Danvers. On my mark--
--FIRE!
PTOOM
PTOOM
PTOOM

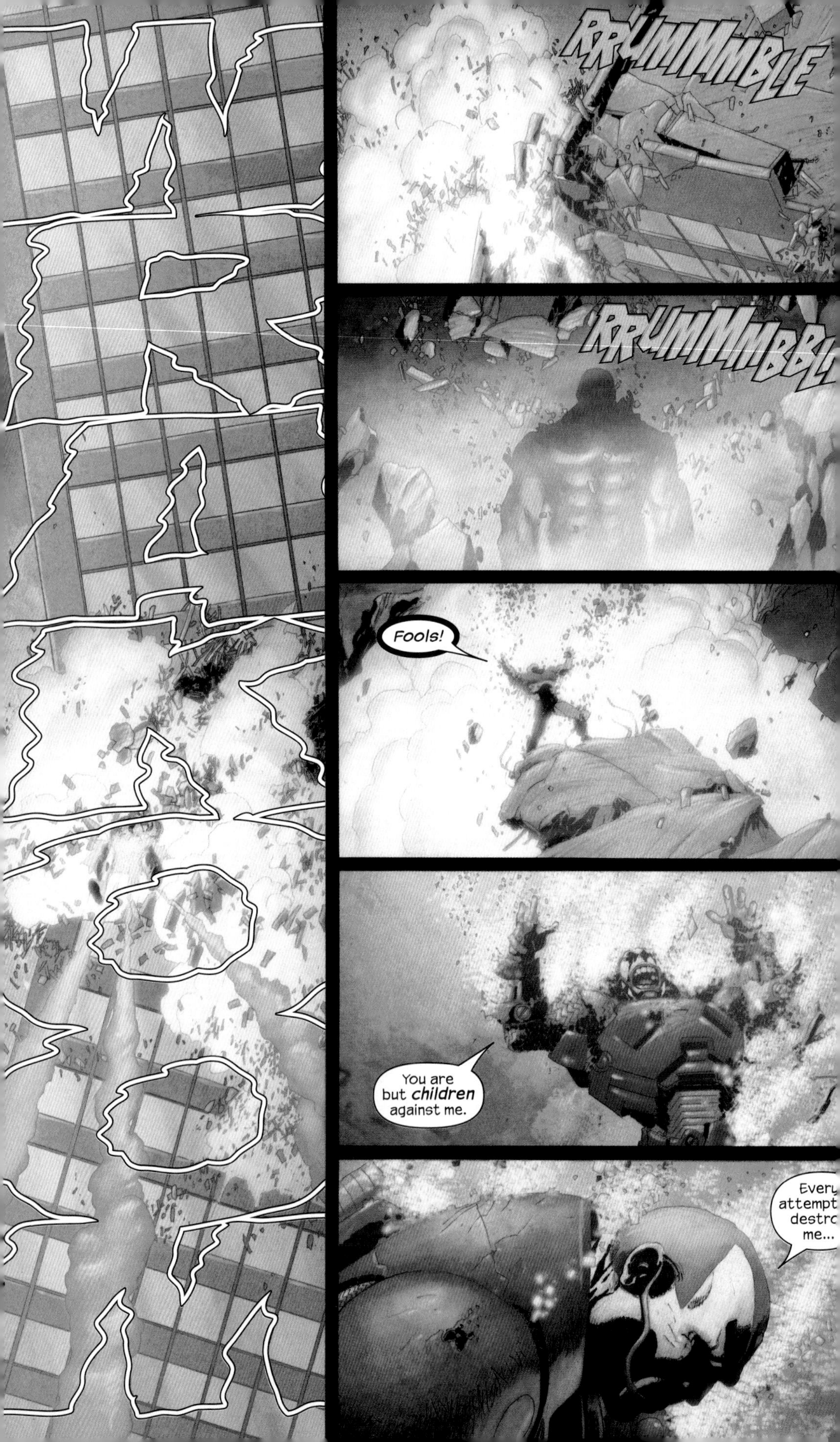
RRUMMMMBLE
RRUMMMMBBL
Fools!
You are but children against me.
Every attempt destro me...

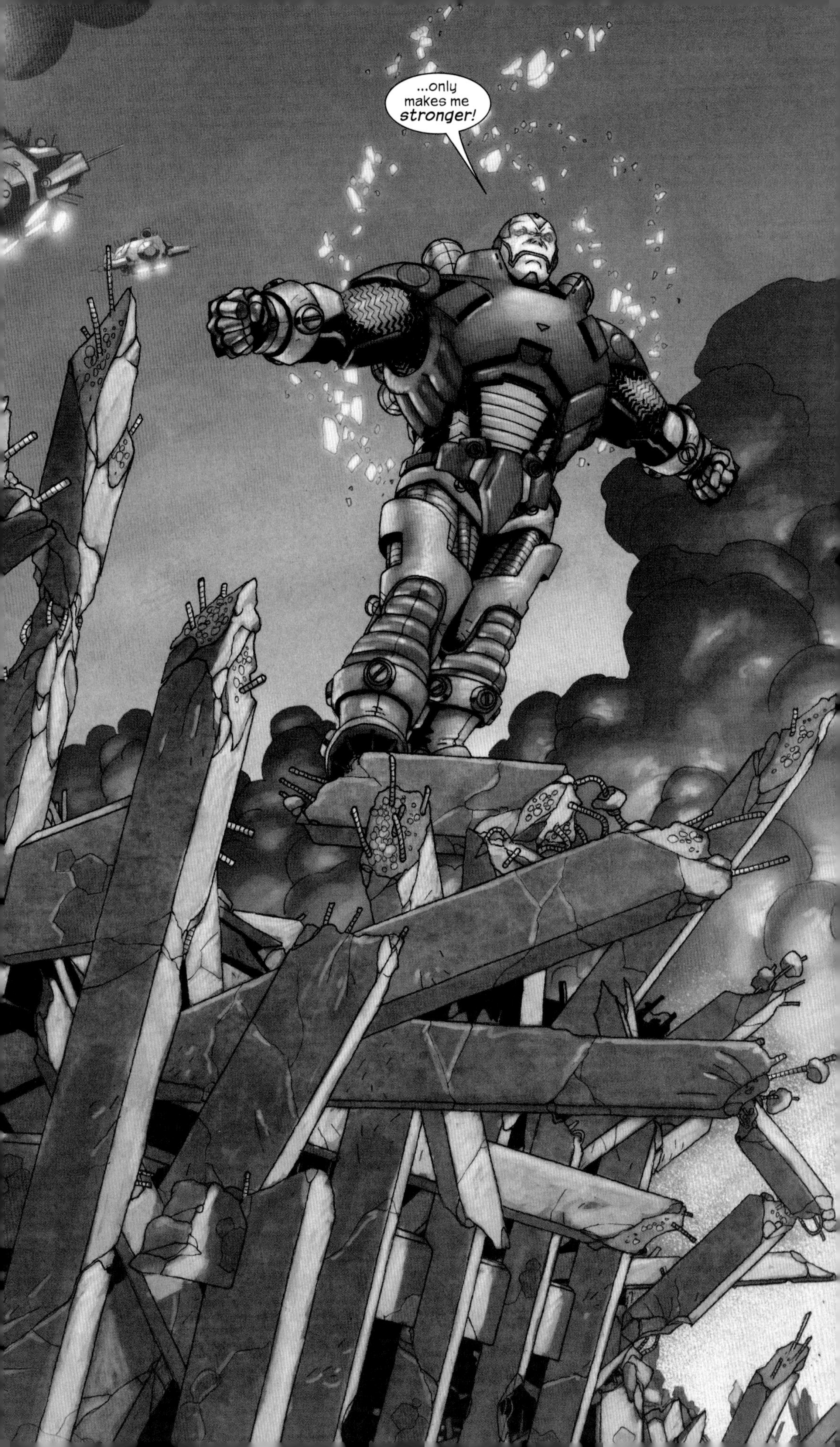
...only makes me *stronger!*

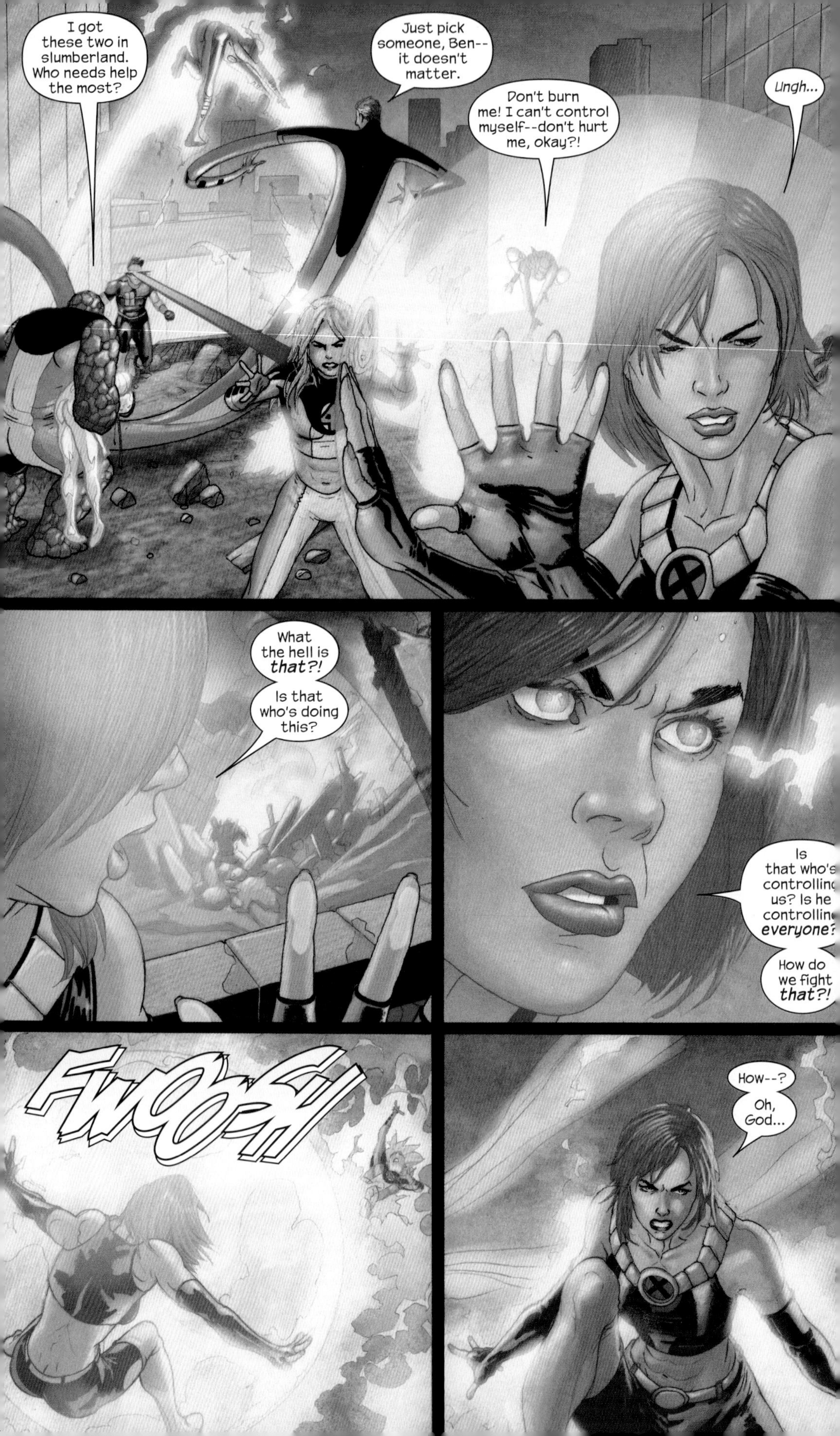
I got these two in slumberland. Who needs help the most?
Just pick someone, Ben-- it doesn't matter.
Don't burn me! I can't control myself--don't hurt me, okay?!
Ungh...
What the hell is *that?!*
Is that who's doing this?
Is that who's controllin
us? Is he controllin
everyone?
How do we fight *that?!*
FWOOSH
How--?
Oh, God...

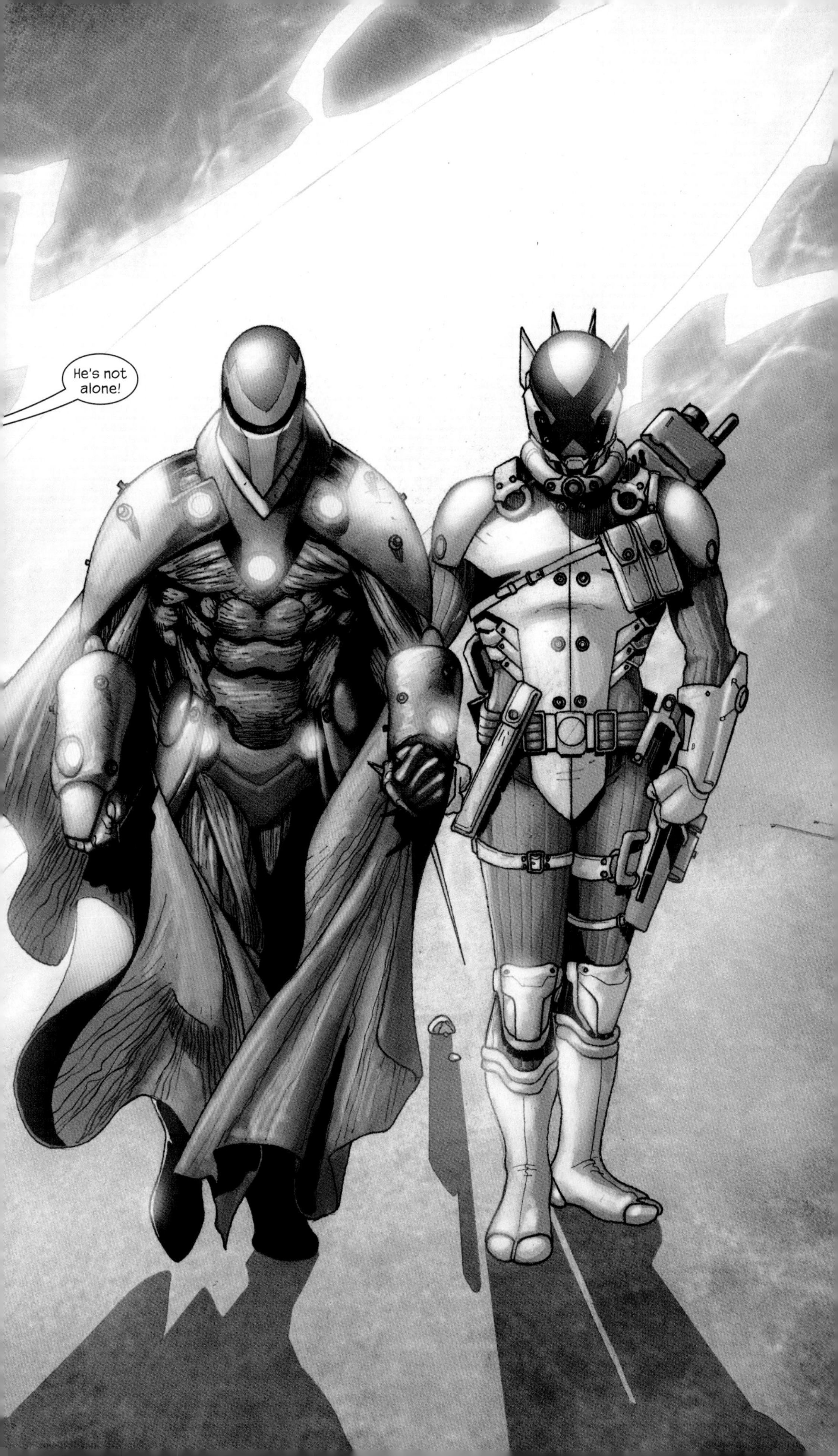
He's not alone!

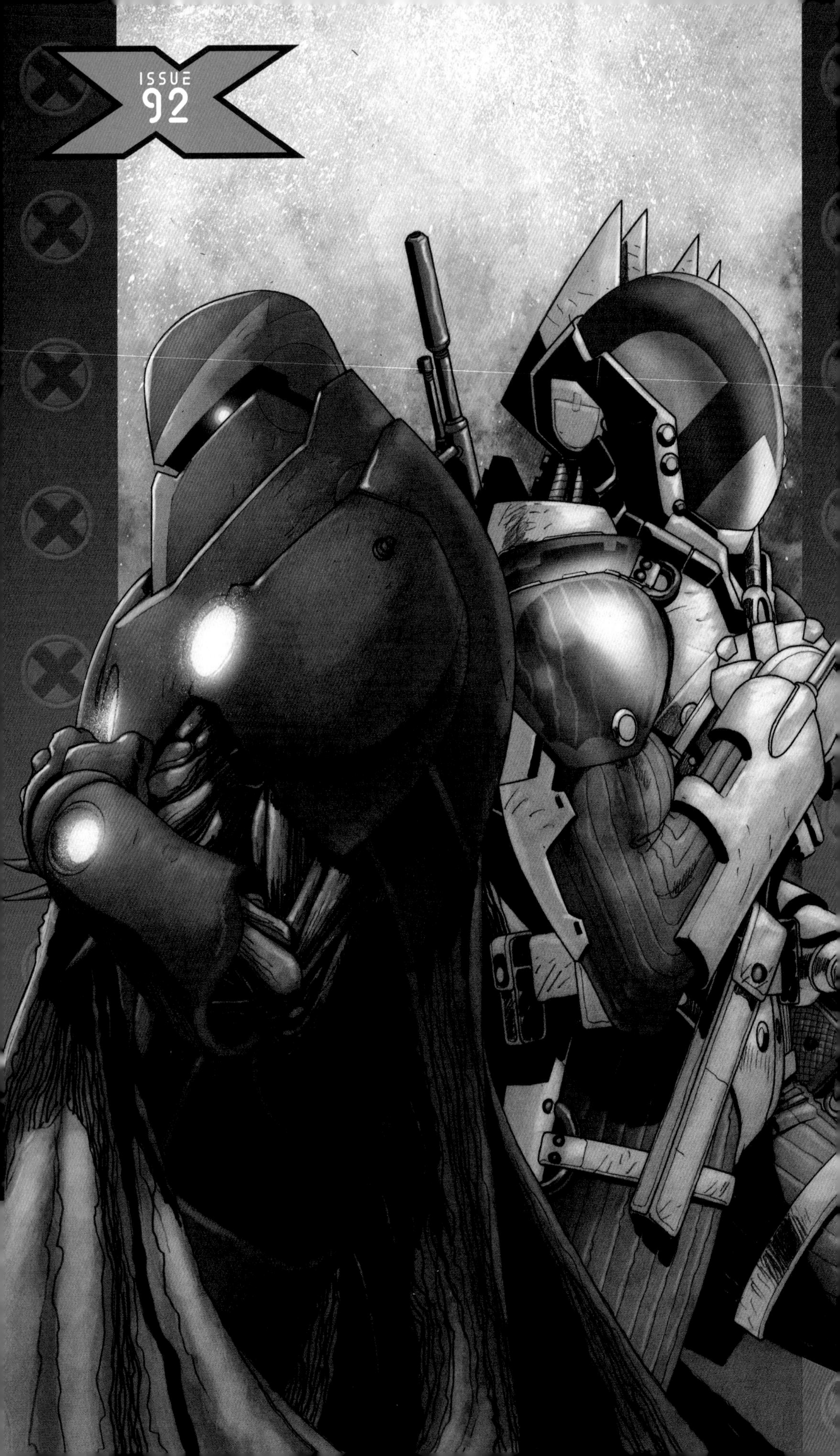
ISSUE
92

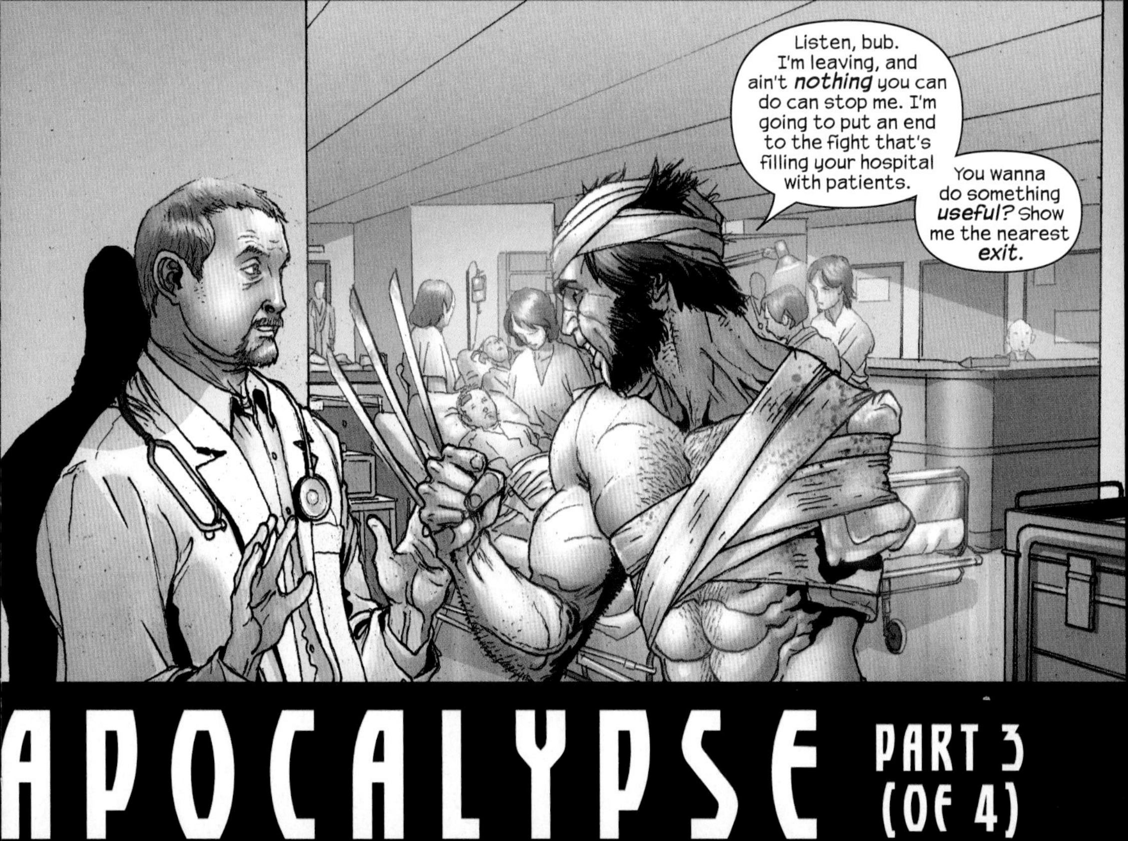
Listen, bub. I'm leaving, and ain't nothing you can do can stop me. I'm going to put an end to the fight that's filling your hospital with patients.
You wanna do something useful? Show me the nearest exit.
APOCALYPSE PART 3 (OF 4)

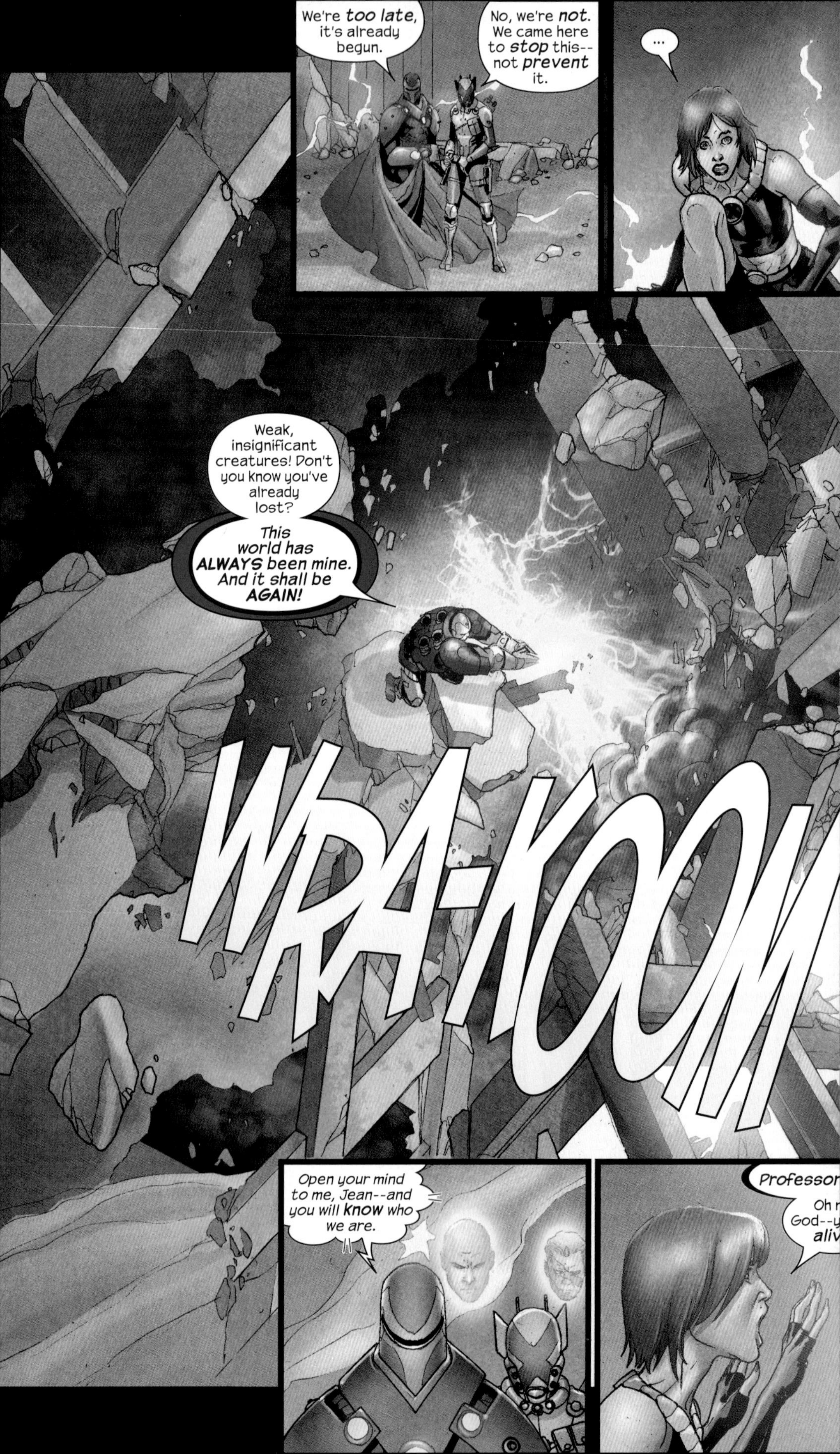
We're too late, it's already begun.
No, we're not. We came here to stop this-- not prevent it.
...
Weak, insignificant creatures! Don't you know you've already lost?
This world has ALWAYS been mine. And it shall be AGAIN!
WRA-KOOM
Open your mind to me, Jean--and you will KNOW who we are.
Professor
Oh God--y aliv

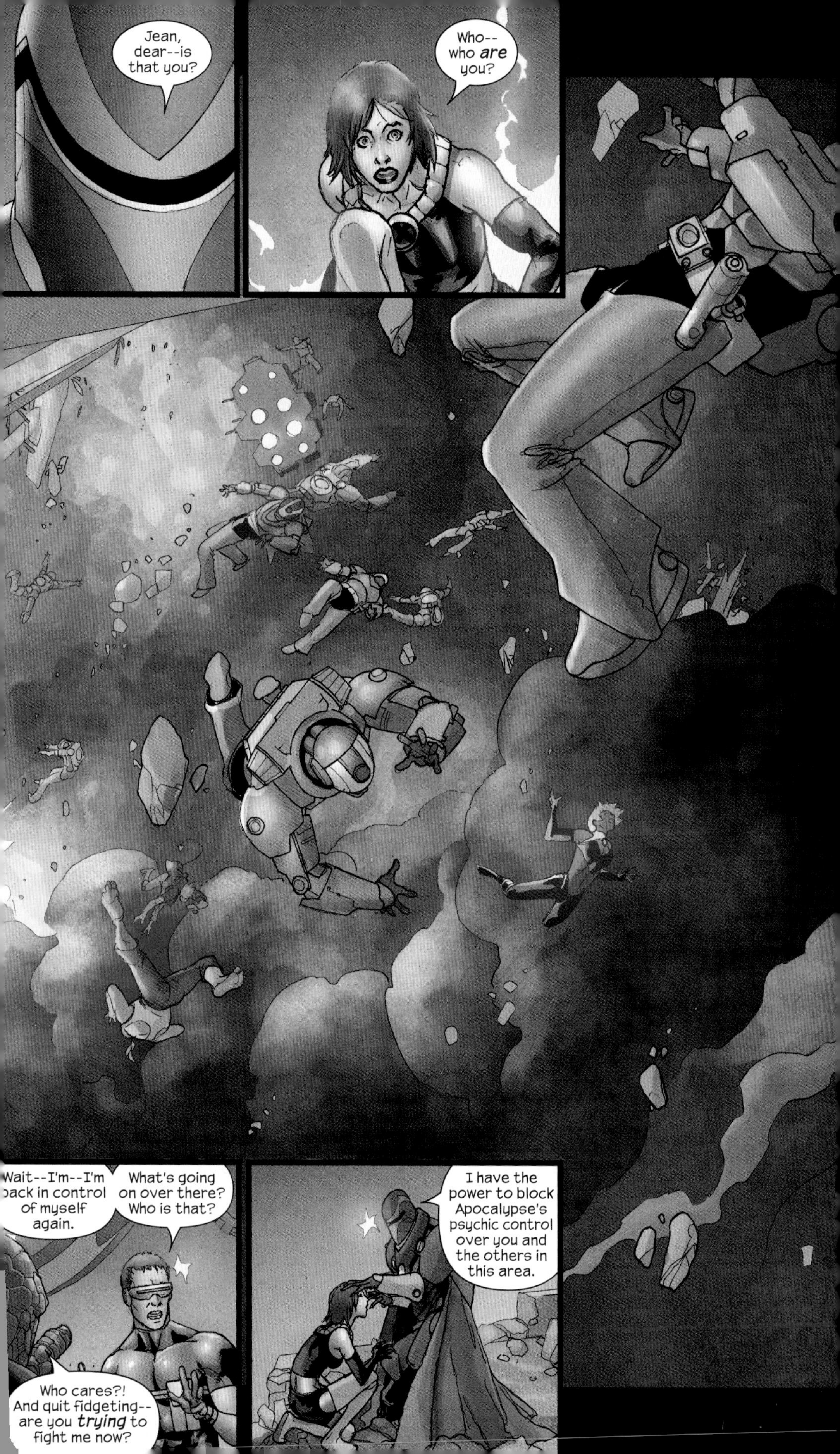
Jean, dear--is that you?
Who-- who **are** you?
Wait--I'm--I'm back in control of myself again.
What's going on over there? Who is that?
Who cares?! And quit fidgeting-- are you ***trying*** to fight me now?
I have the power to block Apocalypse's psychic control over you and the others in this area.

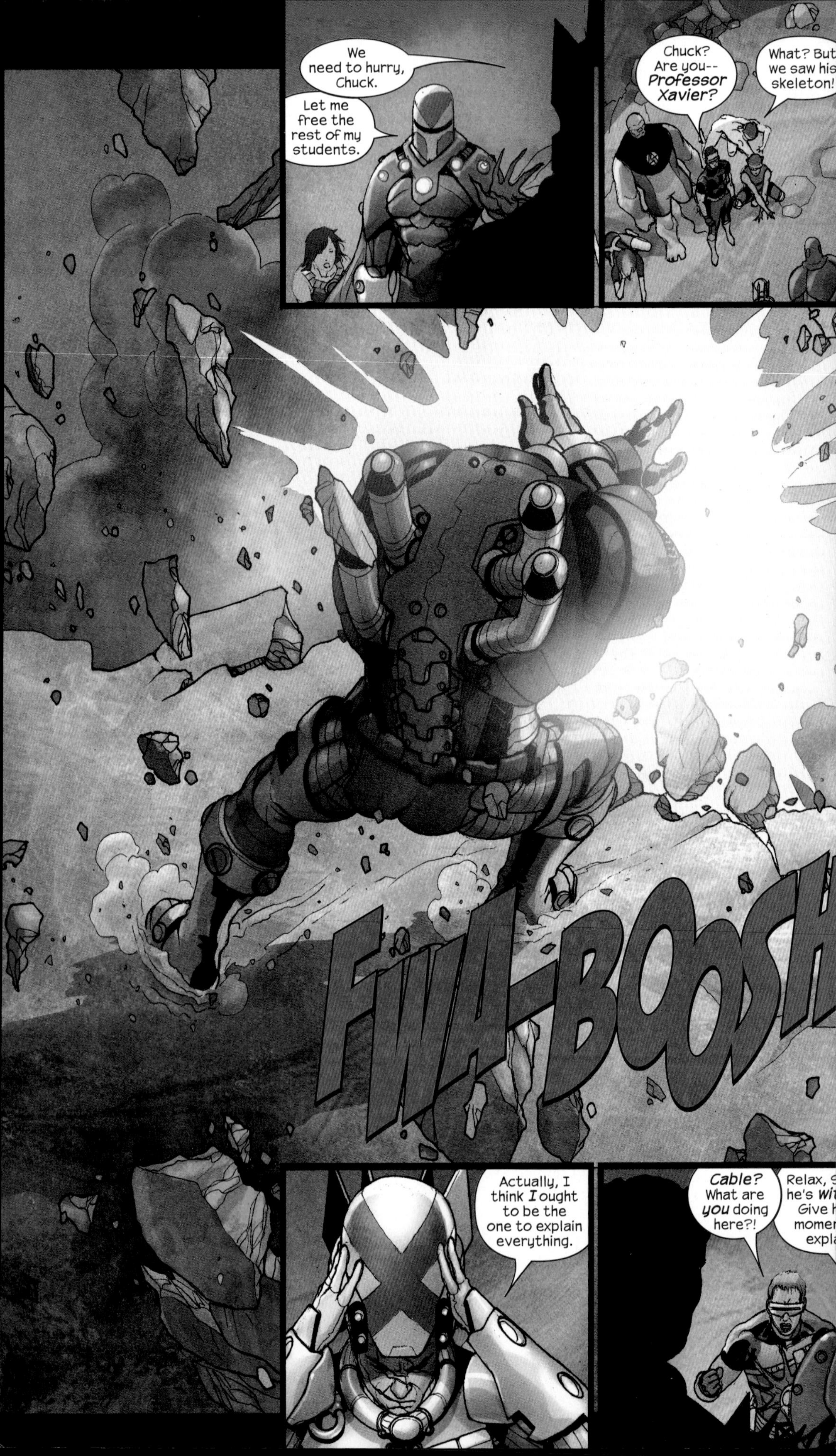

We need to hurry, Chuck.
Let me free the rest of my students.
Chuck? Are you-- *Professor Xavier?*
What? But we saw his skeleton!
FWA-BOOSH
Actually, I think *I* ought to be the one to explain everything.
Cable? What are *you* doing here?!

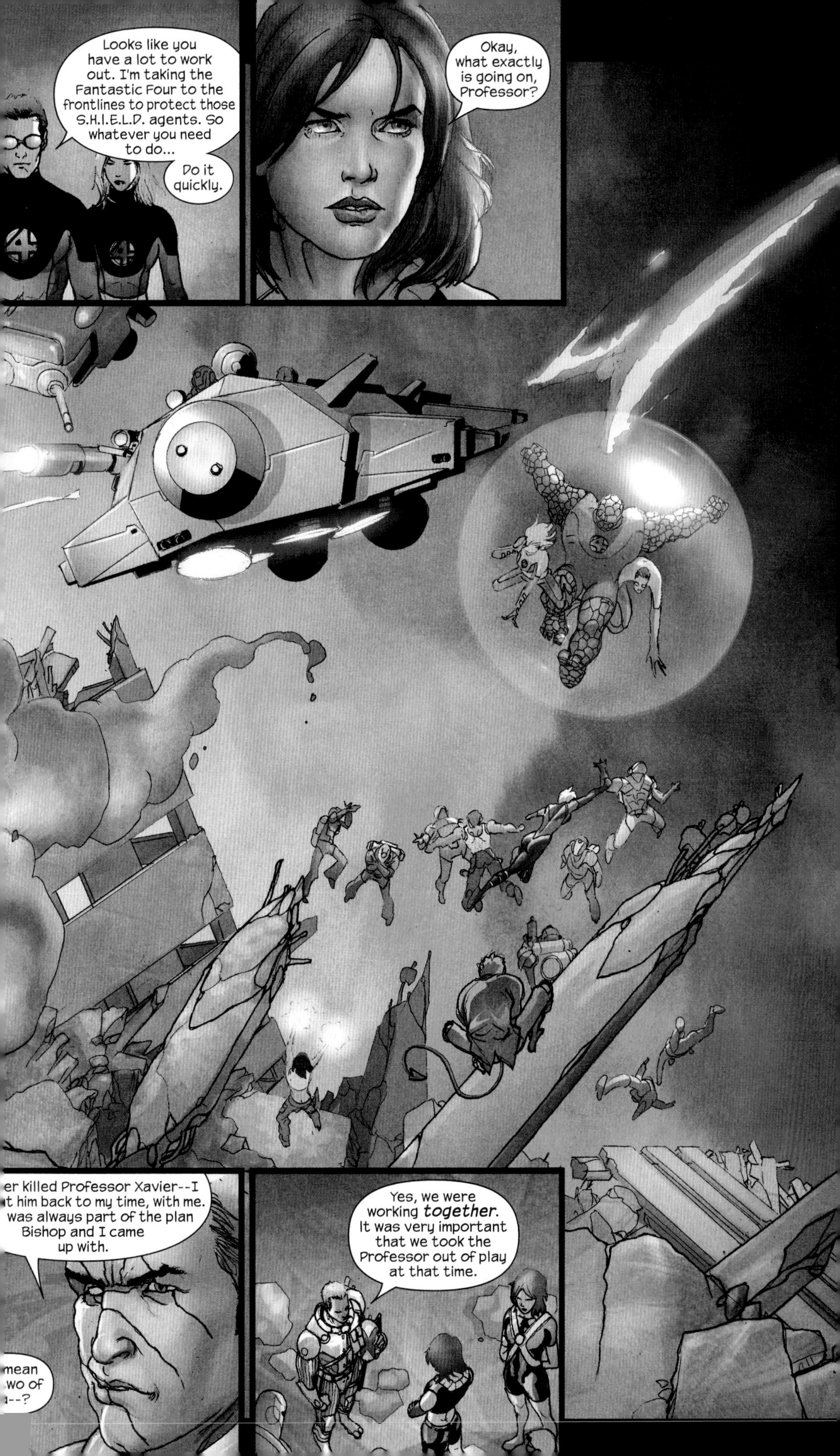

Looks like you have a lot to work out. I'm taking the Fantastic Four to the frontlines to protect those S.H.I.E.L.D. agents. So whatever you need to do...
Do it quickly.
Okay, what exactly is going on, Professor?
er killed Professor Xavier--I t him back to my time, with me. was always part of the plan Bishop and I came up with.
mean wo of --?
Yes, we were working *together*. It was very important that we took the Professor out of play at that time.

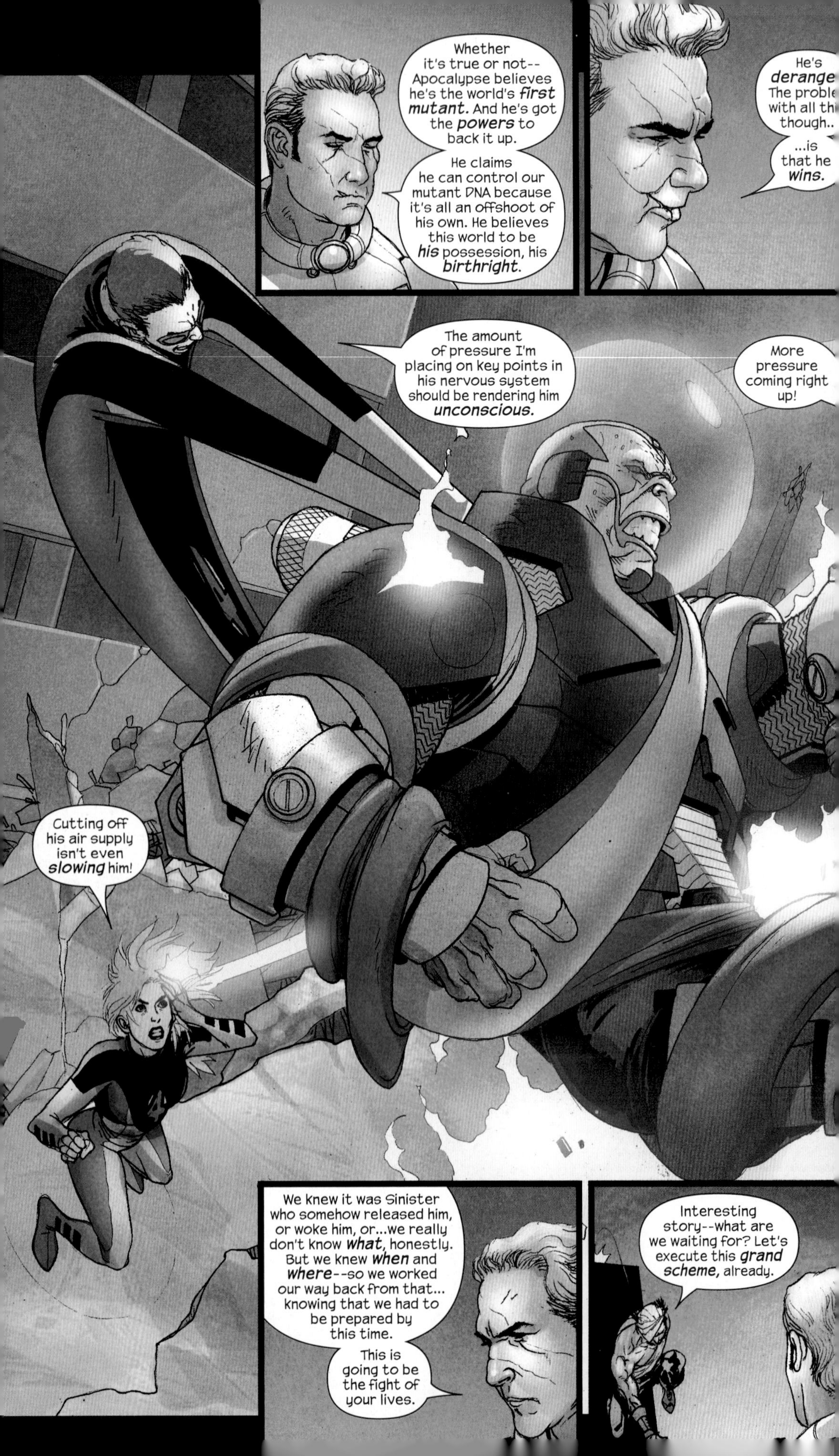

Whether it's true or not--Apocalypse believes he's the world's *first mutant*. And he's got the *powers* to back it up.
He claims he can control our mutant DNA because it's all an offshoot of his own. He believes this world to be *his* possession, his *birthright*.
He's *derange* The proble with all th though..
...is that he *wins*.
The amount of pressure I'm placing on key points in his nervous system should be rendering him *unconscious*.
More pressure coming right up!
Cutting off his air supply isn't even *slowing* him!
We knew it was Sinister who somehow released him, or woke him, or...we really don't know *what*, honestly. But we knew *when* and *where*--so we worked our way back from that... knowing that we had to be prepared by this time.
This is going to be the fight of your lives.
Interesting story--what are we waiting for? Let's execute this *grand scheme*, already.

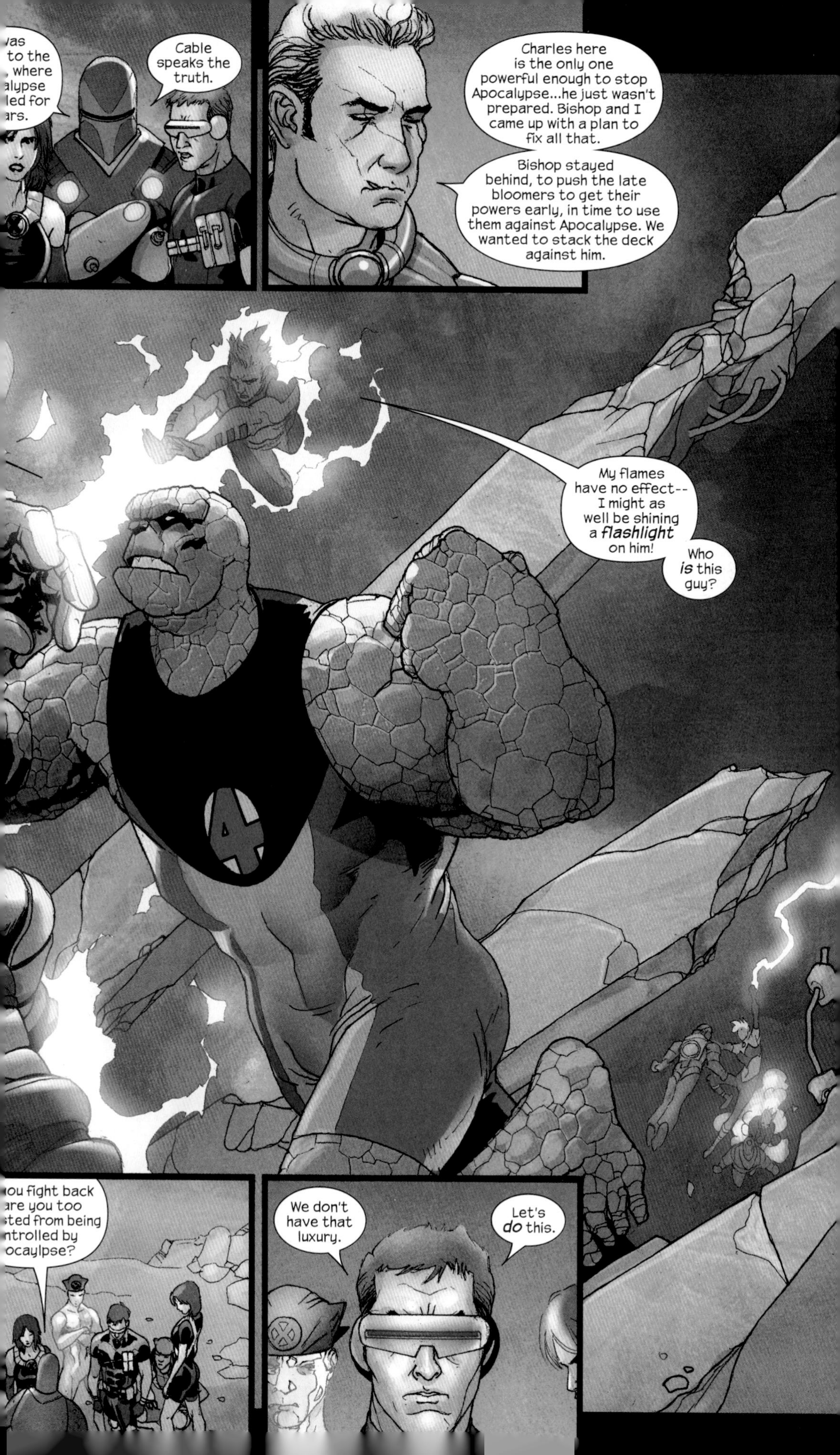

/as
to the
, where
alypse
led for
ars.
Cable speaks the truth.
Charles here is the only one powerful enough to stop Apocalypse...he just wasn't prepared. Bishop and I came up with a plan to fix all that.
Bishop stayed behind, to push the late bloomers to get their powers early, in time to use them against Apocalypse. We wanted to stack the deck against him.
My flames have no effect-- I might as well be shining a *flashlight* on him!
Who *is* this guy?
ou fight back
are you too
sted from being
ntrolled by
ocaylpse?
We don't have that luxury.
Let's *do* this.

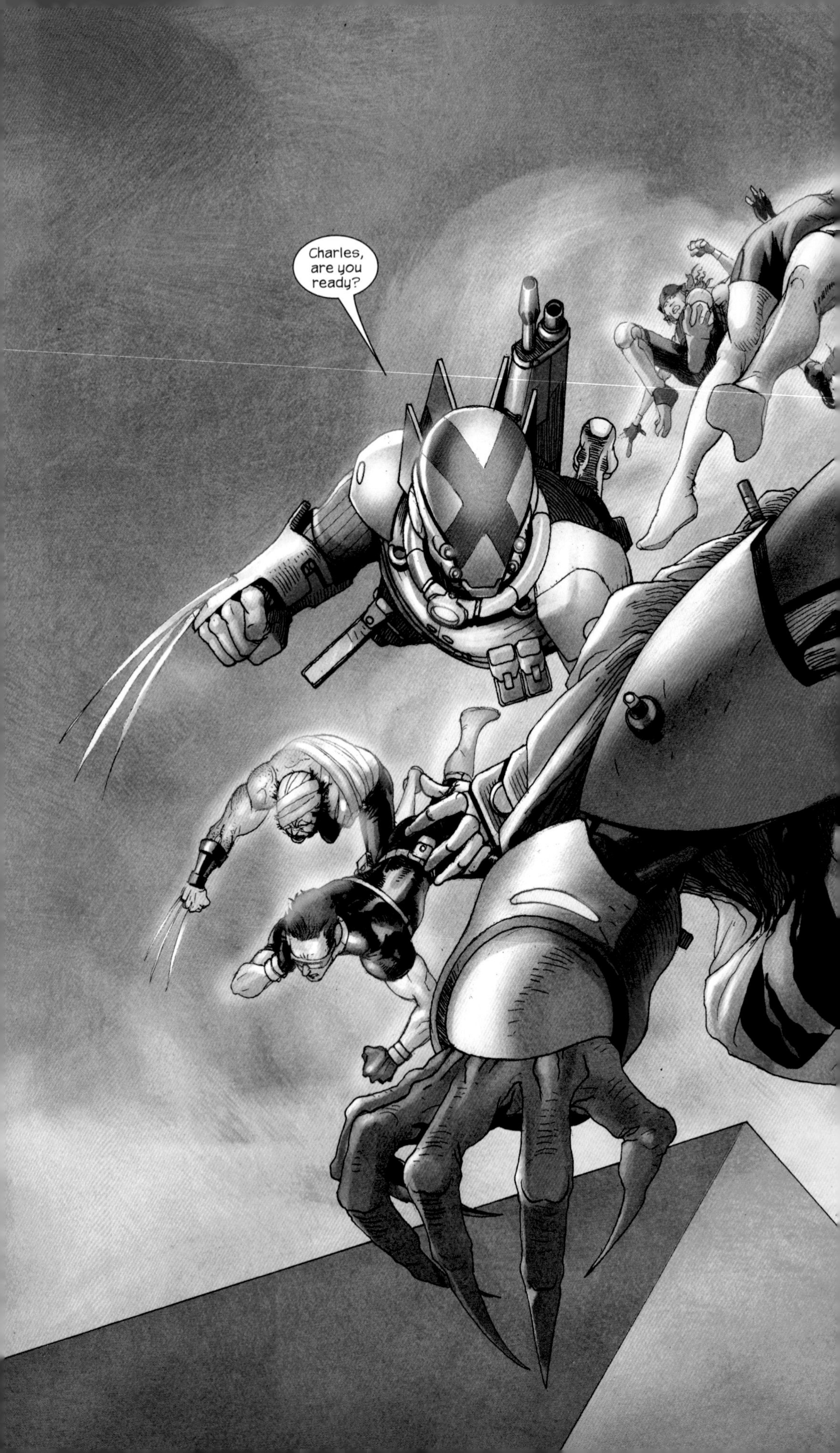
Charles, are you ready?

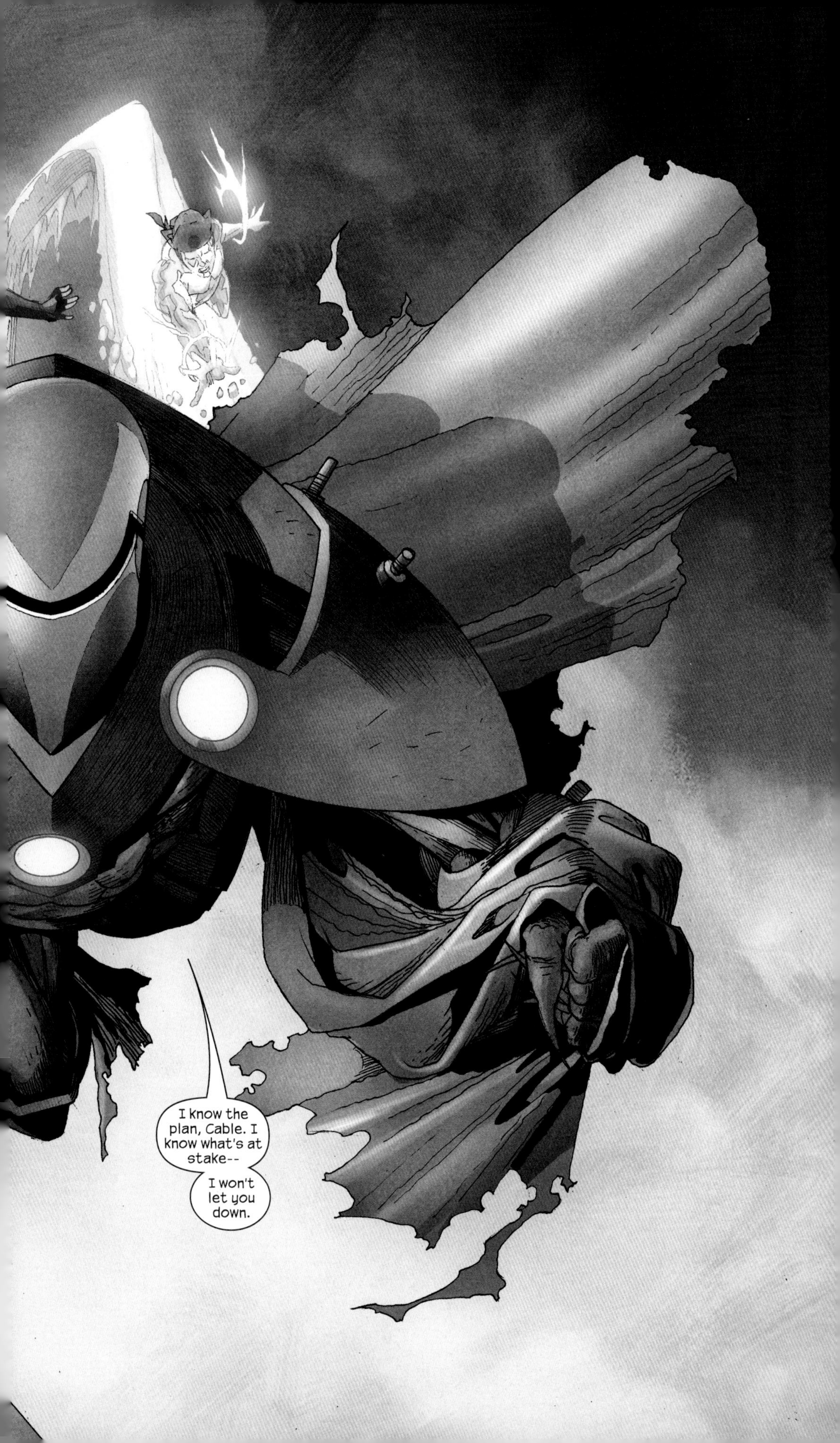
I know the plan, Cable. I know what's at stake--
I won't let you down.

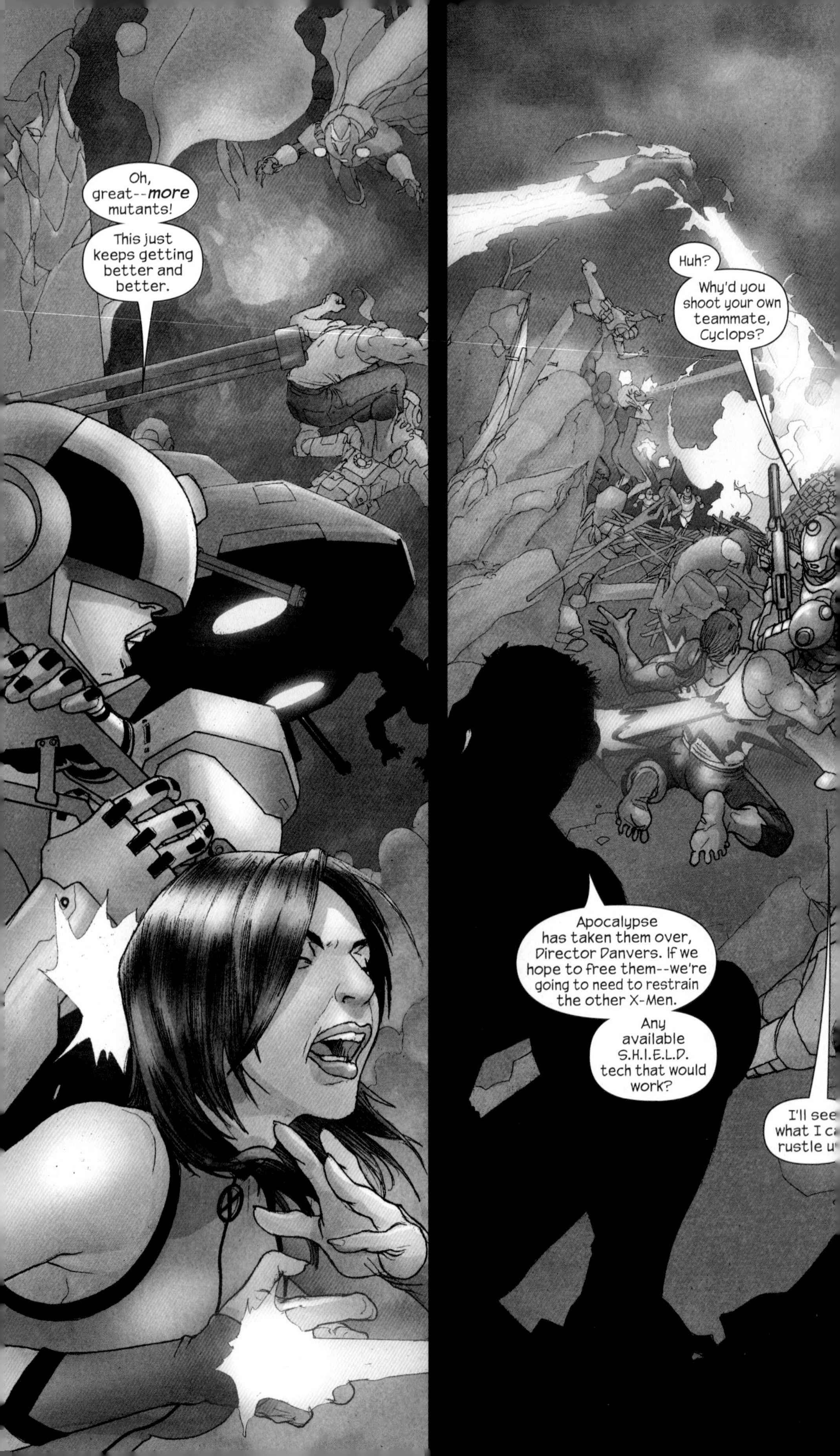

Oh, great--*more* mutants!
This just keeps getting better and better.
Huh?
Why'd you shoot your own teammate, Cyclops?
Apocalypse has taken them over, Director Danvers. If we hope to free them--we're going to need to restrain the other X-Men.
Any available S.H.I.E.L.D. tech that would work?

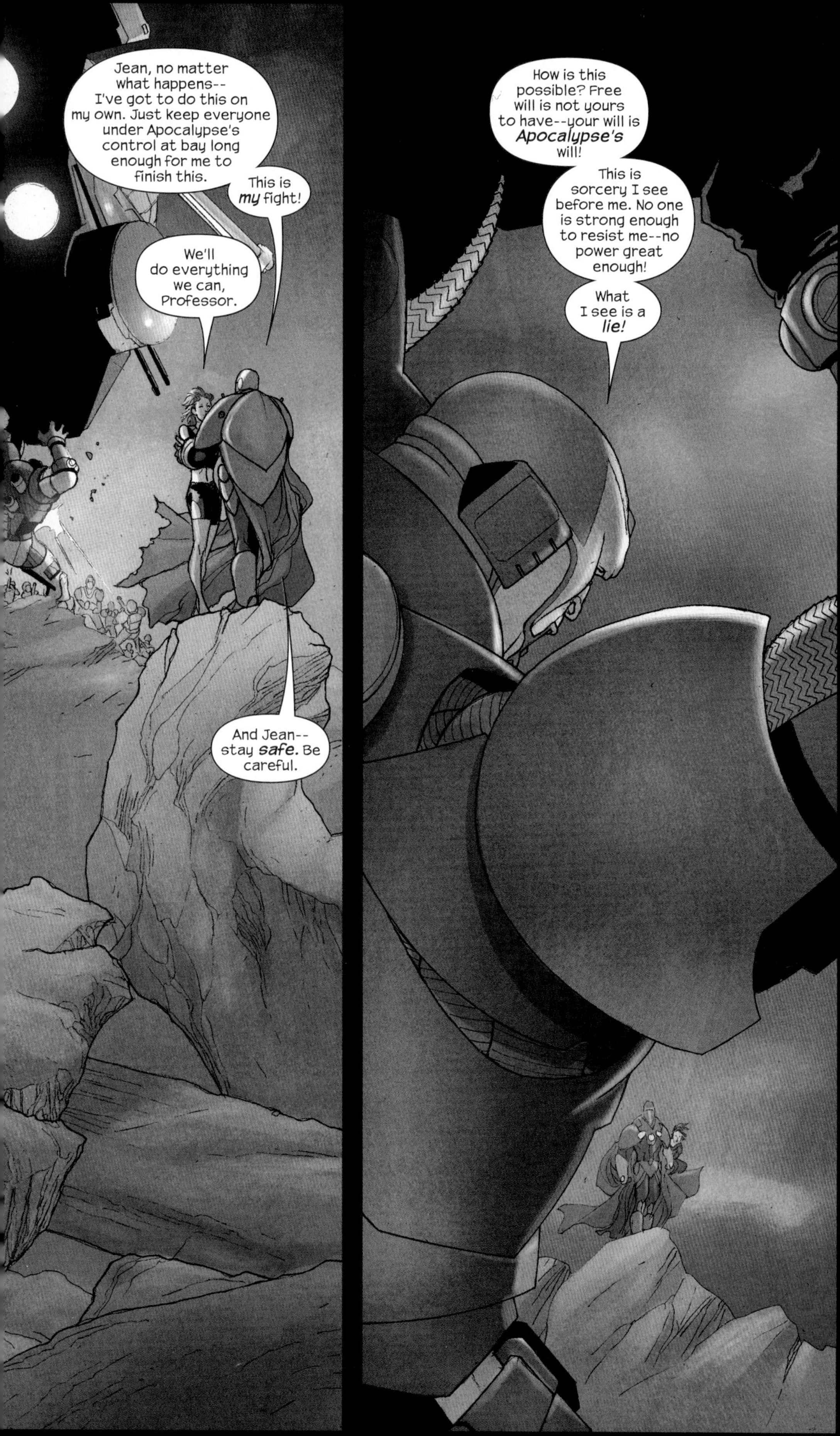

Jean, no matter what happens-- I've got to do this on my own. Just keep everyone under Apocalypse's control at bay long enough for me to finish this.
This is *my* fight!
We'll do everything we can, Professor.
And Jean-- stay *safe.* Be careful.
How is this possible? Free will is not yours to have--your will is *Apocalypse's* will!
This is sorcery I see before me. No one is strong enough to resist me--no power great enough!
What I see is a *lie!*

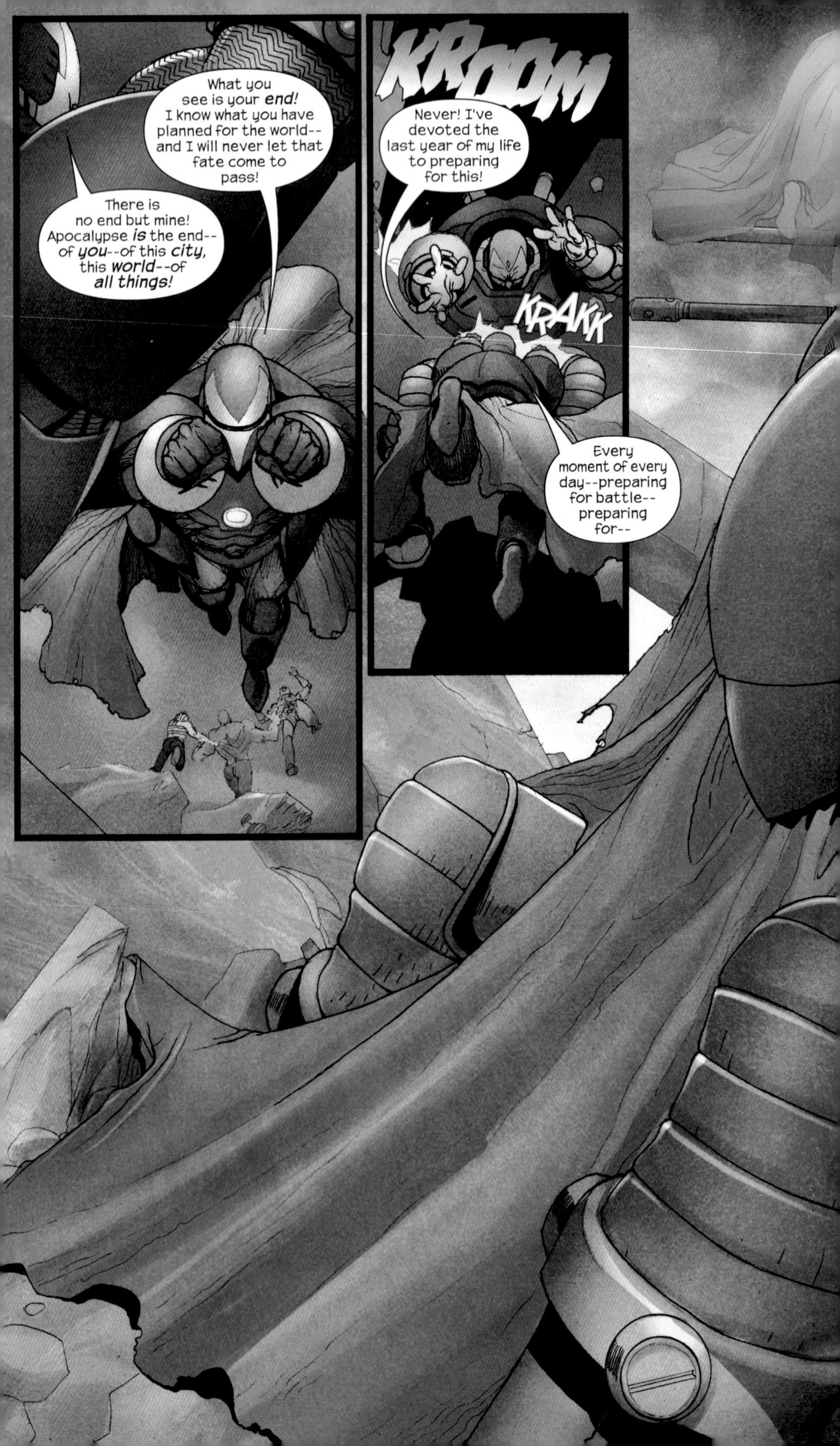
What you see is your end! I know what you have planned for the world-- and I will never let that fate come to pass!
There is no end but mine! Apocalypse is the end-- of you--of this city, this world--of all things!
KROOM
Never! I've devoted the last year of my life to preparing for this!
KRAKK
Every moment of every day--preparing for battle-- preparing for--

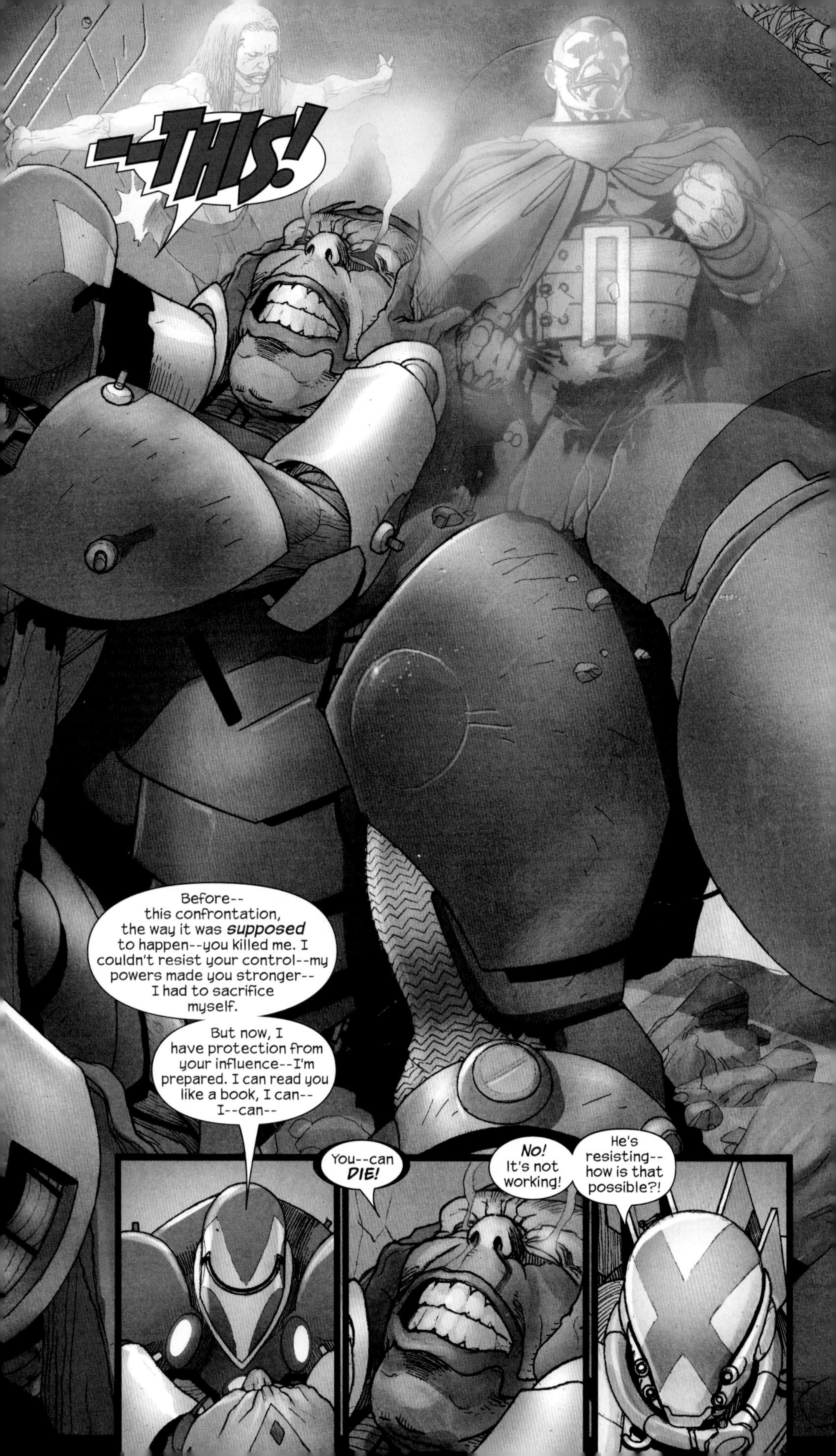
--THIS!
Before-- this confrontation, the way it was *supposed* to happen--you killed me. I couldn't resist your control--my powers made you stronger-- I had to sacrifice myself.
But now, I have protection from your influence--I'm prepared. I can read you like a book, I can-- I--can--
You--can *DIE!*
NO! It's not working!
He's resisting-- how is that possible?!

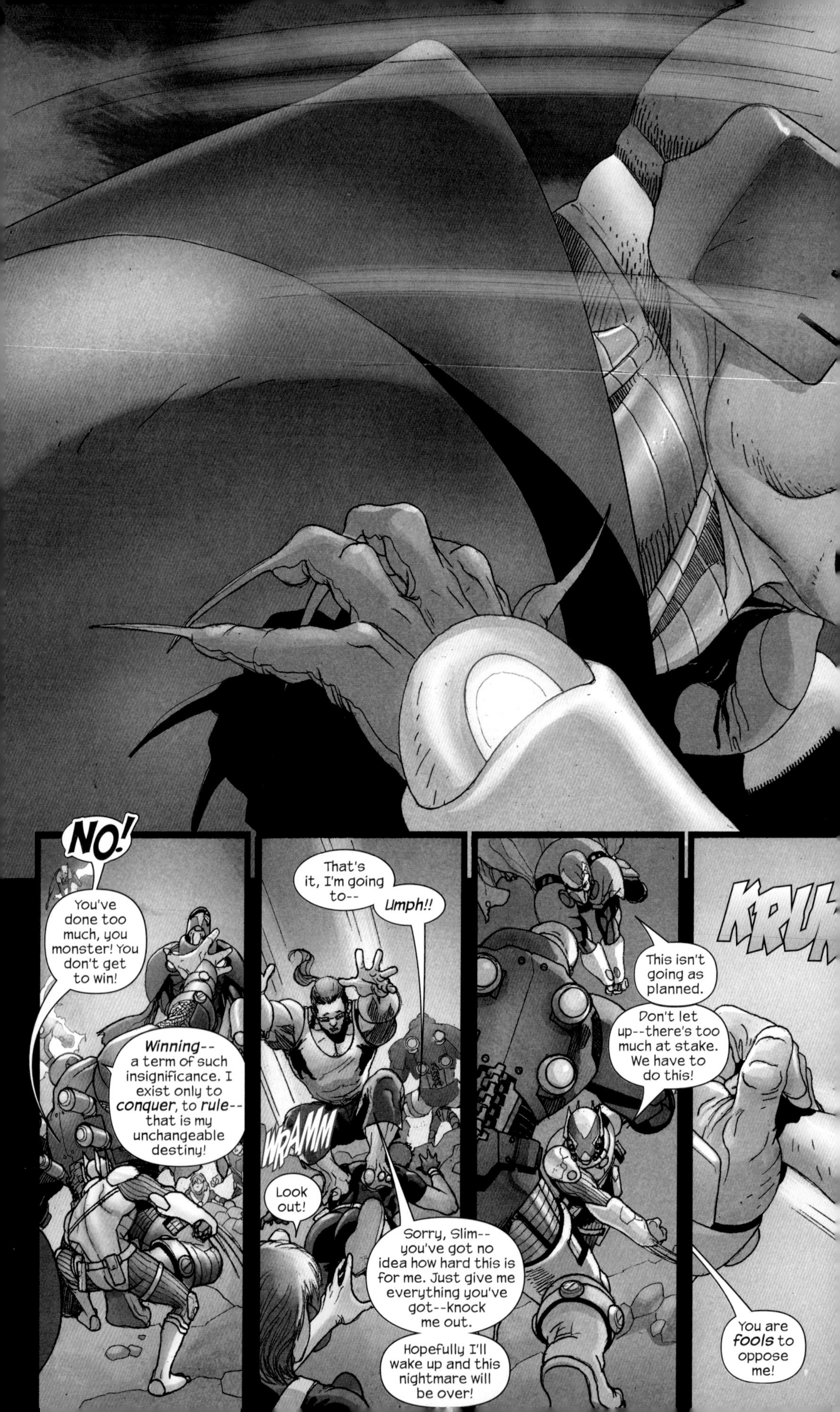

NO!
You've done too much, you monster! You don't get to win!
Winning-- a term of such insignificance. I exist only to conquer, to rule-- that is my unchangeable destiny!
That's it, I'm going to--
Umph!!
WRAMM
Look out!
Sorry, Slim-- you've got no idea how hard this is for me. Just give me everything you've got--knock me out.
Hopefully I'll wake up and this nightmare will be over!
This isn't going as planned.
Don't let up--there's too much at stake. We have to do this!
KRUN
You are fools to oppose me!

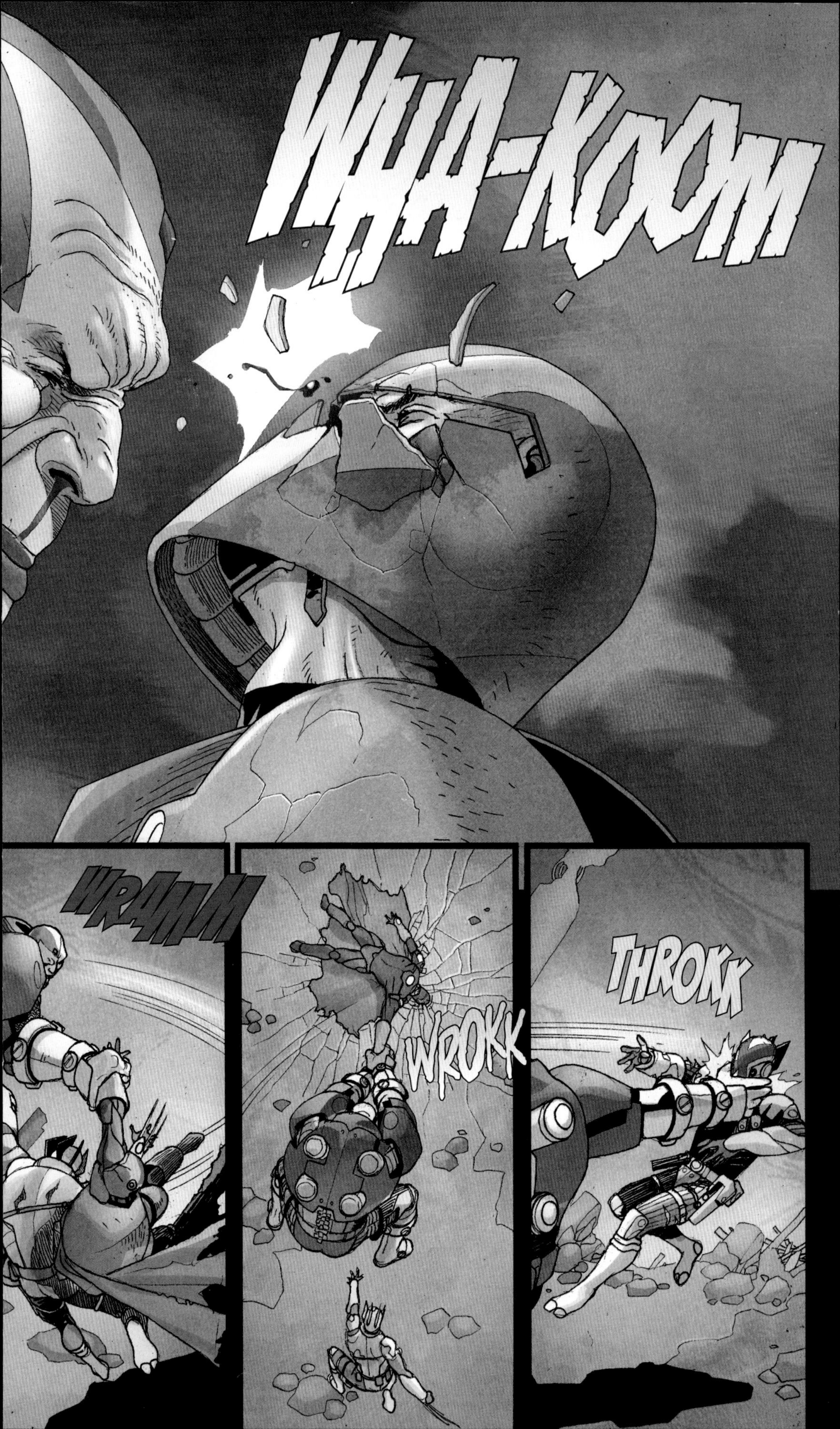
WHA-KOOM
WRAMM
WROKK
THROKK

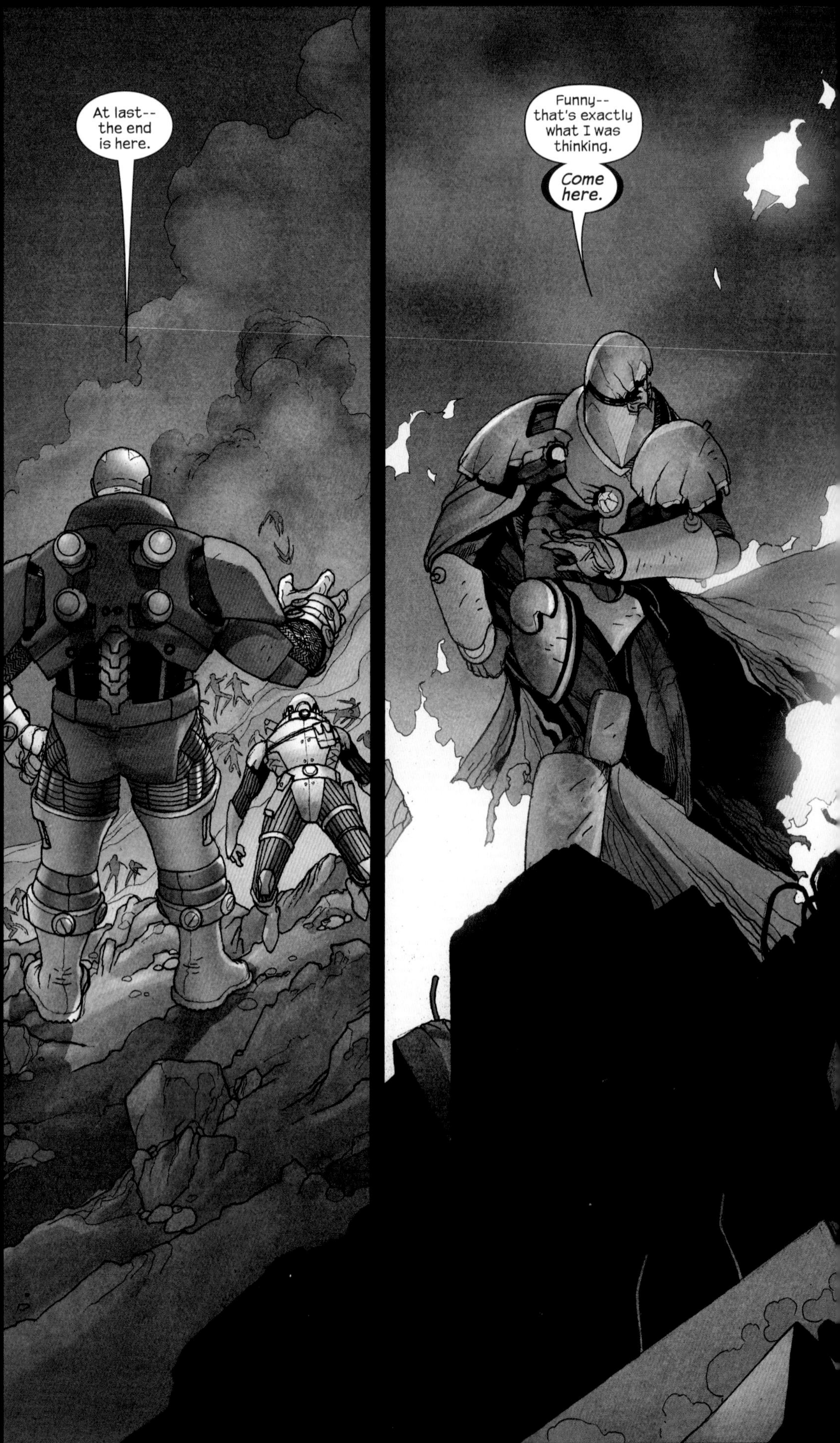
At last-- the end is here.
Funny-- that's exactly what I was thinking.
Come here.

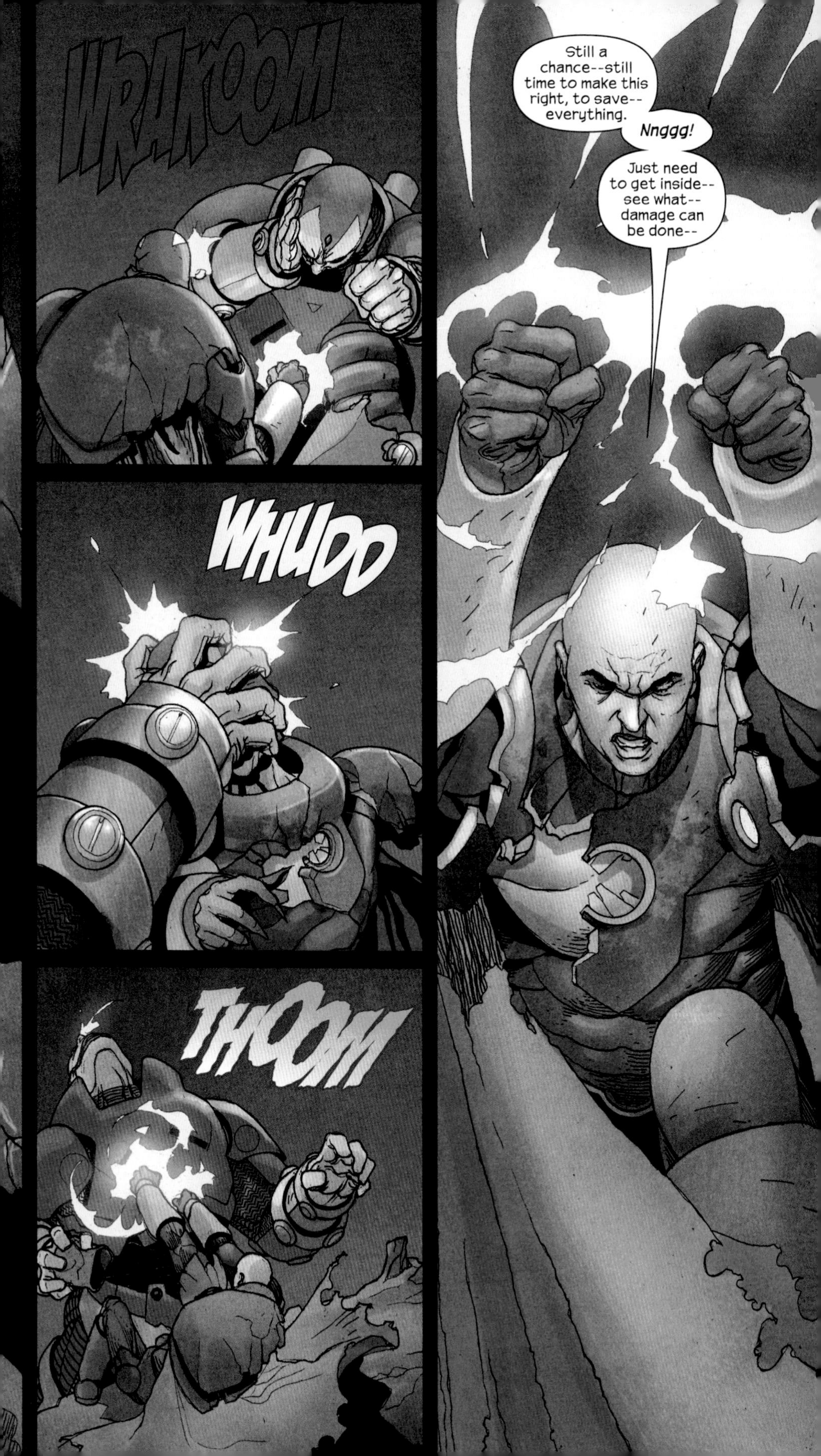
WRAKOOM
WHUDD
THOOM
Still a chance--still time to make this right, to save--everything.
Nnggg!
Just need to get inside--see what--damage can be done--

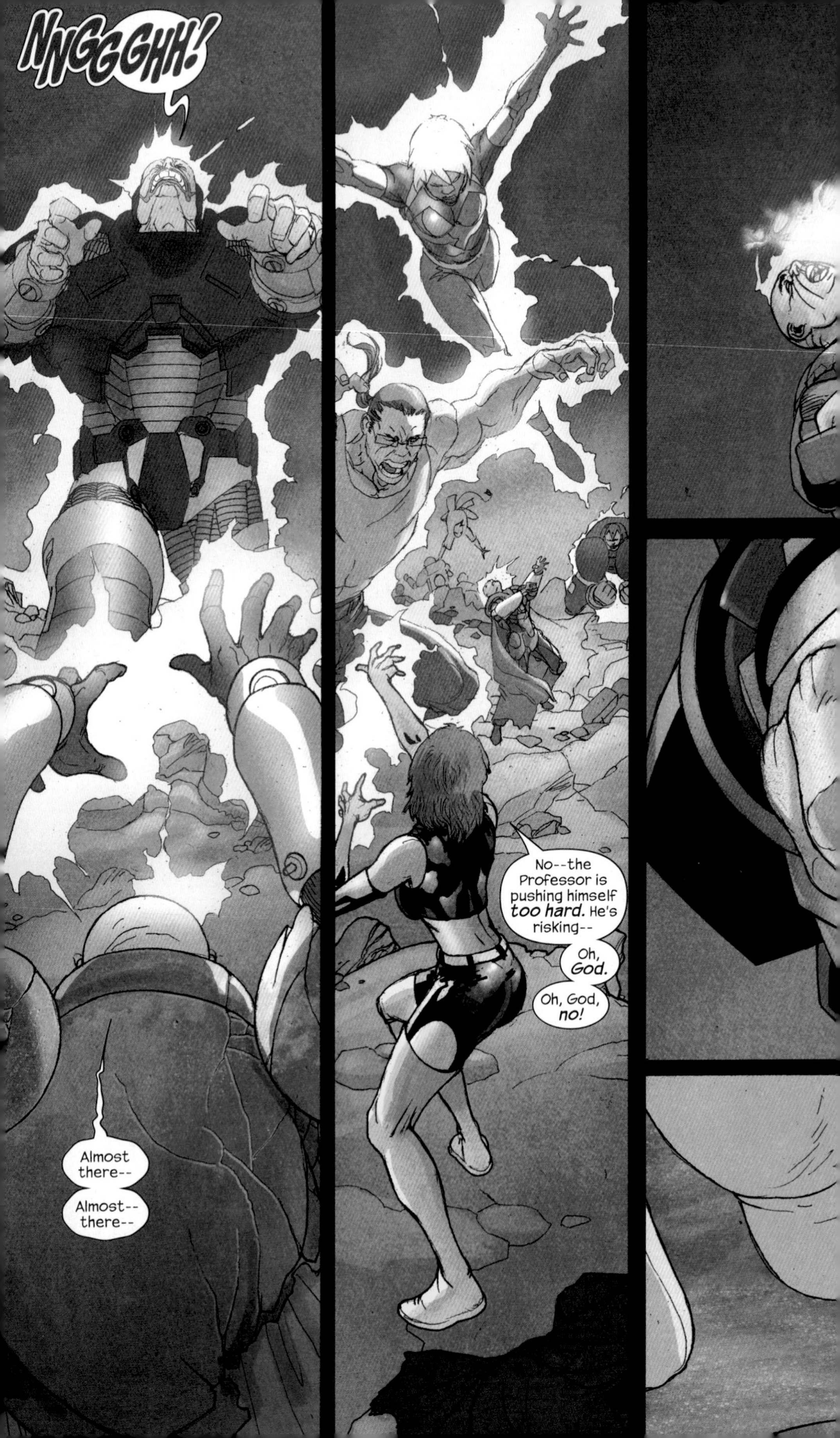
NNGGGHH!
Almost there--
Almost-- there--
No--the Professor is pushing himself *too hard.* He's risking--
Oh, *God.*
Oh, God, *no!*

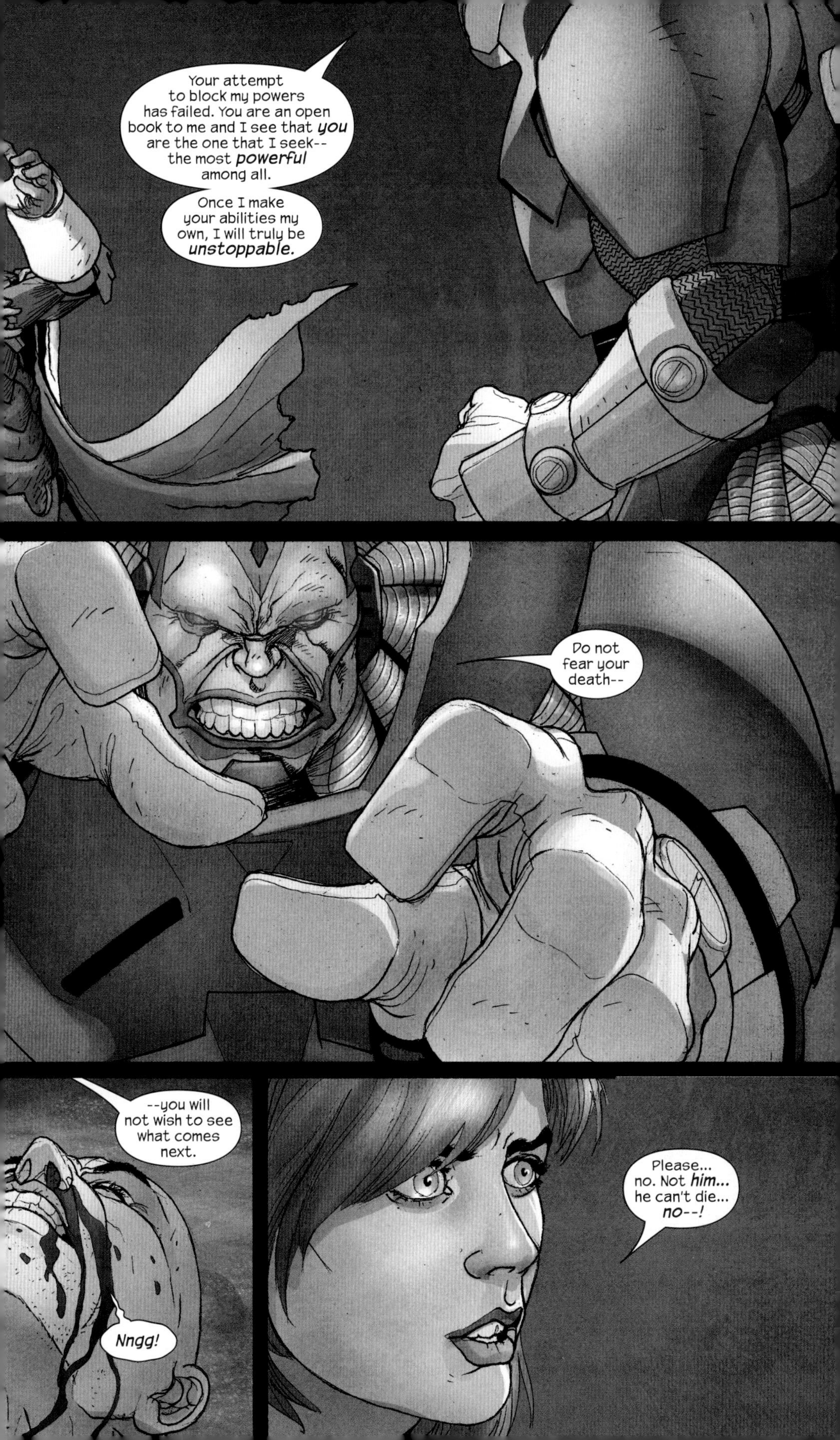
Your attempt to block my powers has failed. You are an open book to me and I see that *you* are the one that I seek-- the most *powerful* among all.
Once I make your abilities my own, I will truly be *unstoppable.*
Do not fear your death--
--you will not wish to see what comes next.
Nngg!
Please... no. Not *him...* he can't die... *no--!*

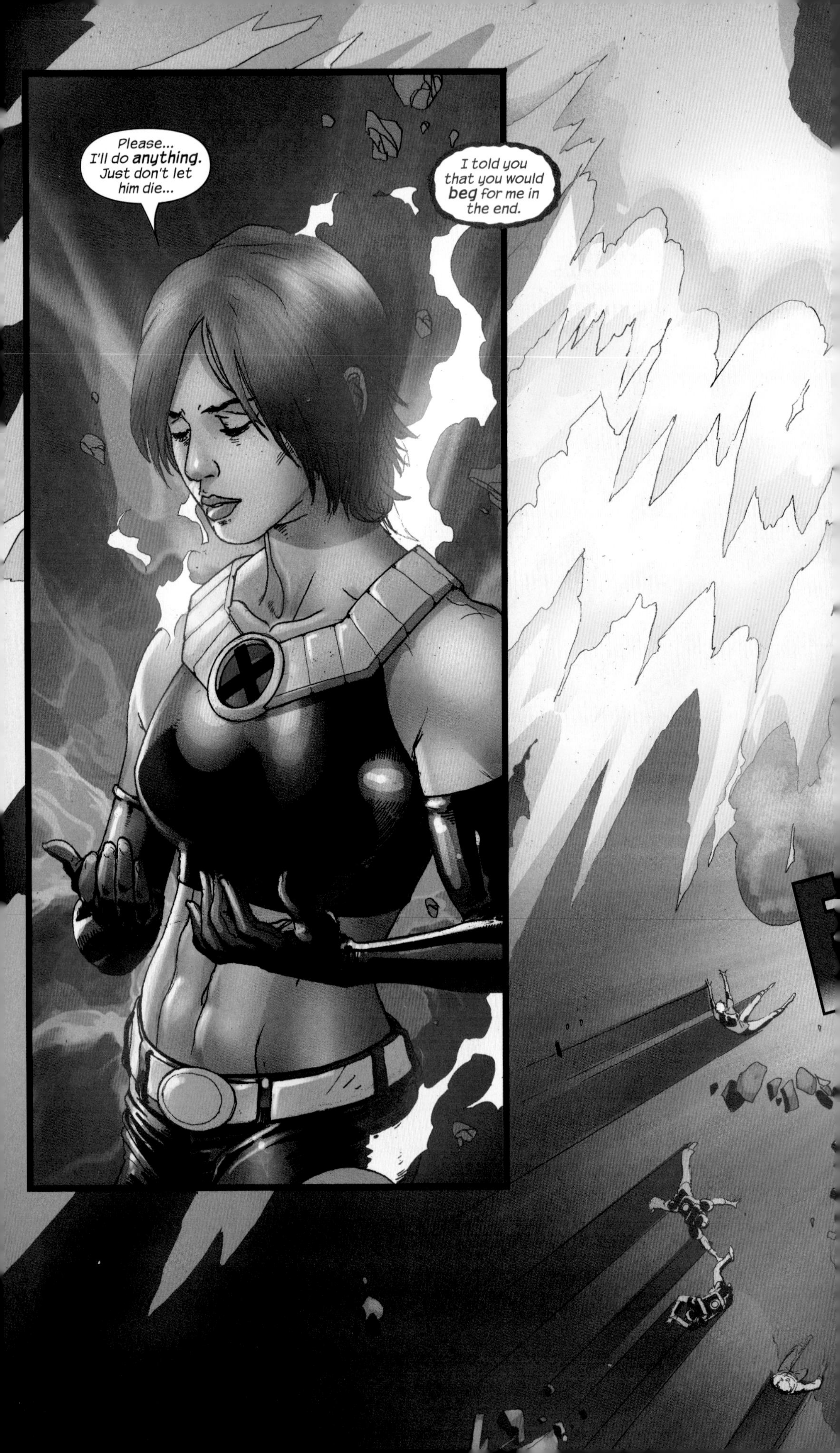
Please... I'll do **anything.** Just don't let him die...
I told you that you would **beg** for me in the end.

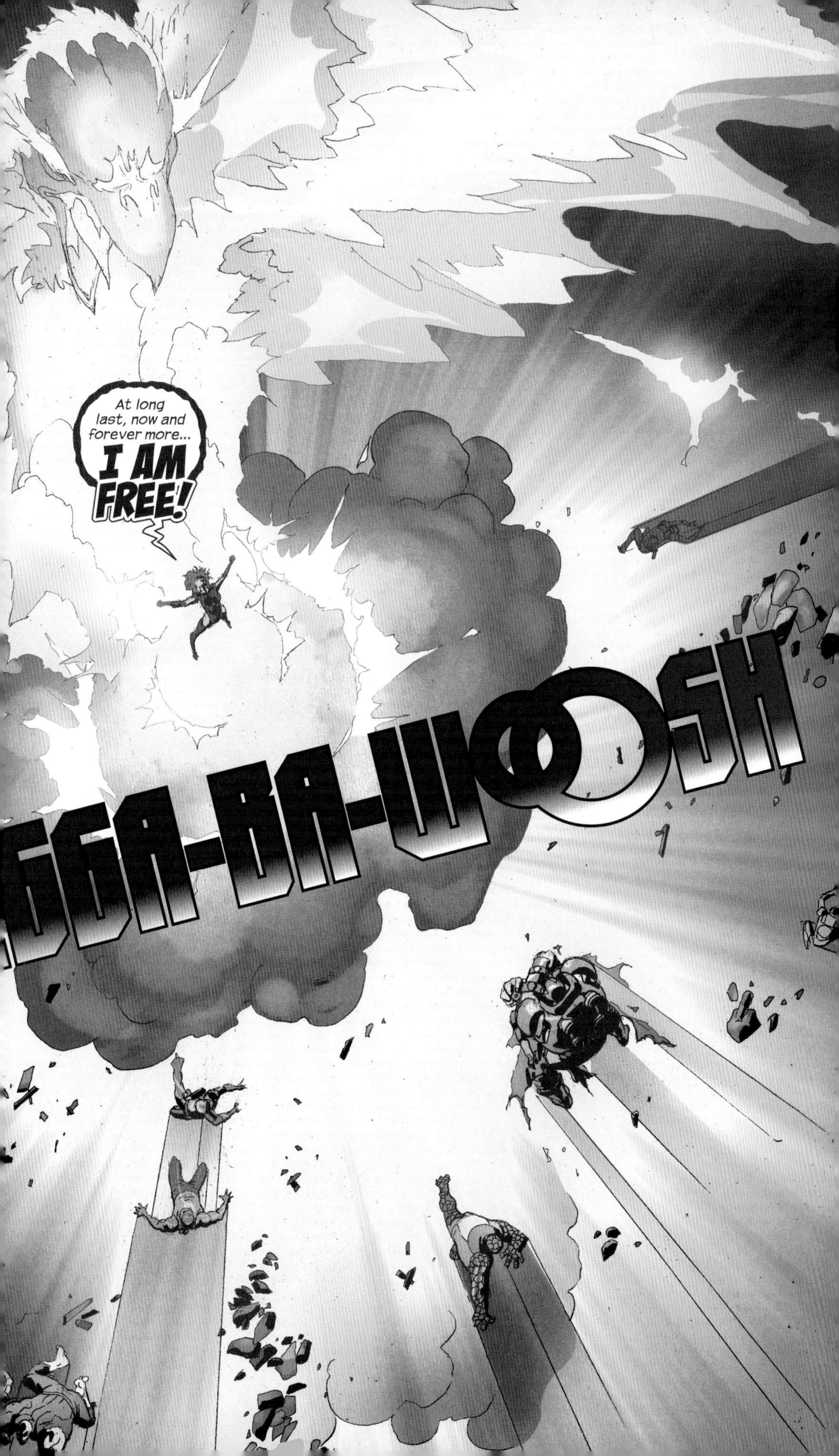
At long last, now and forever more... I AM FREE!
GGA-BA-WOOSH

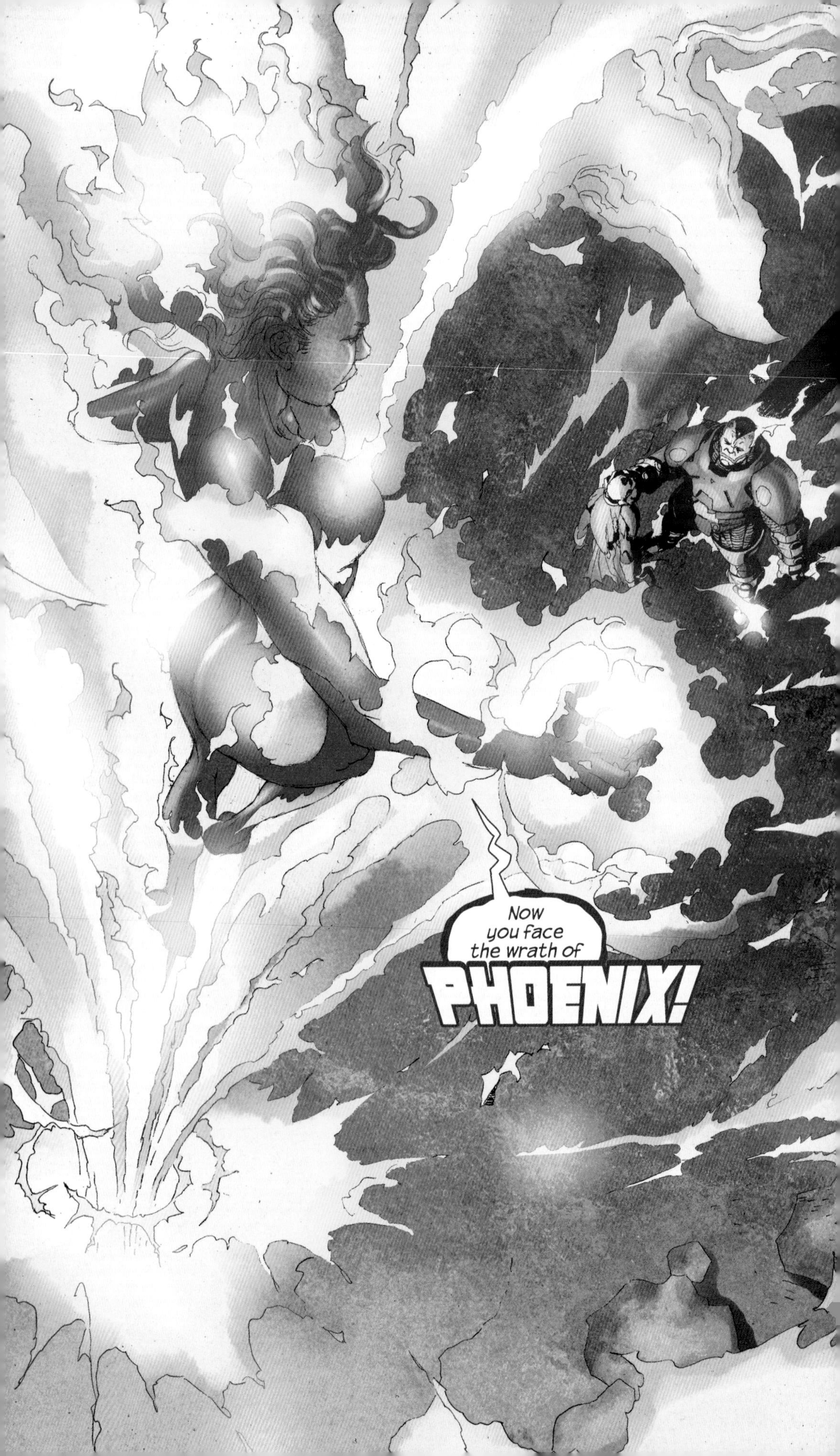

Now you face the wrath of
PHOENIX!

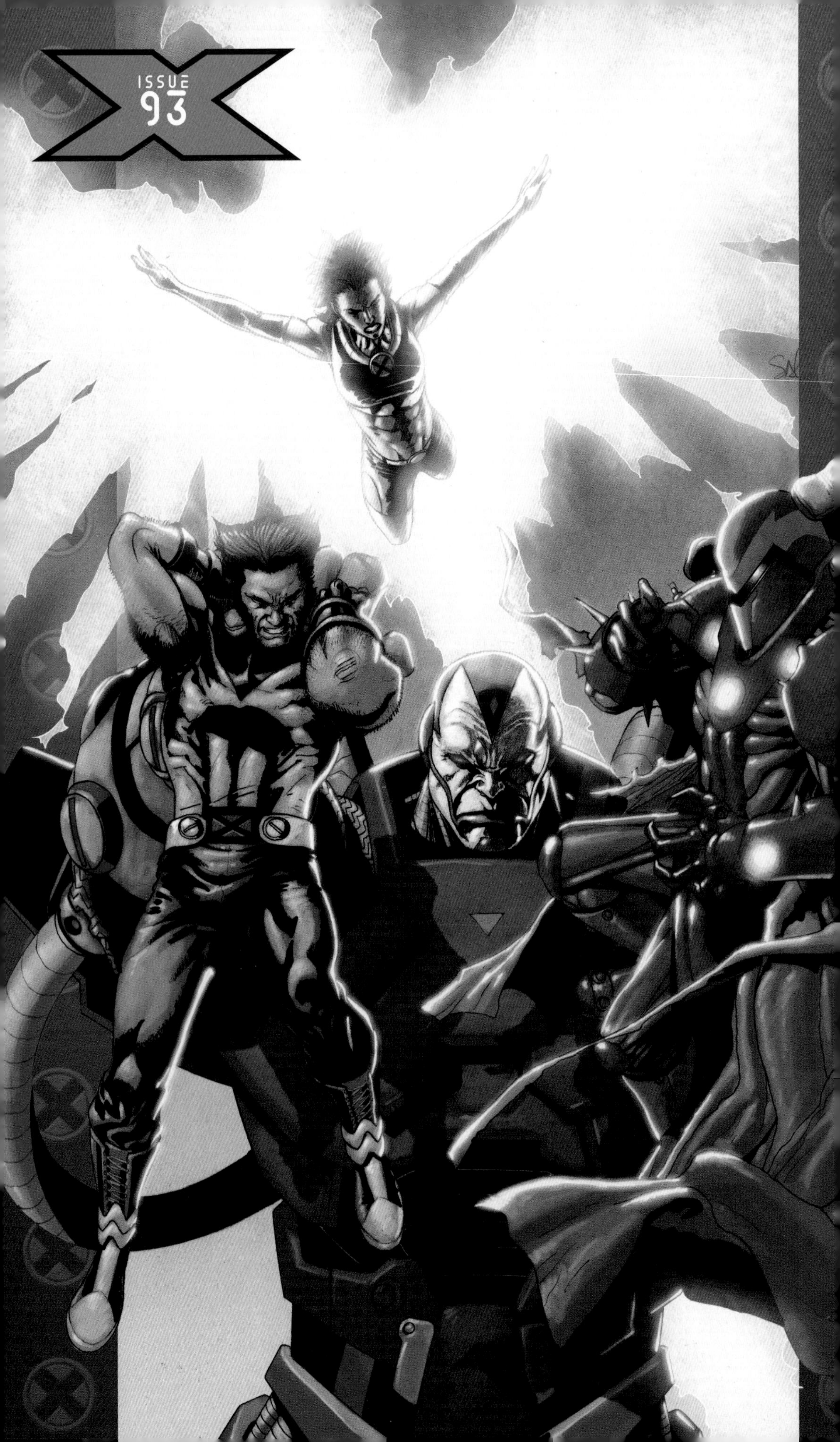
ISSUE
93

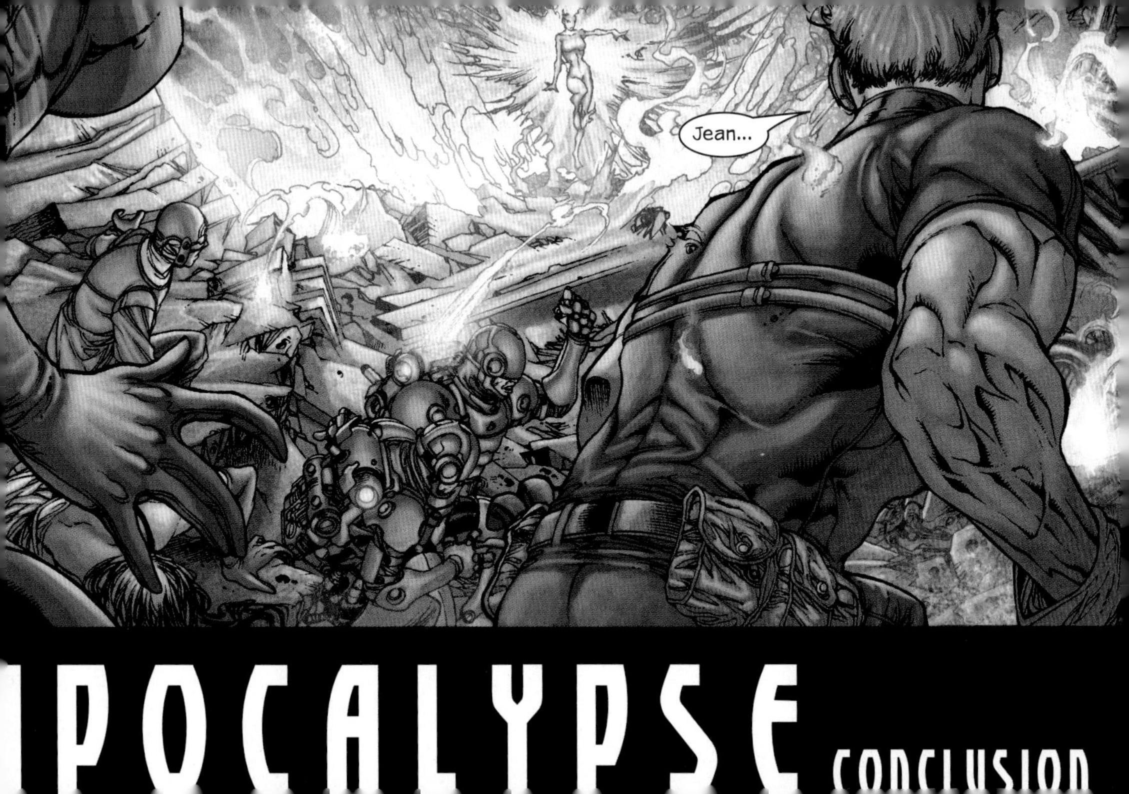
Jean...
POCALYPSE
CONCLUSION

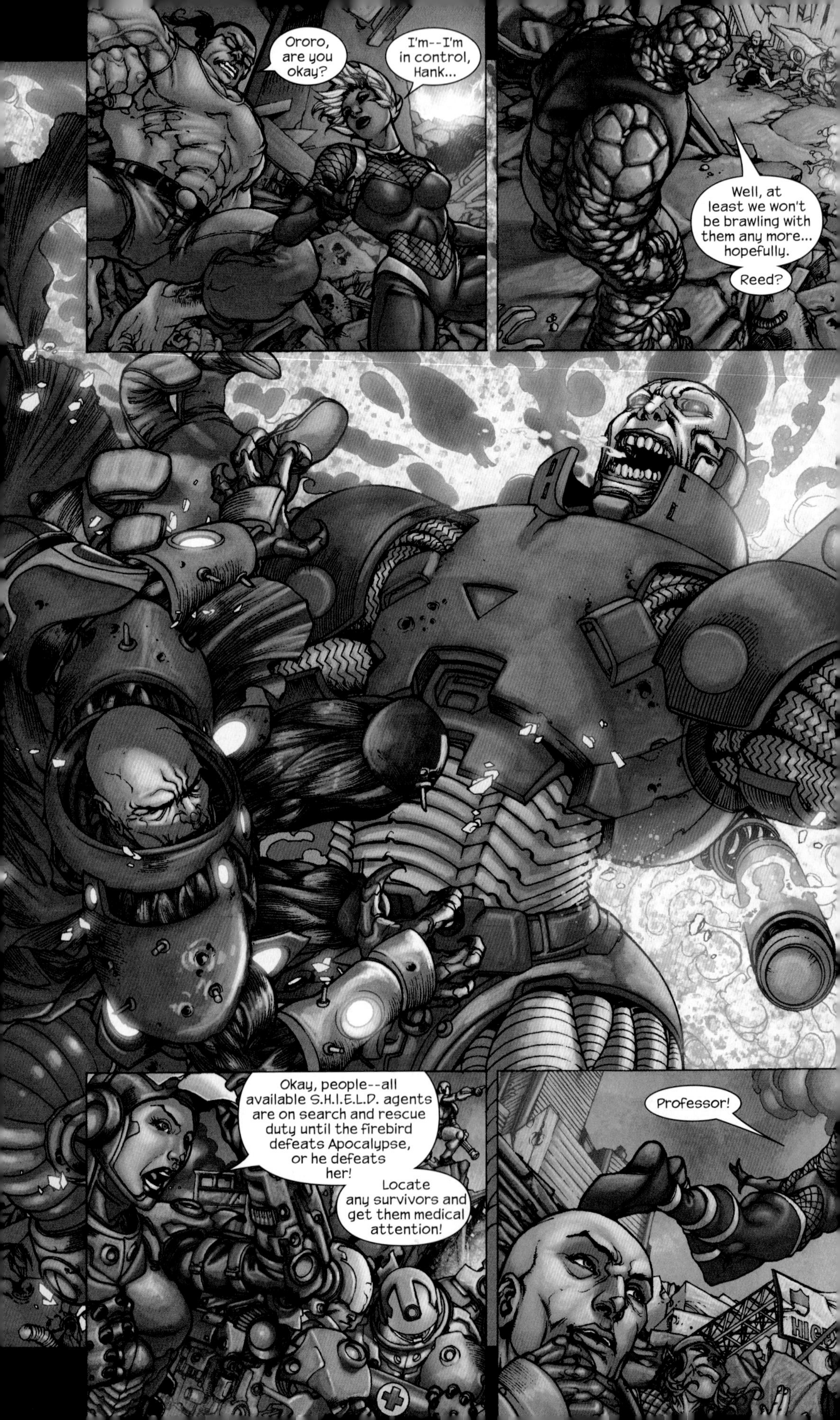
Ororo, are you okay?
I'm--I'm in control, Hank...
Well, at least we won't be brawling with them any more... hopefully.
Reed?
Okay, people--all available S.H.I.E.L.D. agents are on search and rescue duty until the firebird defeats Apocalypse, or he defeats her!
Locate any survivors and get them medical attention!
Professor!

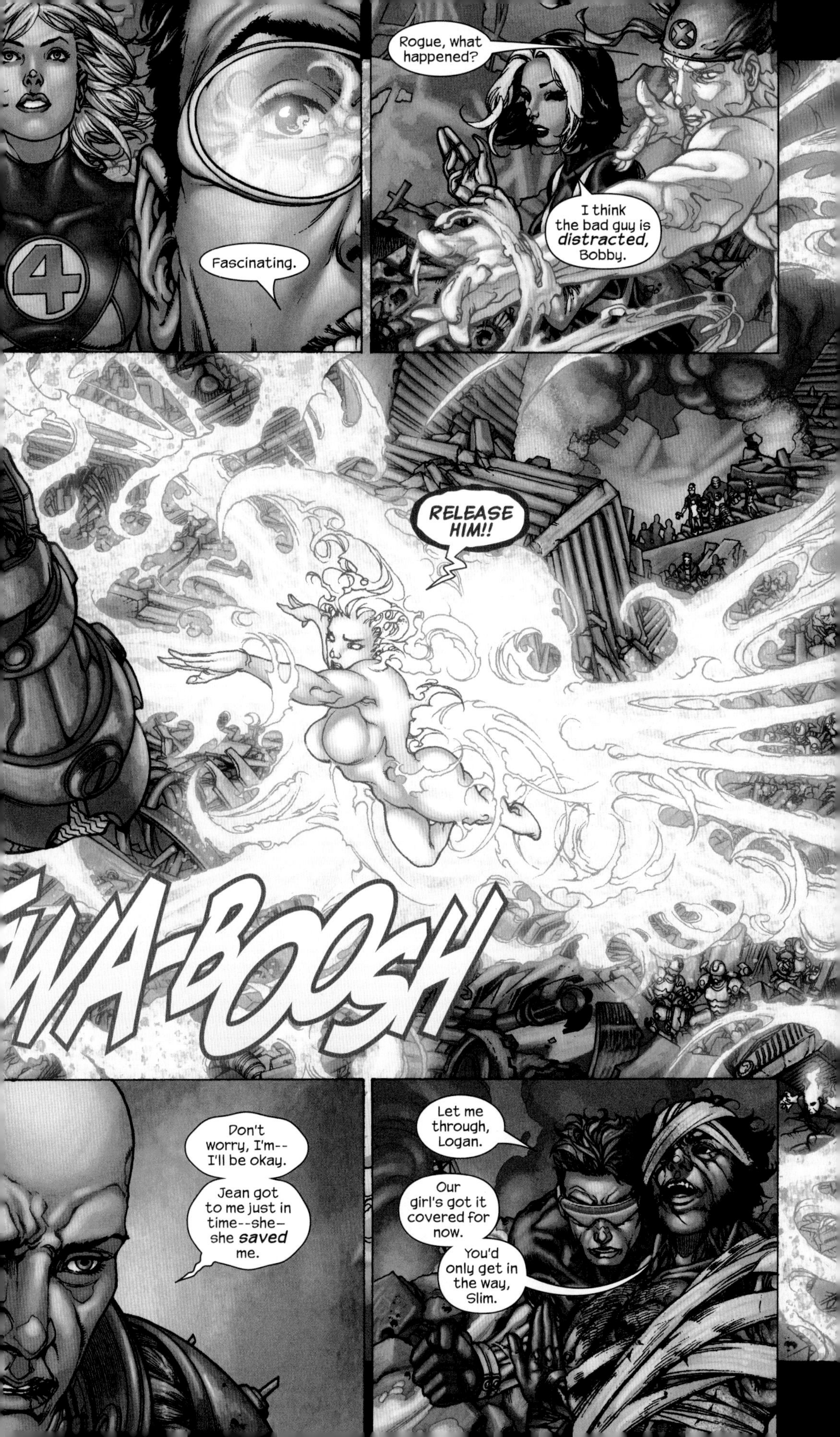
Fascinating.
Rogue, what happened?
I think the bad guy is *distracted,* Bobby.
RELEASE HIM!!
WA-BOOSH
Don't worry, I'm-- I'll be okay.
Jean got to me just in time--she-- she *saved* me.
Let me through, Logan.
Our girl's got it covered for now.
You'd only get in the way, Slim.

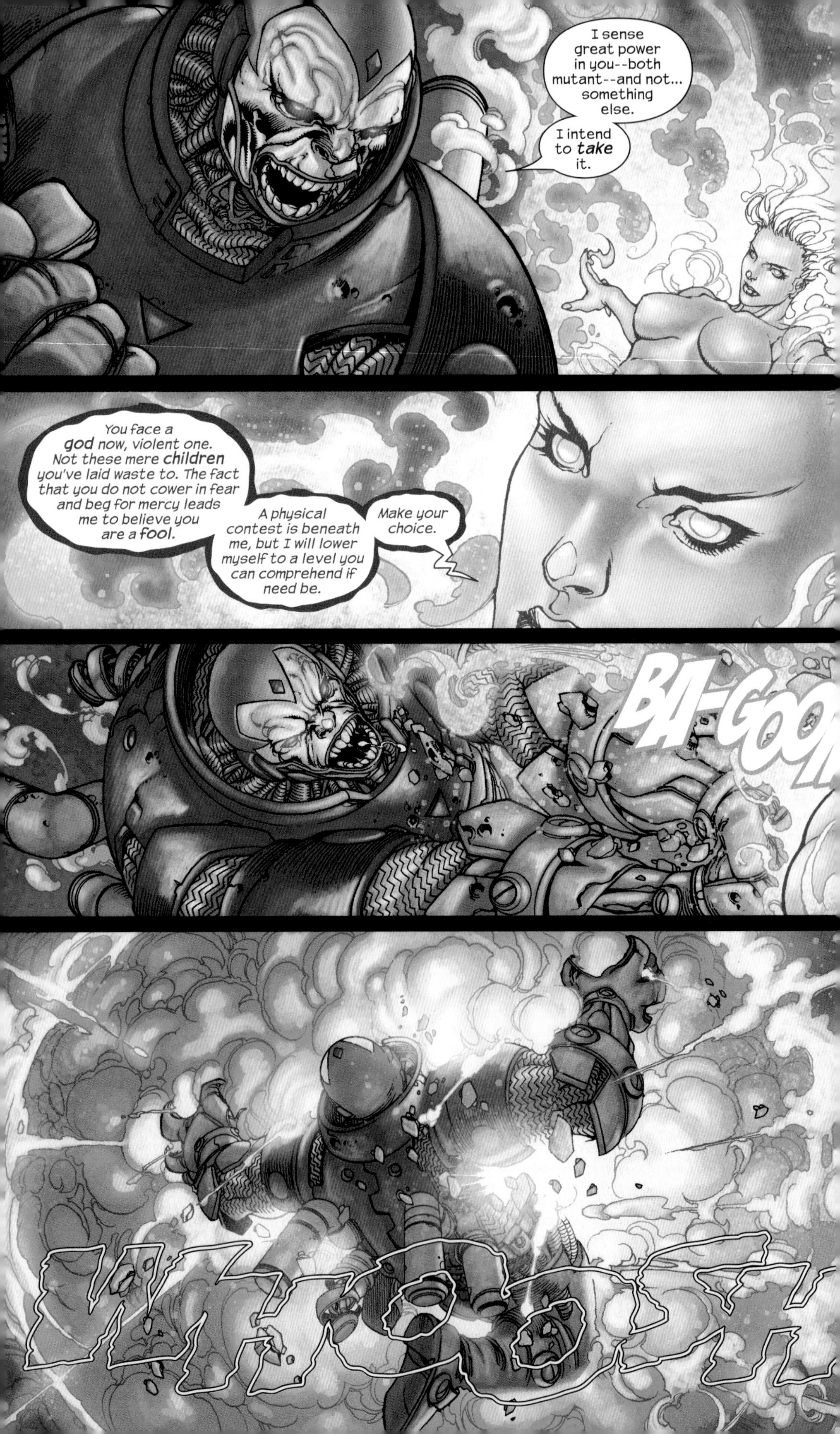
I sense great power in you--both mutant--and not... something else.
I intend to *take* it.
You face a **god** now, violent one. Not these mere **children** you've laid waste to. The fact that you do not cower in fear and beg for mercy leads me to believe you are a **fool**.
A physical contest is beneath me, but I will lower myself to a level you can comprehend if need be.
Make your choice.
BA-GOO

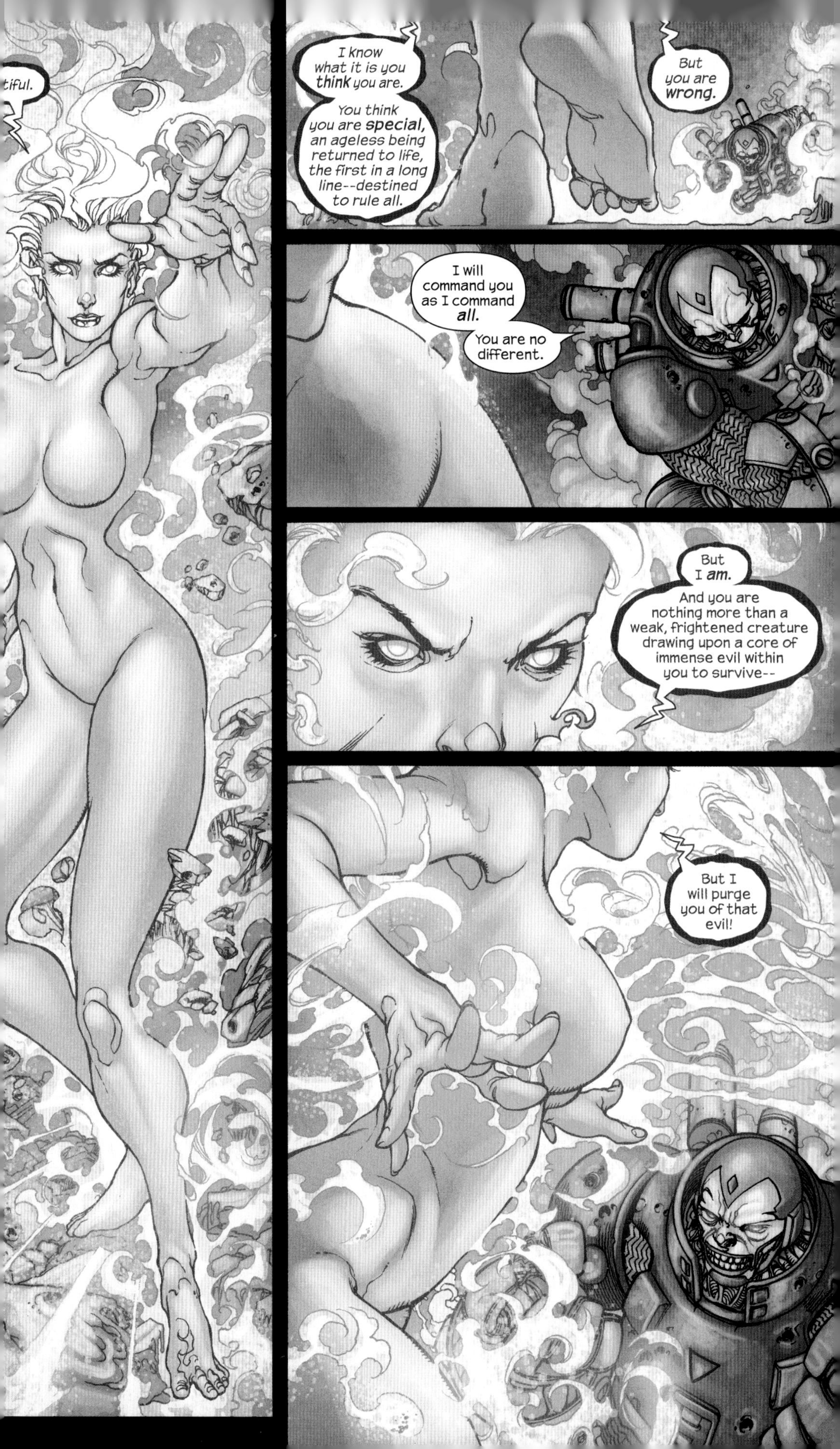
tiful.
I know what it is you think you are.
You think you are special, an ageless being returned to life, the first in a long line--destined to rule all.
But you are wrong.
I will command you as I command all.
You are no different.
But I am.
And you are nothing more than a weak, frightened creature drawing upon a core of immense evil within you to survive--
But I will purge you of that evil!

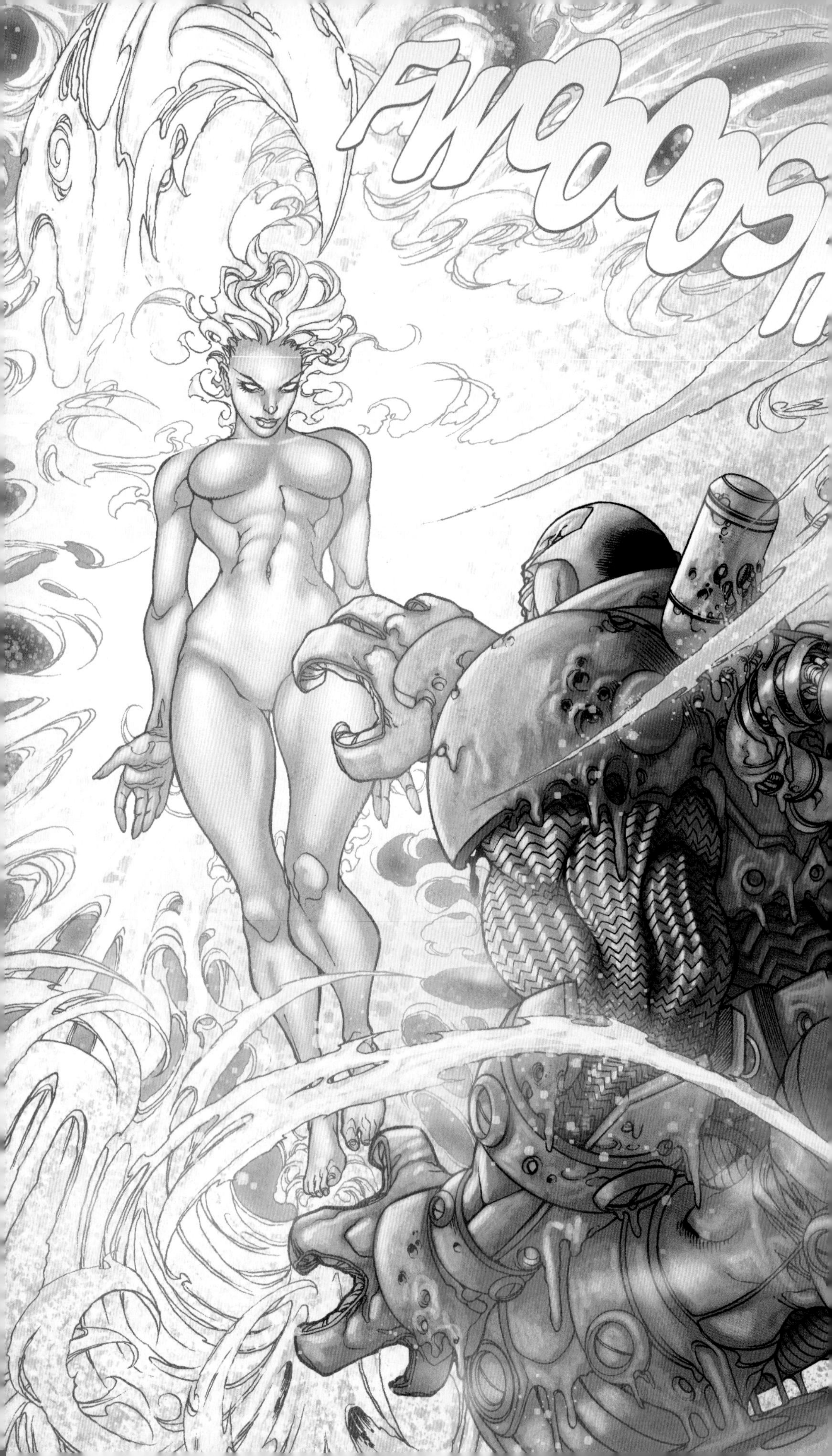
FWOOOS

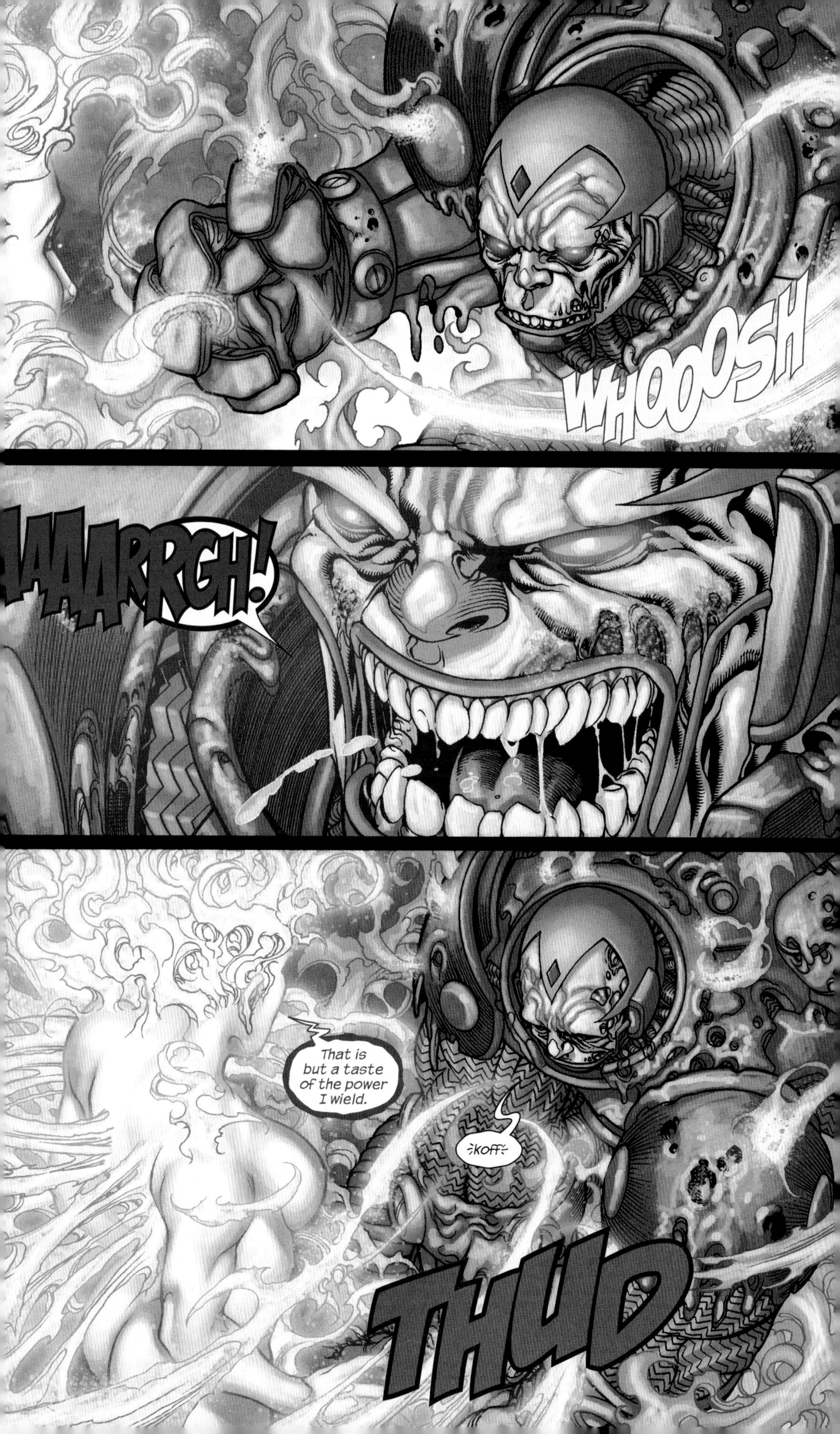
WHOOOSH
AAAARRGH!
That is but a taste of the power I wield.
koff
THUD

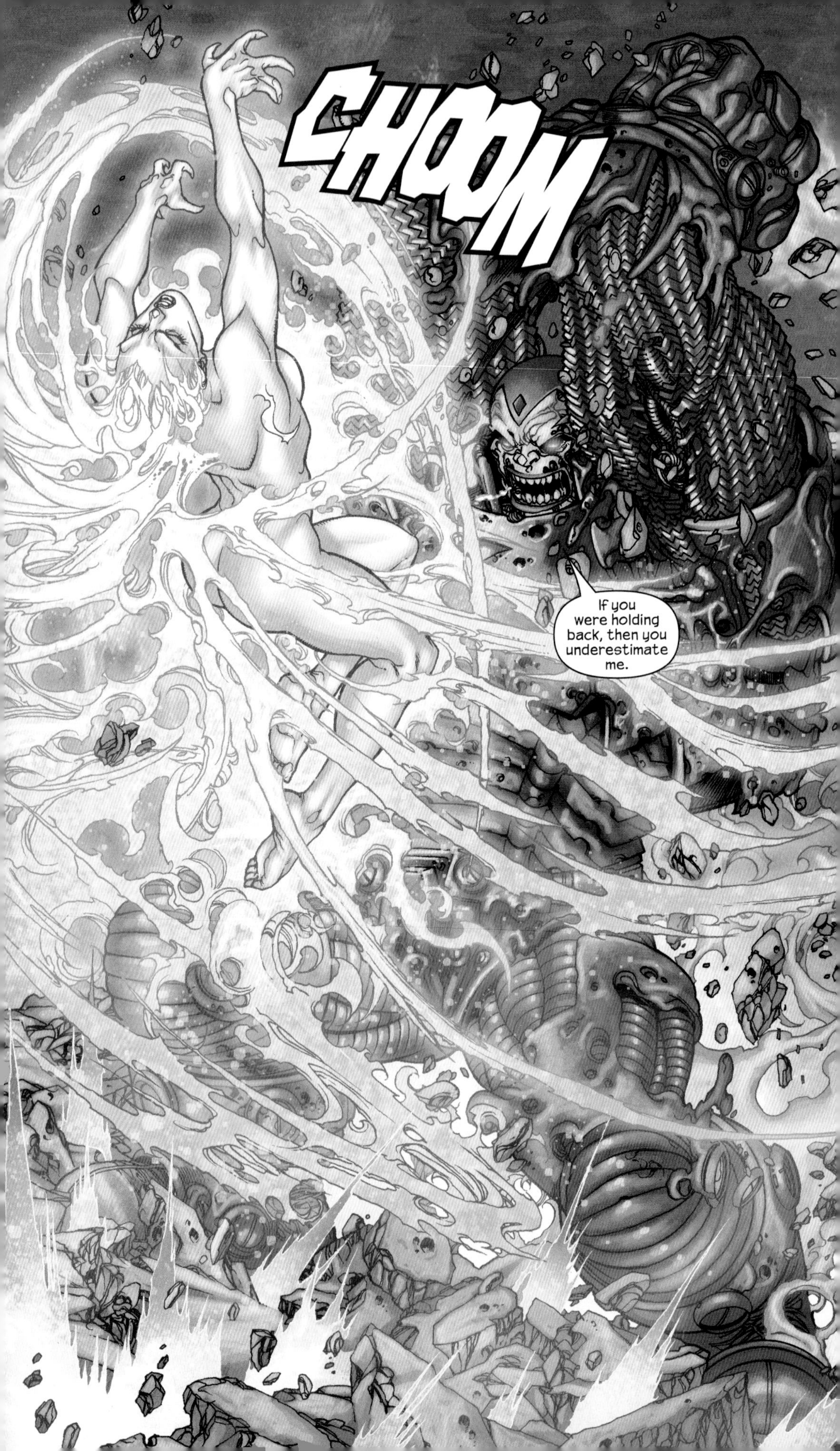
CHOOM
If you were holding back, then you underestimate me.

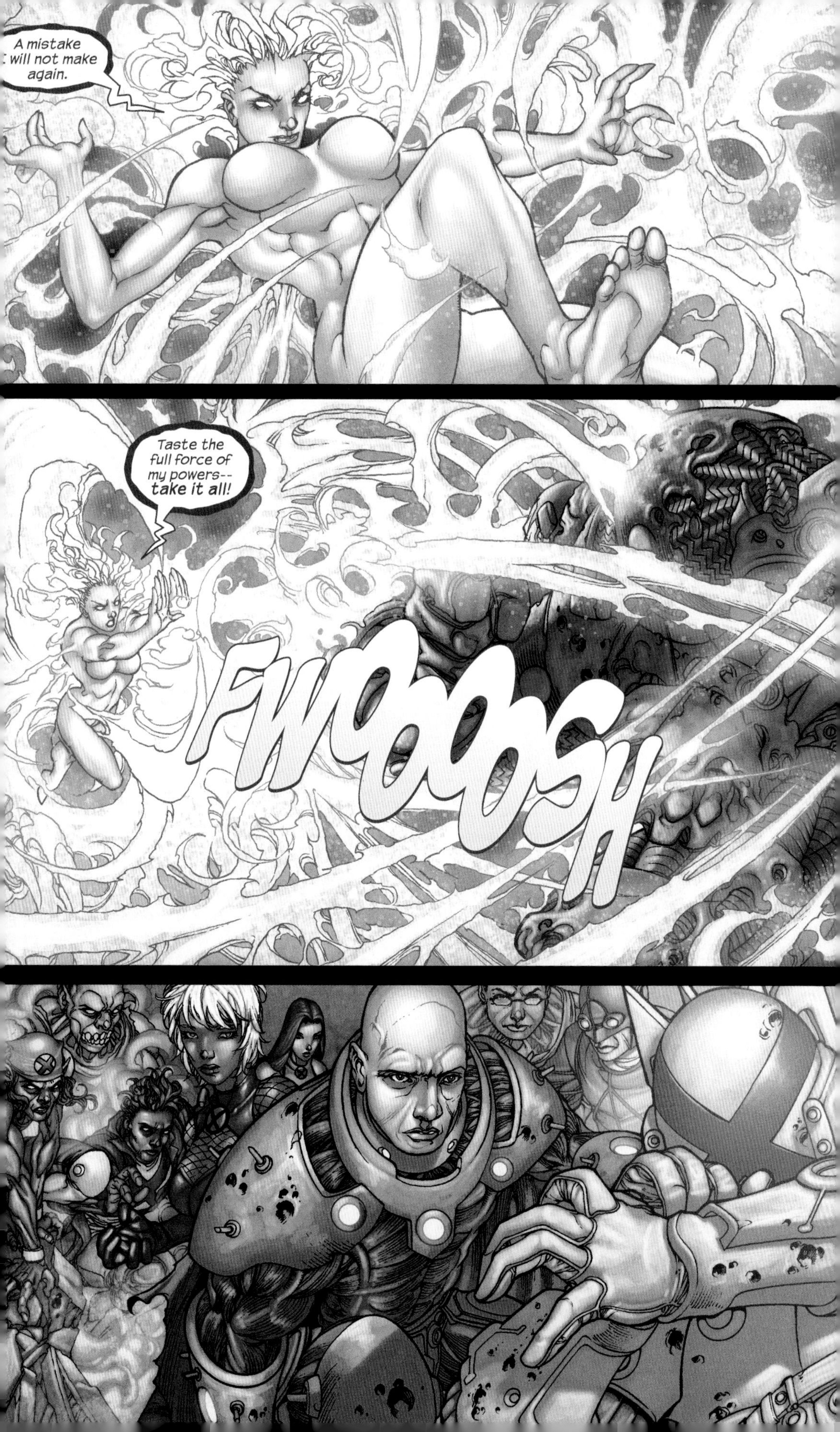
A mistake I will not make again.
Taste the full force of my powers-- take it all!
FWOOOSH

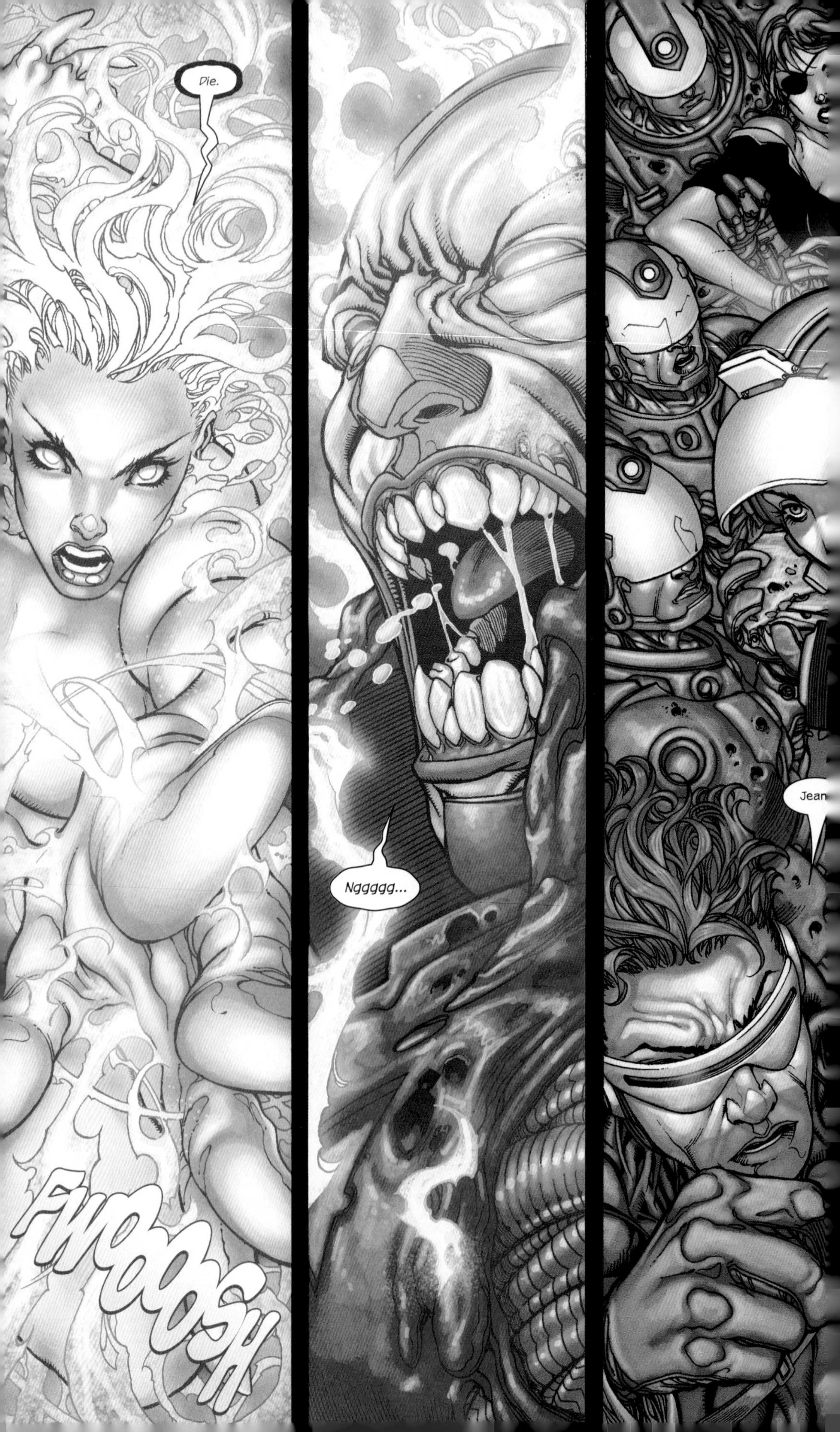
Die.
FWOOOSH
Ngggg...
Jean

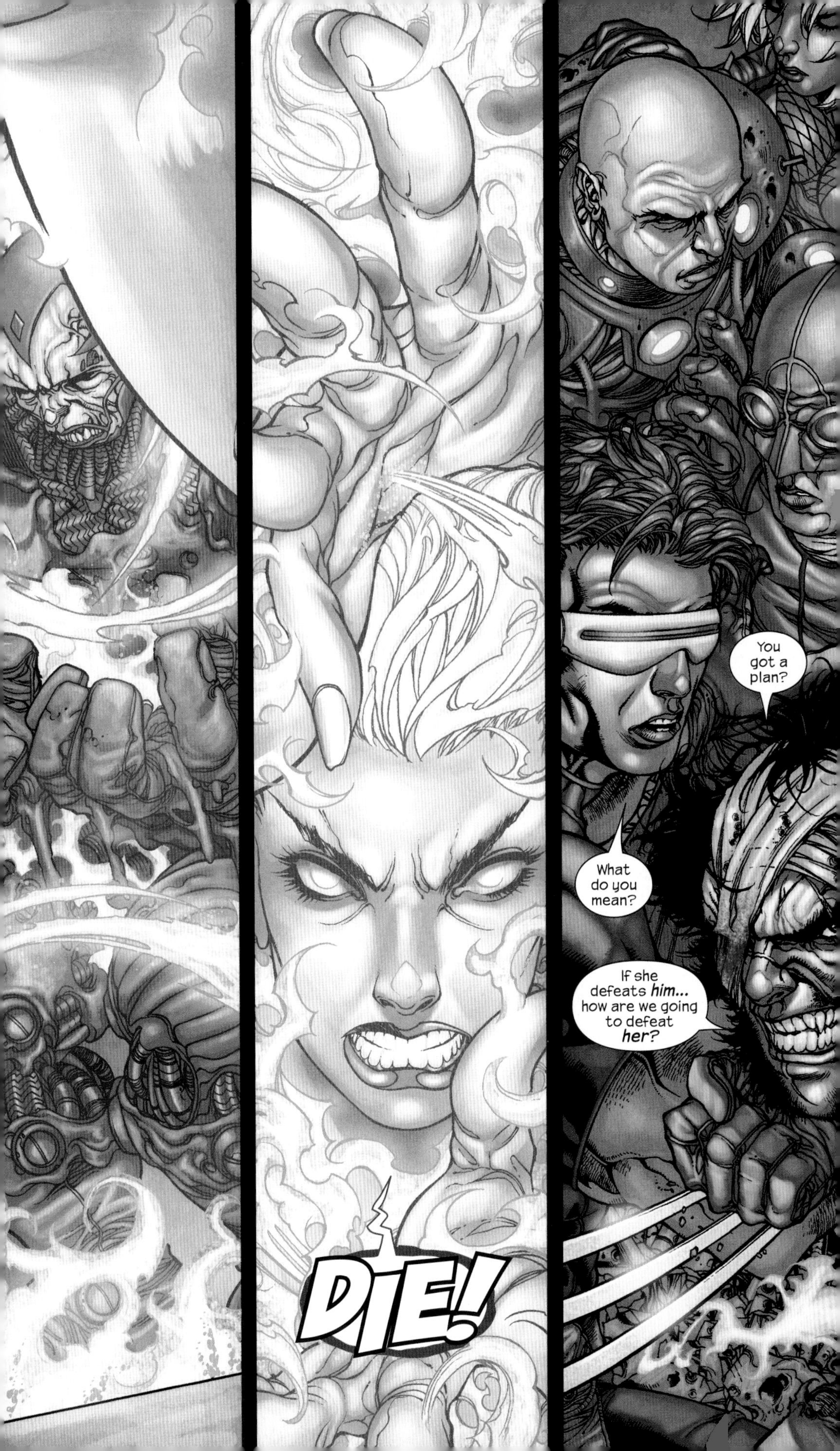
DIE!
You got a plan?
What do you mean?
If she defeats *him*... how are we going to defeat *her*?

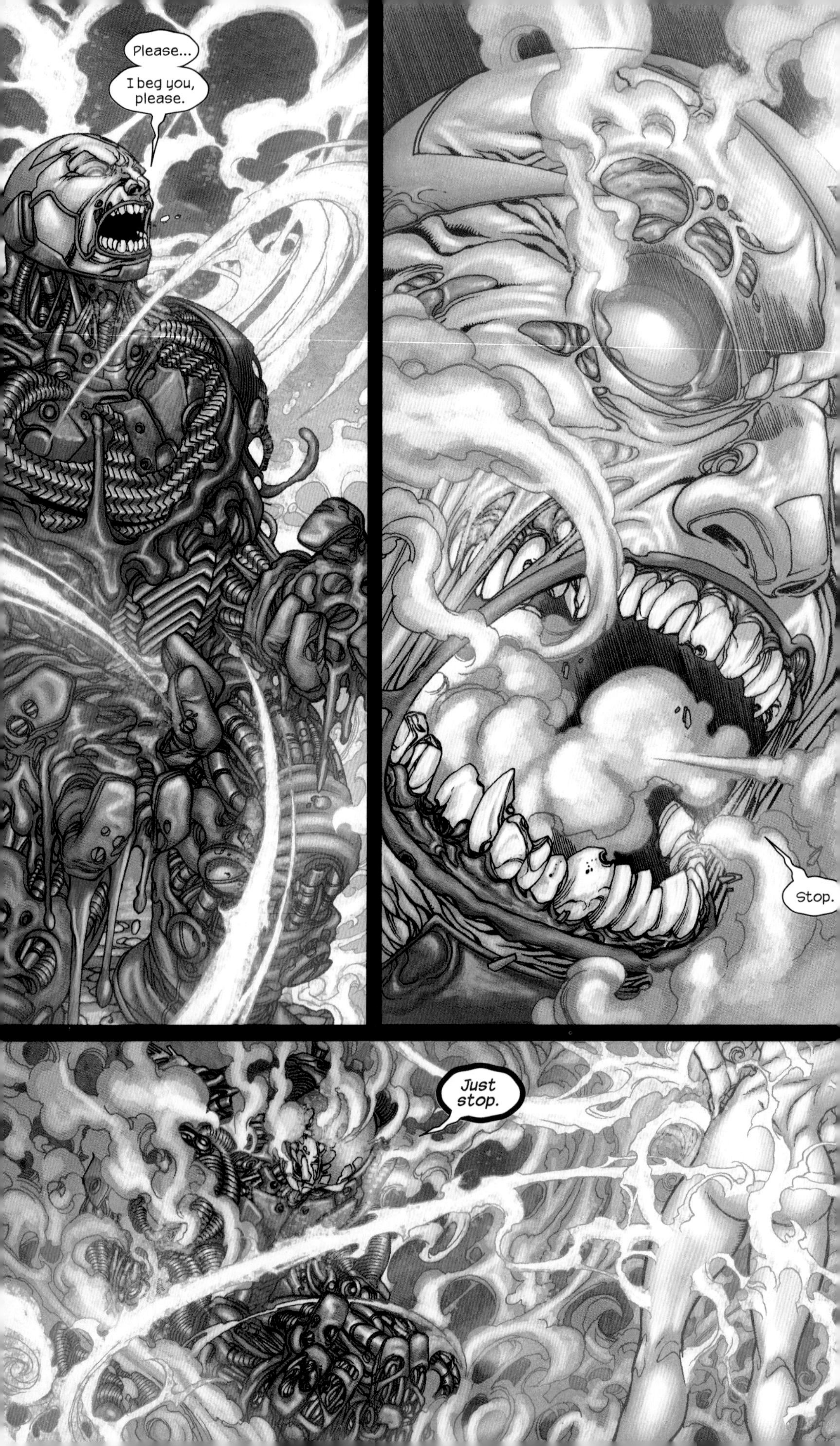
Please...
I beg you, please.
Stop.
Just stop.

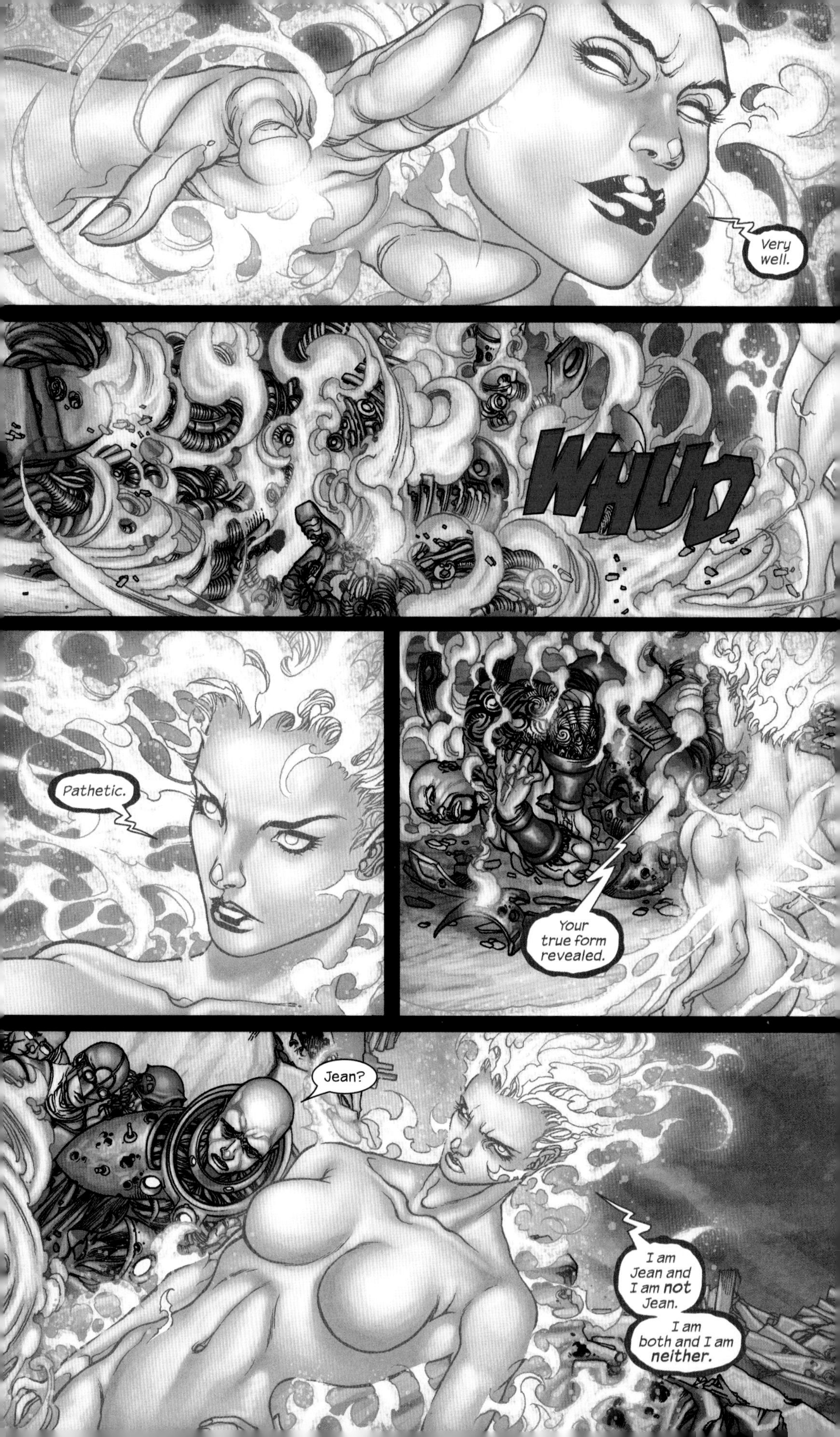
Very well.
WHUD
Pathetic.
Your true form revealed.
Jean?
I am Jean and I am **not** Jean.
I am both and I am **neither**.

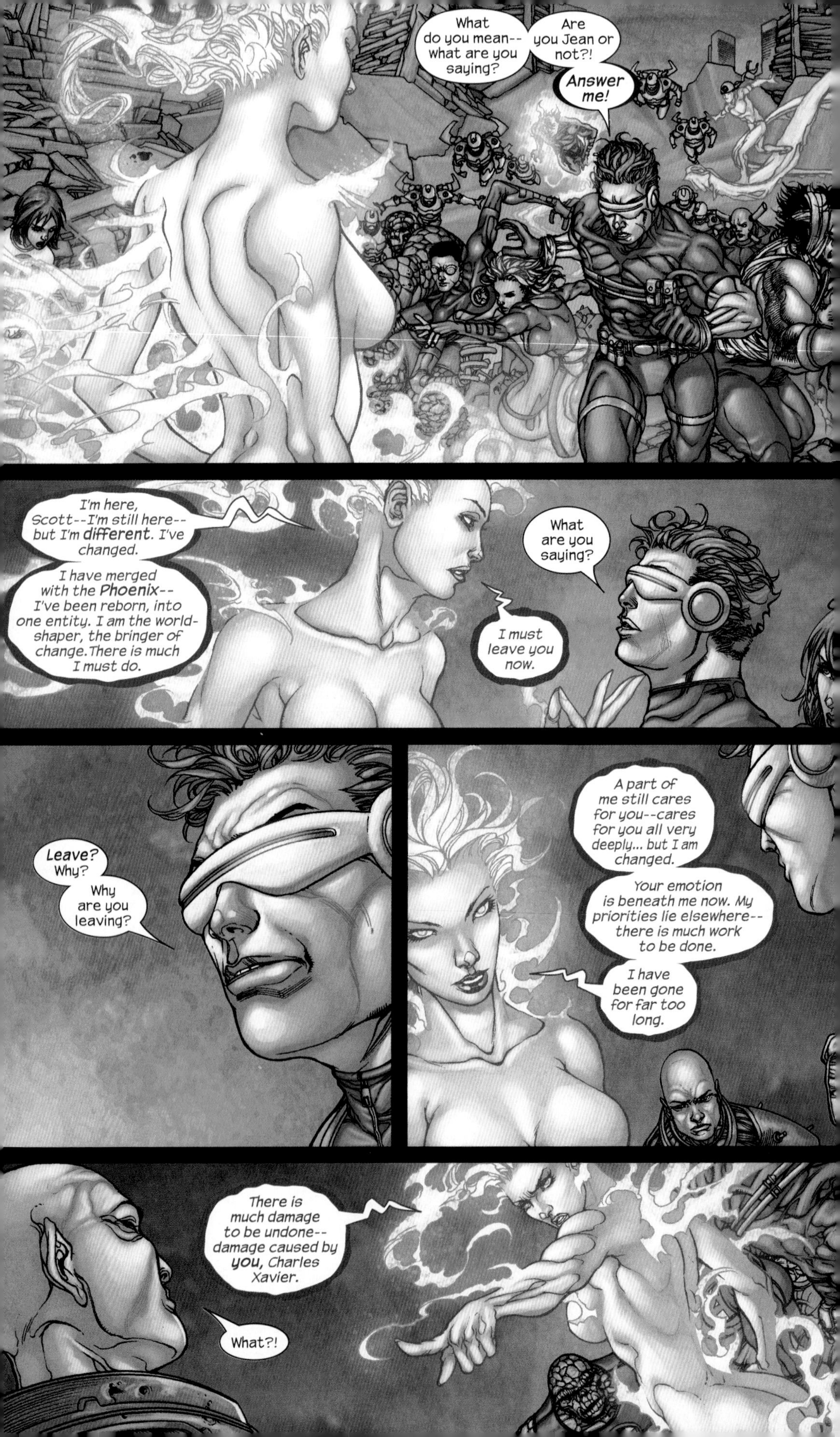

What do you mean-- what are you saying?
Are you Jean or not?!
Answer me!
I'm here, Scott--I'm still here-- but I'm different. I've changed.
I have merged with the Phoenix-- I've been reborn, into one entity. I am the world-shaper, the bringer of change. There is much I must do.
What are you saying?
I must leave you now.
Leave? Why?
Why are you leaving?
A part of me still cares for you--cares for you all very deeply... but I am changed.
Your emotion is beneath me now. My priorities lie elsewhere-- there is much work to be done.
I have been gone for far too long.
There is much damage to be undone-- damage caused by you, Charles Xavier.
What?!

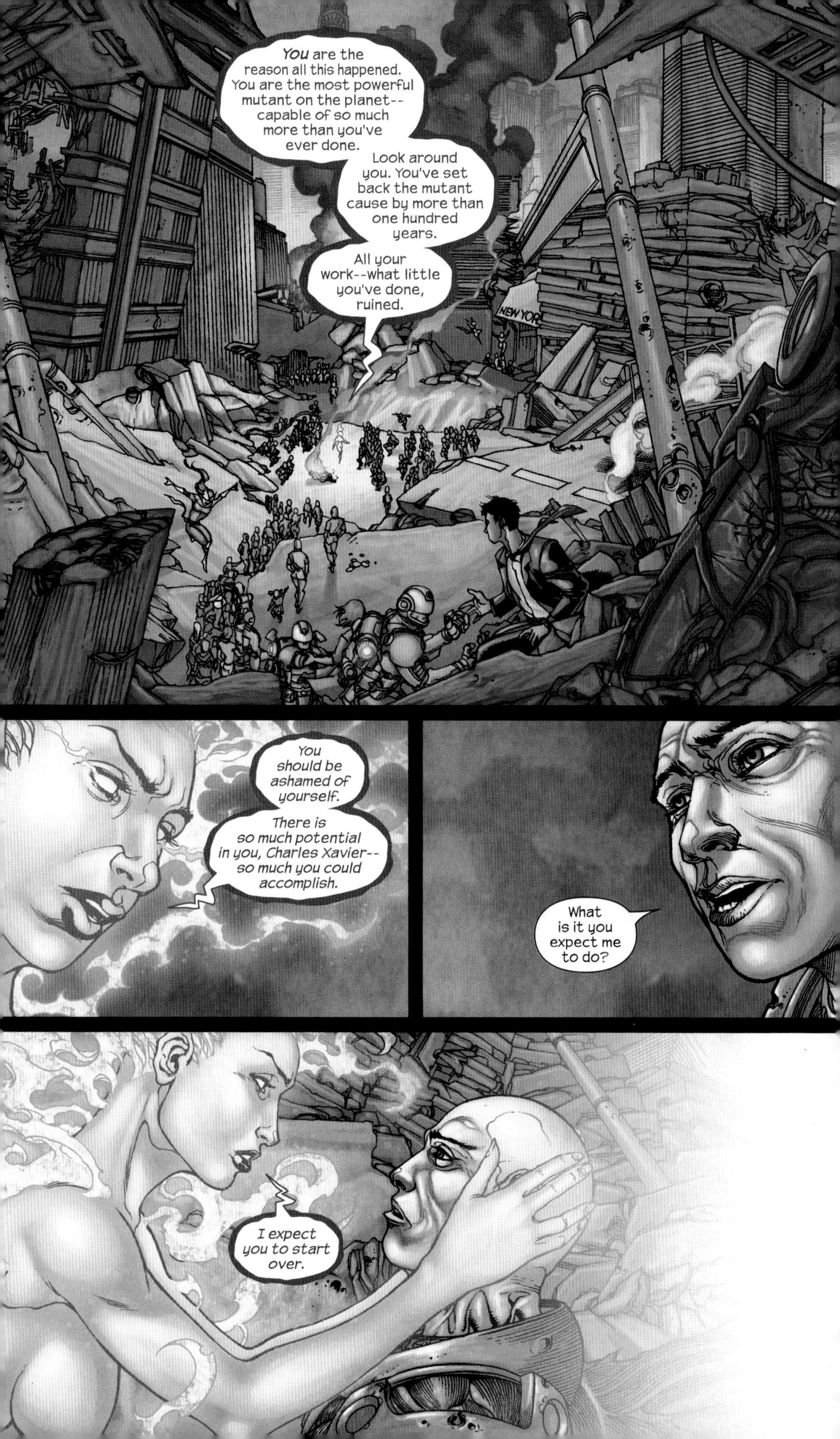
YOU are the reason all this happened. You are the most powerful mutant on the planet--capable of so much more than you've ever done.
Look around you. You've set back the mutant cause by more than one hundred years.
All your work--what little you've done, ruined.
NEW YOR
You should be ashamed of yourself.
There is so much potential in you, Charles Xavier--so much you could accomplish.
What is it you expect me to do?
I expect you to start over.

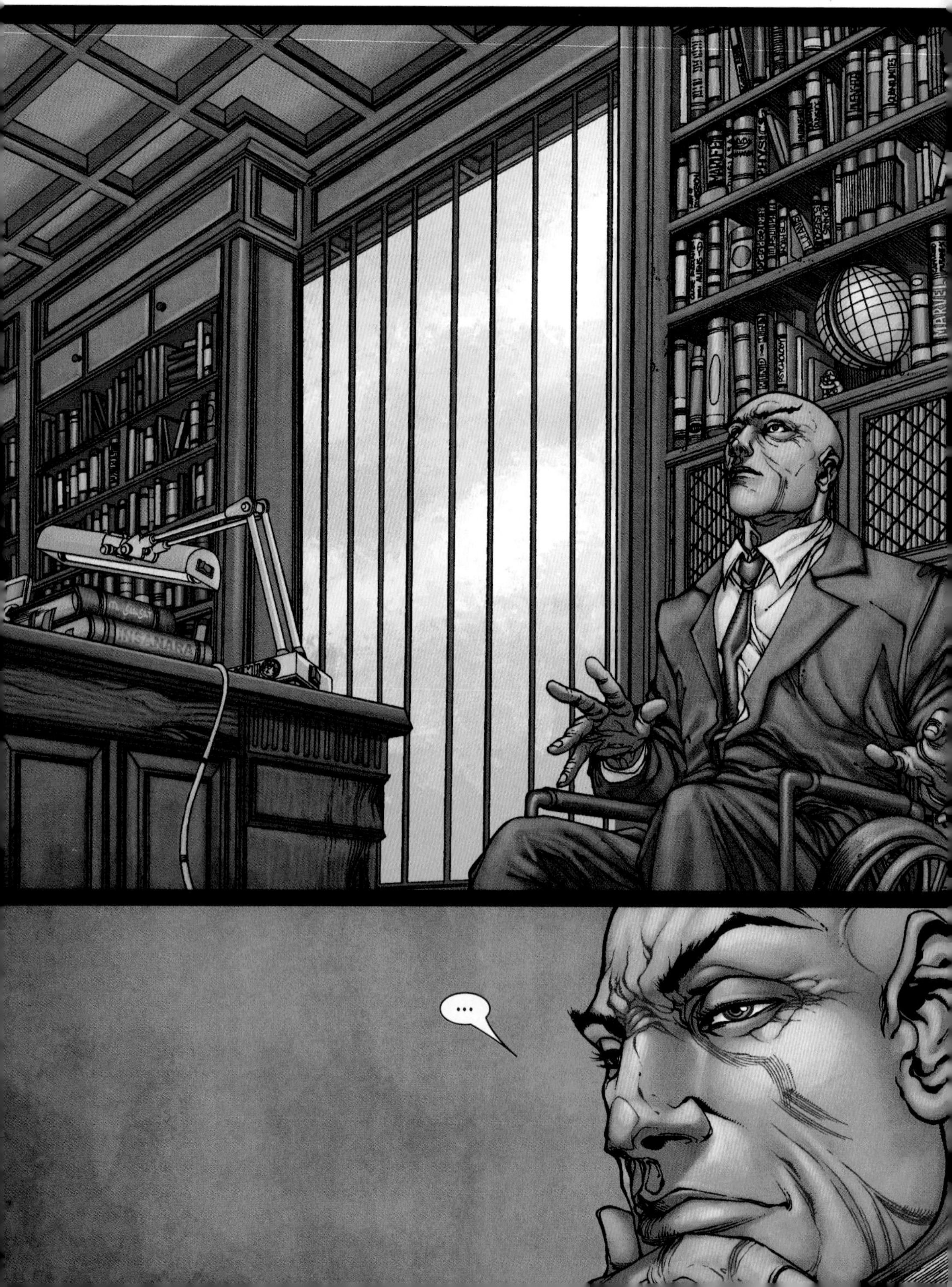
...

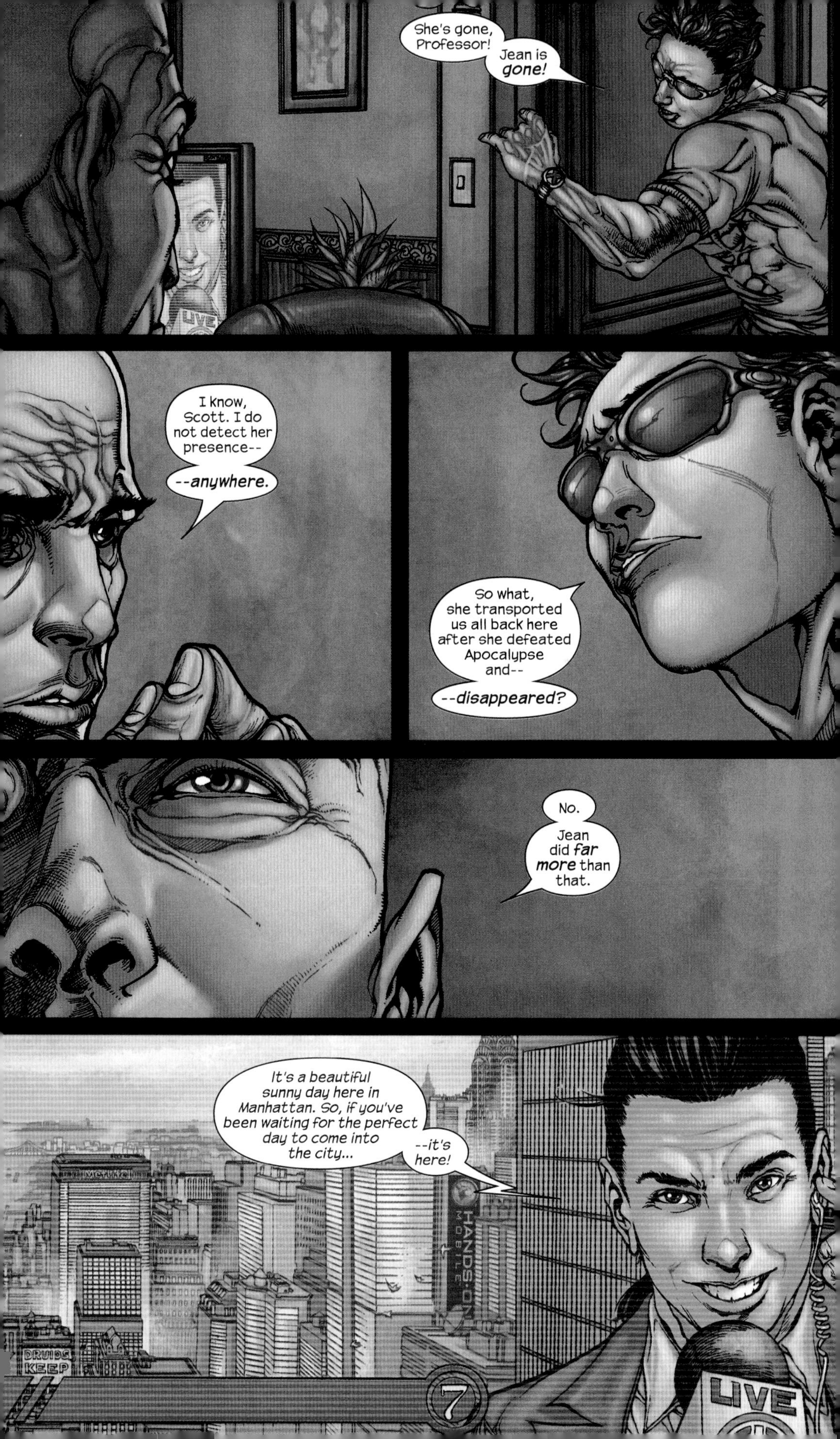
She's gone, Professor!
Jean is *gone!*
I know, Scott. I do not detect her presence--
--*anywhere.*
So what, she transported us all back here after she defeated Apocalypse and--
--*disappeared?*
No.
Jean did *far more* than that.
It's a beautiful sunny day here in Manhattan. So, if you've been waiting for the perfect day to come into the city...
--it's here!
HANDS-ON MOBILE
DRUIDS KEEP
7
LIVE

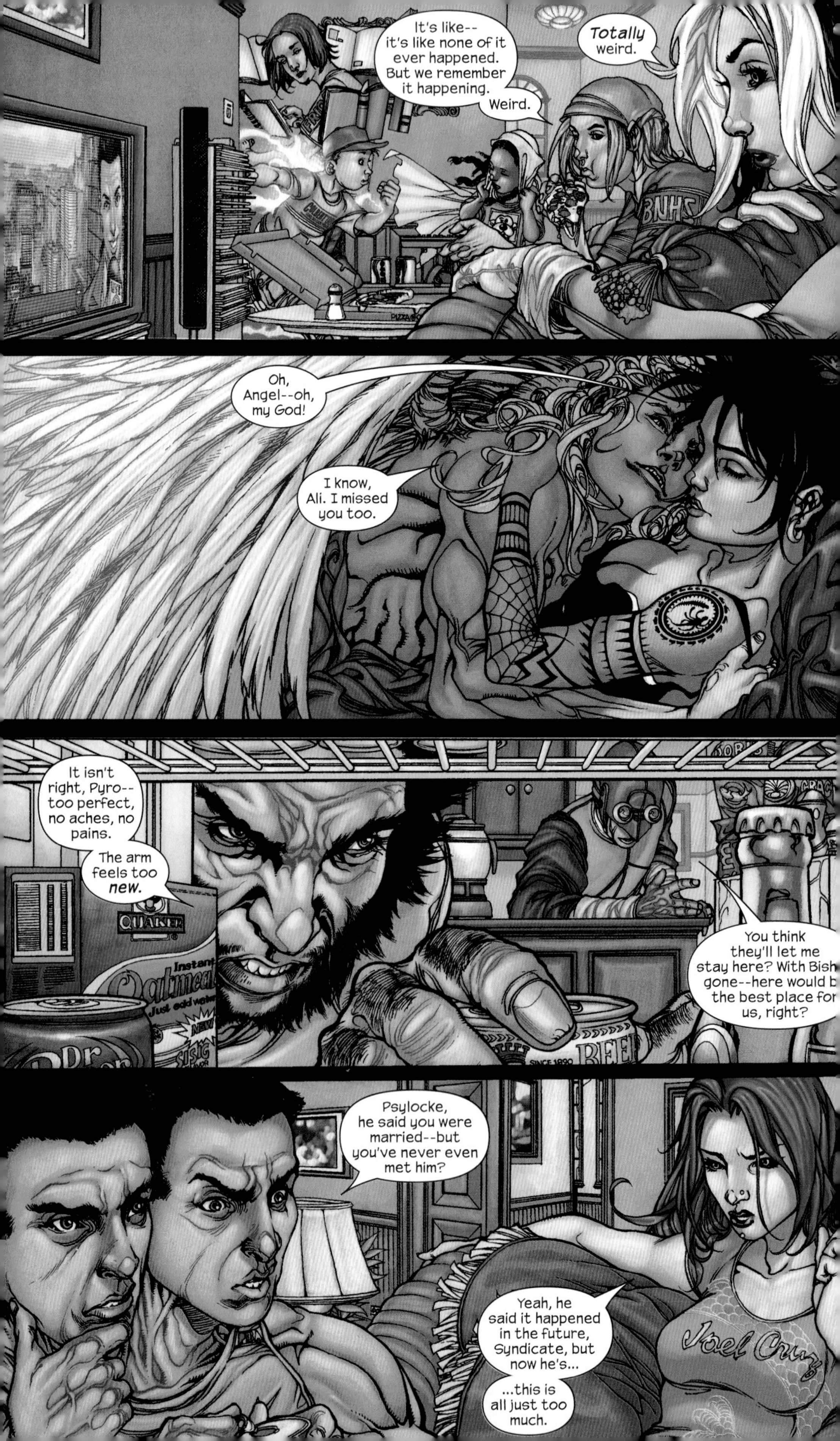

It's like-- it's like none of it ever happened. But we remember it happening.
Weird.
Totally weird.
Oh, Angel--oh, my God!
I know, Ali. I missed you too.
It isn't right, Pyro-- too perfect, no aches, no pains.
The arm feels too new.
QUAKER
Instant Oatmeal
Just add water
NEW
BEER
SINCE 1890
You think they'll let me stay here? With Bish gone--here would b the best place for us, right?
Psylocke, he said you were married--but you've never even met him?
Yeah, he said it happened in the future, Syndicate, but now he's...
...this is all just too much.
Joel Cruz

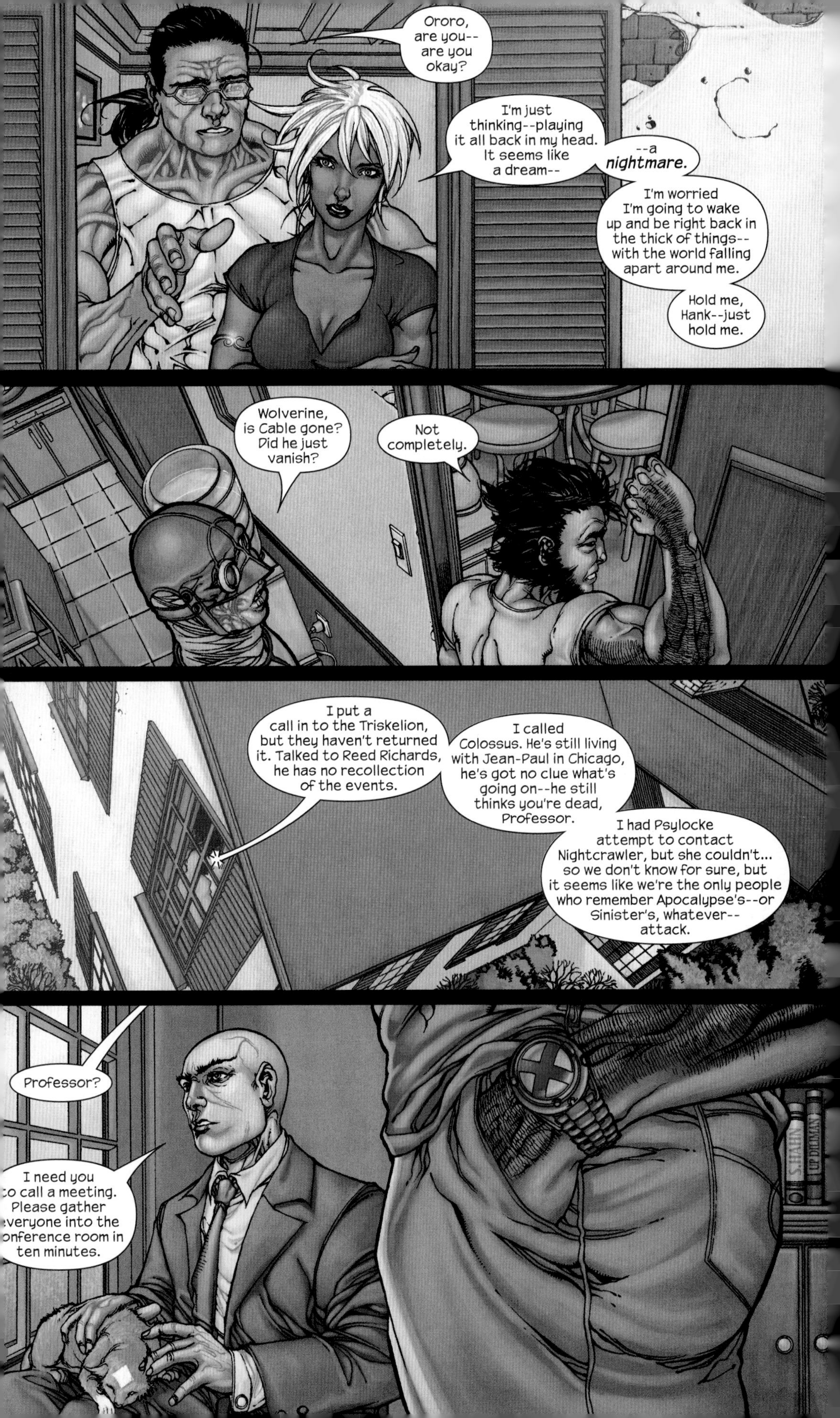
Ororo, are you-- are you okay?
I'm just thinking--playing it all back in my head. It seems like a dream--
--a *nightmare.*
I'm worried I'm going to wake up and be right back in the thick of things-- with the world falling apart around me.
Hold me, Hank--just hold me.
Wolverine, is Cable gone? Did he just vanish?
Not completely.
I put a call in to the Triskelion, but they haven't returned it. Talked to Reed Richards, he has no recollection of the events.
I called Colossus. He's still living with Jean-Paul in Chicago, he's got no clue what's going on--he still thinks you're dead, Professor.
I had Psylocke attempt to contact Nightcrawler, but she couldn't... so we don't know for sure, but it seems like we're the only people who remember Apocalypse's--or Sinister's, whatever-- attack.
Professor?
I need you o call a meeting. Please gather veryone into the onference room in ten minutes.

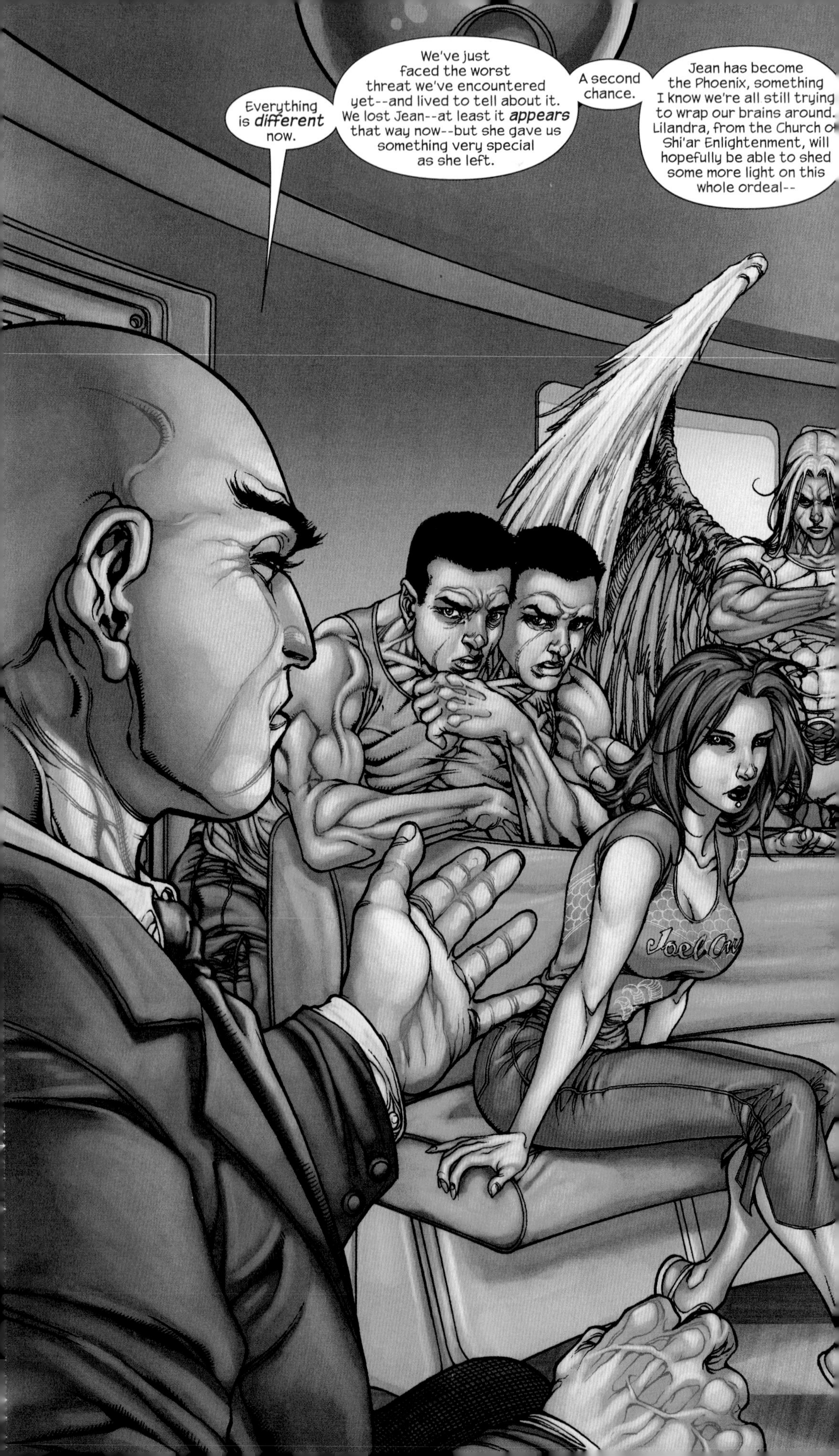
Everything is *different* now.
We've just faced the worst threat we've encountered yet--and lived to tell about it. We lost Jean--at least it *appears* that way now--but she gave us something very special as she left.
A second chance.
Jean has become the Phoenix, something I know we're all still trying to wrap our brains around. Lilandra, from the Church of Shi'ar Enlightenment, will hopefully be able to shed some more light on this whole ordeal--

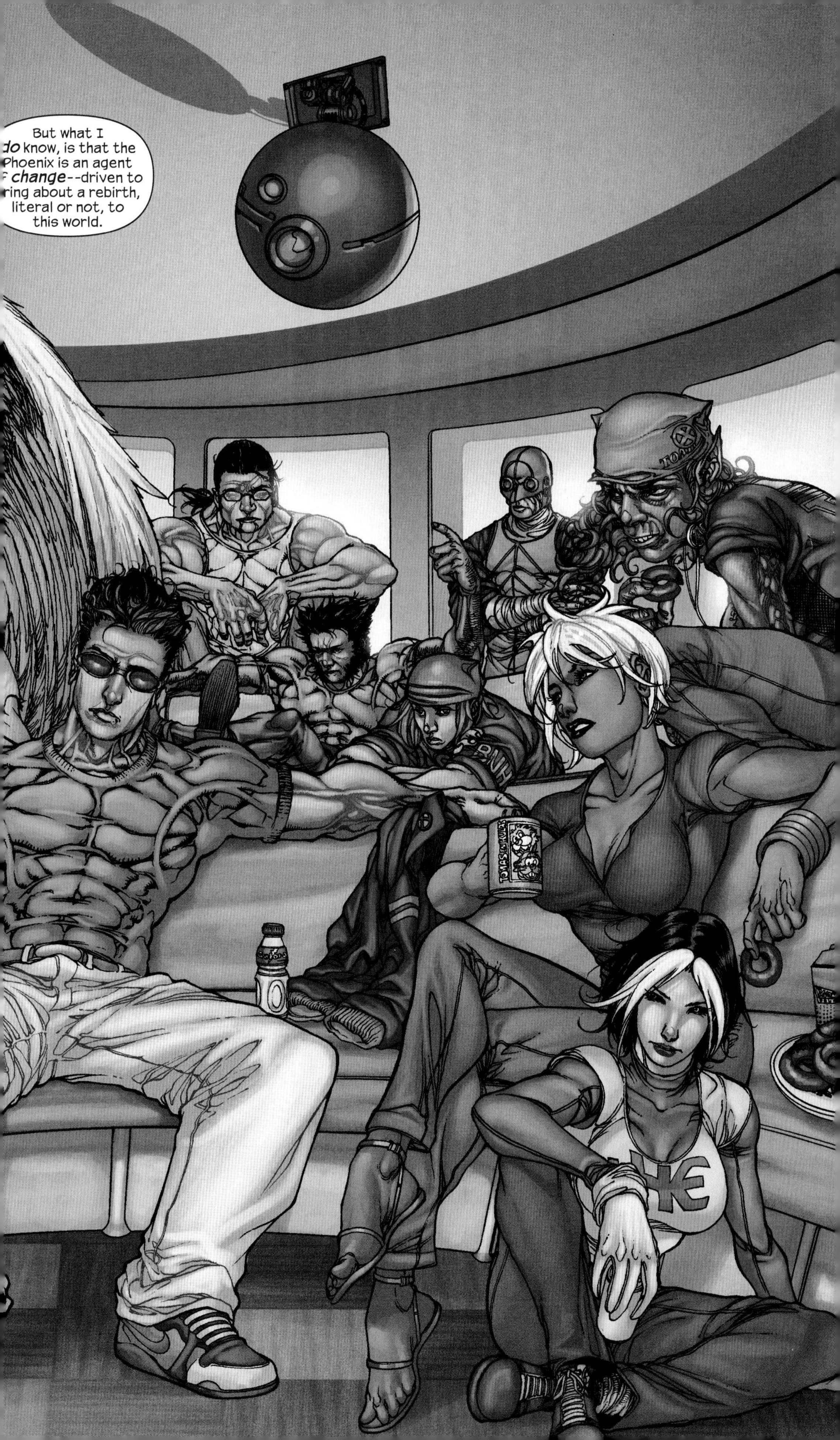
But what I *do* know, is that the Phoenix is an agent of *change*--driven to bring about a rebirth, literal or not, to this world.

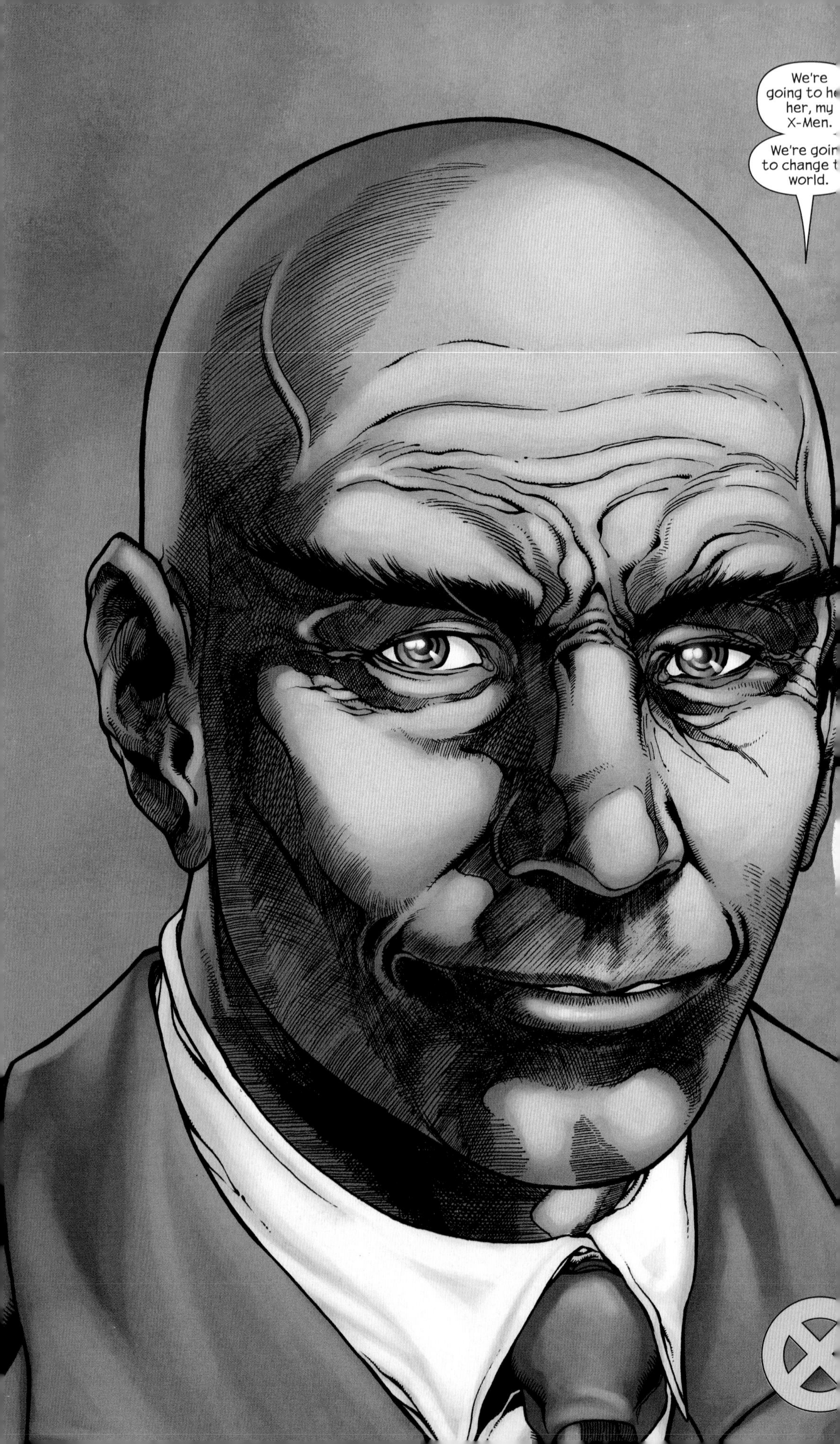
We're going to h her, my X-Men.
We're goin to change t world.